Pluralism: The Future of Religion

Pluralism: The Future of Religion

Kenneth Rose

BLOOMSBURY
NEW YORK • LONDON • NEW DELHI • SYDNEY

Bloomsbury Academic
An imprint of Bloomsbury Publishing Inc

1385 Broadway
New York
NY 10018
USA

50 Bedford Square
London
WC1B 3DP
UK

www.bloomsbury.com

Bloomsbury is a registered trade mark of Bloomsbury Publishing Plc

First published 2013
This paperback edition first published 2014

Library of Congress Cataloging-in-Publication Data
Rose, Kenneth, 1951-
Pluralism: the future of religion/Kenneth Rose.
p. cm.
Includes bibliographical references (p.) and index.
ISBN 978-1-4411-5237-4 (hardcover : alk. paper) 1. Religious pluralism. 2. Religion.
3. Negative theology. 4. Religions–Relations. I. Title.
BL85.R665 2013
201'.5–dc23
2012037399

ISBN: HB: 978-1-4411-5237-4
PB: 978-1-6289-2526-5
ePDF: 978-1-4411-5776-8
ePUB: 978-1-4411-9511-1

Typeset by Deanta Global Publishing Services, Chennai, India

For Beate

Contents

Acknowledgments

I wrote the bulk of this book over the course of a pleasant summer in the lovely old Roman city of Trier in 2011, but I have been reflecting upon the character of religious diversity since embarking upon my own experiments in multiple religious belonging, beginning in the early 1970s and, in the 1980s, during my intensive academic study of multiple religious traditions at Harvard University in the overlapping communities of the Committee on the Study of Religion in the Harvard Graduate School of Arts and Sciences, Harvard Divinity School, and the Harvard Center for the Study of World Religions. At Harvard, I remain grateful to John Carman, Hilary Putnam, Diana Eck, Gordon Kaufman, and Harvey Cox, all of whom humanely sought to discern the enduring worth of religion through searching critical analysis and sympathetic comparison. I owe my first awareness of religious pluralism as the most appropriate response to the multiple religious belonging that had plunged me into a sea of apparently irresolvable dilemmas when, as a philosophy student at Ohio State University (OSU), in the early 1980s, I read John Hick's epochal "The Copernican Revolution in Theology." After a long life dedicated to exploring the deepest truths of life in a spirit of interreligious pluralism, Professor Hick has now departed, but the pluralist revolution that he ignited with this lecture and furthered with numerous iconic publications is now irrevocably engraved upon the face of all subsequent serious interreligious reflection about religion. I also remain grateful for his encouragement of my work in this area over the last two decades.

I would like, long after my days as an undergraduate in the philosophy department of OSU, to acknowledge the formative influence over my then awakening interest in Western philosophy of Bernard Rosen, Robert Kraut, and Tamar Rudavsky. It was through the influence of these excellent professors in the philosophy department at OSU that I realized that I could go the distance in graduate school.

Of the many fellow graduate students from my time at Harvard, one has continued as a departmental colleague at Christopher Newport University (CNU), Graham Schweig. Graham and I have shared countless hours of discussion over the matters great and small that go into the delightful work of the scholar of religious studies since our first conversation by the back entrance of Andover Hall in Cambridge in 1983.

In the years since I first began to teach at CNU, I have been surrounded by a congenial group of philosophers and religious studies scholars who are passionately dedicated to illumining the quandaries of life with charity, critical acumen, and unimpeachable openness. They vividly represent the virtues of pluralistic and nonabsolutistic thought. I especially want to call attention in this regard to the late John Hoaglund, George Teschner, Deborah Campbell, Lori Underwood, Hussam Timani, and John Thompson. I am also grateful to the Faculty Senate of CNU and to Provosts Richard Summerville and Mark Padilla and to Deans Jouett Powell, Douglas Gordon, and Steven Breese for the awarding of faculty development grants, sabbatical leave, and course reductions over the years, which have helped me find the time to write this book.

Without the impressively rapid and flawless delivery of the tower of books and articles that I requested through interlibrary loan (ILL) at the Paul and Rosemary Trible Library at CNU, I could not so easily have pursued the research that forms the foundation of this book. I am especially thankful to Jesse Spencer, ILL Librarian, for cheerfully fulfilling these requests and for chasing down some of the more difficult to trace items that I requested, and to Mary Sellen, University Librarian, for supporting the robust and highly effective ILL services in Trible Library. For last-minute help in tracking down missing information in the bibliography, I am indebted to Amy W. Boykin, Instruction Librarian, at Trible Library.

I would like to thank Steven Rosen at the *Journal of Vaishnava Studies*, and, at the *Journal of Ecumenical Studies*, Paul Mozjes, Nancy E. Krody, Julia Sheetz-Willard, Maria Kaplun, Lilian Sigal, and Meliani Murtiningsih for invitations to publish articles and reviews in these journals. It was in the pages of these journals that the seeds of this book, which have been sown in countless lectures and presentations over the last two decades, fructified and made their first appearance in print.

At Continuum Books, I found a supportive editor in Haaris Naqvi, who promptly and affirmatively fielded my query and guided my proposal to acceptance by his editorial board. In an age when the future of traditional publishing houses appears imperiled, Haaris and Continuum continue to represent the venerable, author-friendly qualities of traditional publishing.

I am grateful to Birgit Roser, Leiterin des Akademischen Auslandsamts, Universität Trier, for providing me with facilities in the University's library to conduct research there in the summer of 2011. It was a delight to write many of the pages of this book in the large and bright reading hall of the Bibliothek, which overlooks the Hunsrück, while reading books efficiently delivered to me through Fernleihe.

Among my many family members, my brother Robert Rose has most closely shared in the exchange of ideas and experiences that form the biographical background to a scholarly production such as this. His is a pluralism that has been tested in his own experiences of multiple religious attraction and in his ongoing and ever-renewed colloquy with the great masters of humanity's spiritual and intellectual life. I am also grateful to my brother Richard Rose for his unswerving commitment to truth and his integrity as a journalist.

In Trier, I have happily availed myself of the continuous hospitality and kindly solicitude of the extended Boost and Raltschitsch families, whose dedication to the arts and pleasures of life in an ancient European city, enriched by a wide network of family and friends, has shown this Amerikaner a way of life richer than that lived by walled-off individualists.

Above all, without the love and enthusiastic support of my wife, Beate Boost Rose, not only would this book not have been written, but it would also have meant far less to me than it does. In a spirit of thankfulness for our shared life of travel, yoga, and deep companionship, I dedicate this book to her.

I am grateful to the following publishers for granting permission to incorporate revised sections of the listed articles and reviews in this book in the places noted after each item:

Journal of Ecumenical Studies:

- "Toward an Apophatic Pluralism: Beyond Confessionalism, Epicyclism, and Inclusivism in Theology of Religions." *Journal of Ecumenical Studies* 46:1 (Winter 2011), 67–75. Chapters 1–3.
- Review of *Christian Identity and Dalit Religion in Hindu India, 1868–1947*, by Chad M. Bauman, and *Jesus Imandars and Christ Bhaktas: Two Case Studies of Interreligious Hermeneutics and Identity in Global Christianity*, Jonas Adelin Jørgensen. *Journal of Ecumenical Studies* 45:2 (Spring 2010): 319–20. Chapter 4.
- Review of *In Good and Generous Faith: Christian Responses to Religious Pluralism*, by Kenneth Cracknell, and *Is It Insensitive to Share Your Faith? Hard Questions about Christian Mission in a Plural World*, by James R. Krabill. *Journal of Ecumenical Studies* 42:4 (Fall 2008): 640. Chapter 2.

Journal of Vaishnava Studies:

- "Pluralism and the Upaniṣads." *Journal of Vaishnava Studies* 19:1 (Fall 2010): 23–48. Introduction and Chapters 3 and 5.
- Review of *The Song Divine: Christian Commentaries on the Bhagavad Gītā*, edited by Catherine Cornille. *Journal of Vaishnava Studies* 18:1 (Fall 2009): 175–82. Chapter 7.

Hinduism Today:

- "'Interspirituality': When Interfaith Dialogue is but a Disguised Monologue." *Hinduism Today* 29:4 (October/November/December 2007): 54. Chapter 2.

Scottish Journal of Religious Studies:

- "Doctrine and Tolerance in Theology of Religions: On Avoiding Exclusivist Hegemonism and Pluralist Reductionism." Kenneth Rose. *Scottish Journal of Religious Studies* 17 (Autumn 1996): 109–21. Reprinted by permission of the publisher: Taylor & Francis Ltd, www.tandfonline.com. Chapter 7.

Bulletin of the North American Paul Tillich Society:

- "Is Christianity the Most Universal Faith? A Response to Robison B. James's *Tillich and the World Religions: Encountering Other Faiths Today*." *The Bulletin of the North American Paul Tillich Society* 30 (Winter 2004), 15–19. Introduction.

New Blackfriars:

- Although I hold the copyright to the following article, I want to acknowledge *New Blackfriars*, which originally published it: "Keith Ward's Exclusivistic Theology of Revelations." *New Blackfriars* 79 (April 1998): 164–76. Chapter 6.

August 15, 2012
Charlottesville, Virginia

Introduction

After a century in which history seemed at first to be opening into a millennium of social and technological progress but then collapsed amid two devastating wars, the catastrophic contradictions of failed and discredited ideologies, and the dehumanizing effects of amoral, runaway technologies, it is no surprise that the notion of progress is now discredited as a naïve, progressivist fantasy. So a book presuming to speak about the future of religion may seem as dated as the hope of many Western Christian theologians and idealist philosophers a century ago that the twentieth century would be a liberal Christian century fulfilling a millennialist vision of cooperating sciences, philosophies, theologies, and religions. Contrary to that fervent hope, the twentieth century closed with stalemated progressive theologies, regression to inclusivist, confessionalist, and constructivist approaches to religion, and the resurgence (except, for the most part, in the academy) of traditionalist and sometimes fundamentalist theologies.[1]

Karl Barth prophetically foretold the logic of this unanticipated antimodernist shift in Christian theology when he turned against his liberal teachers at the onset of the Great War and, in an abrupt return to revelation, created an abrasive, antithetical theological language that became a template for the many antiliberal theological movements that have since undercut liberalism and progressivism with sharp rhetorical language rather than reasoned argument. It may seem anachronistic, then, in this postideological, postliberal, posthistorical, postnarrativist, postmodern, posttheoretical, and postsecular era to speak about pluralism as the future of religion and theology.[2] A claim like this will seem implausibly ambitious to those who remain enthralled by these counterrevolutionary movements. Even more odd to some readers, in an era when the currently dominant particularism in theology and constructivism in the study of mysticism has turned attention to what divides religions rather than unites them, will be my claim in this book that theological and philosophical stances espousing religious pluralism are the only responsible bases for comparative thought about religion. It may appear naïve or arrogant to speak of pluralism as religion's future, but now, when mainstream Christian theologies of religions are dominated by stubbornly parochial expressions of religious particularism, the call to move forward into a more promising, religiously pluralist future is not merely a vain hope but an unavoidable step guaranteed by religious change and the passage of time.

Pluralism and the overcoming of inclusivism

This historical optimism that sees pluralism as inevitable is grounded not in a progressivist philosophy of history but in the irrevocable law of change. This law applies in our daily lives, in history, in biology, and in the rise and fall of universes. It applies in our neighborhoods and families, and also in the affairs of nations and empires, as well as to the supposedly unchanging truths of philosophy and religion. Nothing remains the same, and the eternal verities of one age are curiosities for another. This is not merely a skeptical, historicistic, and evolutionary view of things, for it is inscribed within the heart of critical religious thought itself, which turns upon the interplay of positive, cataphatic attempts to articulate a vision of life and negative, apophatic criticism of the inadequacies of these visions of life. The inevitable limitations of religious and philosophical visions of life guarantee change and pluralism, since no set of formulas, practices, or teachings devised in the language of one time and place can be expected to retain its significance indefinitely or to attain universal acceptance. The limitations that apophatic criticism reveal guarantee, in turn, a pluralism of ever new attempts to present substantive, cataphatic visions of the world. Thus, the passing from the scene of the currently dominant religions as they fade away or slowly morph into their successors is as certain as any other kind of change. So we need not worry—nor can we hope—that any inclusivist strategy for preserving a particular religious tradition will survive deep into the far human future (if we have one).

The claim that pluralism is the future of religion is also based upon the inability of any particular religious teaching to secure for itself universal assent that it is final and normative for all of humanity. This is the central idea grounding what I call "apophatic pluralism," which holds that since no verbal formulas, as products of history and specific contexts and communities, can be final or normative, religious pluralism should be the default stance of responsible religious thought. For no matter how internally coherent a body of religious teachings may seem to convinced insiders, it will inevitably fail to persuade those who are not inclined to be persuaded by it, even when it puts forward its best arguments or its most forceful claims (or threats).

If religious teachings were truths on the order of basic scientific facts, interreligious agreement would be less elusive than it is. But because no common, nontradition-specific method of validating specific bodies of religious teachings is available, religious truth, when seen as identical with the doctrines of this or that religion, will remain a local matter, like the mores of different cultures. Consequently, if the central teachings of the world's religions are taken as making true but contrary and nonnegotiable claims about history and the unfolding of life in the cosmos, then no doctrinal resolution of these conflicting claims will be possible at the level of doctrine. (Other solutions, including seeing these teachings as noncognitive, symbolic, or as expressions of cultural arrangements or biological causes are possible but are not the focus of this book.)

All theologizing conducted as if a specific body of religious doctrine, taken literally, were adequate to reality and thus irreformable inevitably leads to impasses and dead ends. No exit is possible from these impasses through more doctrinal argument, more open inclusivisms, more refined apologetics, renewed appeals to authority or revelation, or calls for greater faith or deeper commitment. Since none of these doctrinal systems can evade the inevitable dethroning of absolutist pretensions that occurs through what I call "departicularization,"[3] only temporary refuge can be found in inclusivism, as is seen in the increasingly implausible *ex post facto* and *ad hoc* arguments developed to defend the finality of favored bodies of doctrines by leading inclusivist theologians of religions. In the end, no one remains persuaded by these inclusivistic evasions of the truth of pluralism, including later inclusivists in inclusivistic traditions. Consequently, no form of inclusivism can hold out forever against departicularization. It must either retreat into an exclusivism that simply repeats doctrine without discussion (but even this stance stands on shifting ground as the flow of history slowly modifies and replaces one religious tradition with others) or it must go forward into a pluralism based on the above principles.

An inclusivist critic of apophatic pluralism might argue that these claims about language and doctrine are themselves hegemonic and inclusivist, which proves that apophatic pluralism is itself just one more expression of inclusivism or exclusivism (a view that I will examine in more depth in the coming chapters). But this criticism fails to distinguish second-order critiques of language from first-order substantive claims. For example, theologian of religions Kristin Beise Kiblinger claims that Buddhist inclusivists and pluralists "want to treat emptiness as an antidote to all positions rather than [as] itself one position alongside others."[4] But in response, a Mahāyāna Buddhist teacher would likely quote Nāgārjuna, who pronounced that

> "the Victors say that Emptiness is the casting aside of all views. But those who hold emptiness as a view are said to be incurable [*asādhya*]."[5]

The significant point here is that the Mahāyāna notion of *śūnyatā*, like other apophatic critical conceptions, refers to the second-order critical activity of evaluating first-order substantive discourse. As with apophatic criticism in any religious tradition of its first-order doctrinal usage in light of the ultimately ineffable character of reality, the Buddhist teaching about śūnyatā is not a doctrinal construction. It is, on the contrary, the application to religious language of the insight that language and reality diverge. Only naïveté or dogmatism would attempt to identify these clearly different uses of language, since they cannot be reduced to each other. To deny the distinction between substantive doctrinal claims and insight into the limits of such claims is to imply the elevation without final negation of a historically conditioned religious language to ultimate status. Such an approach to resolving the inconclusive strife of first-order cataphatic doctrines offers only the prospect of more first-order cataphatic doctrinal strife.

Kiblinger's claim that emptiness is just another position is an error of this sort, since it attempts to annul the distinction between first-order substantive discourse and second-order critical practice even while paradoxically making use of an implicit second-order principle that seems to be something like this: *Any attempt to evaluate doctrinal expressions is hegemonic* (a position that, of course, is itself also hegemonic).

But the distinction between critical, apophatic insight and specific cataphatic claims and teachings is as old as critical thought itself, as can be seen in Socrates's turning the table on Protagoras by demonstrating that relativism is a self-contradictory view.[6] Even if it remains among the oldest of sophomoric moves in philosophy, pointing out that the rejection of general truths is itself a general truth remains true, and to simply insist that this is only Socrates's opinion would be to fall into Socrates's trap even while trying to avoid it.

Thus, to hold that all things change is not a view on the same level as holding the view that the sun never sets on the British Empire. The truth-value of the latter claim has changed, while the former is as uncontroversial a claim as saying that the set of prime numbers is endless. Like anyone else engaged in critical evaluation of first-order discourses, but in conflict with the logic of her stance, Kiblinger writes from a critical, second-order stance about her chosen domain of first-order objects, theologies of religions and comparative theologies, and she would likely reject any attempt to characterize her criticism of comparative theologies that fail to disclose their underlying theology of religions as just another hegemonic comparative theology. A logical mistake of this sort is like saying that evaluating the various ways of traveling from Berlin to Rome is just another way of traveling from Berlin to Rome.

The apparent truism that pluralists are really inclusivists turns out then to be nothing more than a *tu quoque* fallacy devoid of logical force while remaining rhetorically clever, which accounts for its ability to convince the unwary but not the critical reader. Whether deployed with the awareness that it is fallacious or not, it is the last, futile move of inclusivist theologians who explicitly refuse to generalize about religions or to engage in second-order theorizing and criticism. As a short-term survival strategy, this may make sense, but it will inevitably fail, since the slow process of mutation, or departicularization, that transforms religions into their successors is inevitable and is as unstoppable as change.

Apophatic pluralism, which guarantees that pluralism is the future of religion is, like the Mahāyāna critical practice of śūnyatā or the Christian, Jewish, and Islāmic critical practice of apophatic theology, not itself a substantive, cataphatic position. Apophatic pluralism consists of purely negative, or apophatic, critical observations that deflate inclusivist illusions about the epistemic prowess, normativity, and ultimacy of cataphatic religious doctrines. Apophatic pluralism is thus not a new, cataphatic religious teaching, since its practice is essential to the purification of doctrine and revitalization in the ongoing religious life of humanity. Rather than signaling the negation of religion, apophatic pluralism shows how religions continually renew or replace themselves through the rise of new religious forms and movements. Despite postmodern questioning of general theoretical claims and grand views of history, it is clear that pluralism is the future of religion. Not only is the ongoing succession of ever new religious forms guaranteed by the temporal limits of human languages, but the incapacity of any religious tradition to make a final, universally accepted case for itself guarantees that no ancient, contemporary, or future religion will be able to install itself as the one, true religion for all of humanity. Apophatic pluralism, then, will as surely be inscribed in the core of all future religions as it has been in the core of each of the religions that the human mind has until now inspired.

The inevitability of apophatic pluralism does not depend upon the goodwill of exclusivists and inclusivists, or upon pluralists' success at getting others to agree with pluralist views, or even upon the correctness of any specific version of pluralism. This is no more a matter or argument than is the reality of aging and death. The transitoriness of religious forms, like all material, biological, and cultural forms, guarantees that no form of religion will long remain in its current form, thus negating any claim to universal normativity. Even if, as is likely, no inclusivists will credit this view so long as they are focused only on the near future or the imagined future of their tradition, it remains the case that pluralism as an invariable principle governing the succession of historical forms is inevitable. As a subjective and communal experience, inclusivism, at least in the short term, may seem to the inclusivist as solid a reality as a mountain, yet the view from outside these traditions supports the claim that pluralism is as inevitable as the erosion over time of the highest ranges of mountains.

An overview of coming chapters

In the following chapters, I will fill out this argument by first providing an overview of the current antipluralist position in the theology of religions, which has dead-ended in an inclusivist impasse after a bold opening in the 1970s to pluralism. This return to forms of particularism such as exclusivism and inclusivism, as well as the strategy of equating pluralism with particularism, are due, in part, to traditionalism and deference to the limitations of orthodox religion, and in part, to a contrarian opposition to liberal, pluralist theologies that is reminiscent of Barth's antimodernist turn against the liberal theologies of the nineteenth century (and the contrarian, illiberal political and theological mood that prevails as of this writing in parts of the USA, where much of this discussion occurs). Yet, because no orthodoxy can be final given the inevitable changes the passage of time brings and also because of the formal limitations of language, such apparently bold returns to tradition will inevitably involve *ad hoc* and *ex post facto* interpretive strategies (nicknamed "epicycles" by John Hick after the theory-saving devices devised to save Ptolemaic geocentrism[7]). Yet, as I will argue, these flimsy devices can never be anything but unpersuasive to the unpersuaded. Having demonstrated the implausibility of illiberal, antipluralist theologies of religions, I will then present what I think is an indefeasible justification, based on syncretism and departicularization, for the theory of apophatic pluralism. I will then explore the potential of the Upaniṣads and the New Testament as witnesses to apophatic pluralism, with the result that the Upaniṣads are shown to tend toward apophatic pluralism, despite conventional interpretations of them as inclusivistic, and that the New Testament is shown to be essentially an inclusivist text, with a latent pluralism that can serve as the basis of an apophatic pluralist overcoming of its relatively few and contestable exclusivist passages. Finally, I will tease out the logic of apophatic pluralism through a thought experiment that I call the Prisoners' Parable.

In the concluding chapter, I will trace the outlines of an apophatic, pluralist interpretation of the enduring aspects of human religiosity that is both postsecular and postconstructivist. I will suggest that, despite constructivist and reductionist attempts to deny to religion its own independent sphere of competence, religious studies does, in fact, possess its own method for dealing with the intensions[8] that regularly arise in religious traditions. As I develop this claim in light of a glance at the new cognitive science of religion, I will show the inadequacy of the dominant constructivism, which reduces religious traditions to merely local doctrinal formulations devoid of a larger explanatory framework. I will then suggest that the method native to religious studies is both comparative and religious (rather than merely cultural) in that it proposes a religious, or spiritual, interpretation of life that takes its cues from the recurrent ideas that appear ever and again in the world's many religious traditions. Over against a merely secular and cultural view of religion that take scientific explanations as the ultimate arbiter of truth, I will develop the three steps of the method native to religious studies in light of a definition of religion that sees it as pointing to an immaterial realm of beatitude and deathlessness. This method begins with the local, ethnographic studies of religious traditions that are the current staple of the field. It then ranges over these traditions in search of the general features of the sacred upon which a spiritual view of life, as opposed to a merely scientific or cultural understanding of life, can be grounded. Finally, because no such expression, whether local or universal, can evade the limitations placed upon language by finitude, an apophatic negation of these religious teachings will point us toward the ineffable source of the self-generating dynamism that ever and again calls forth new forms of religious life, expression, and practice.

And yet, as I will argue in the concluding pages of this book, authentic spirituality and religion are not merely apophatic, or negative, for the contemporary return of cataphatic, or affirmative, religious views of life, is inevitable after a long period of critical treatment of religion and its subordination to scientific and cultural explanations and interpretations. The dialectical interplay of the apophatic and the cataphatic is as inevitable and inseparable as the interplay of night and day, and just as periods of high, cataphatic theorizing are chastened by succeeding periods of critical, apophatic negation, so this current period of secular and materialistic negation of the spiritual heritage of humanity has necessarily sponsored the rise of new cataphatic quests for ultimate meaning. While the perspective of apophatic pluralism presented in these pages begins from the negative judgment that it is not possible to secure universal assent for any constructed and malleable body of religious teachings, apophatic pluralism is not a mere negativism and skepticism in the service of an antireligious view of life. The ultimate point of origin of apophatic pluralism is a lively sense of the ineffable[9] but vital character of whatever is ultimately real, along with a genuine but not servile openness to its plural expressions in the languages, rituals, laws, and spiritual practices of the world's many religious and philosophical traditions. Rather than spelling the end of religion—a hope that will remain empty as long as human beings remain marked by finitude and deficiency—apophatic pluralism is a sign that, as in the present and the past, new religious movements will continue to spring up as if miraculously from the ineffable depth of life to guide us on our planetary journey to wholeness.

An excursus on terminology

Before taking up the argument of this book in the coming chapters, it may be helpful to the reader to clarify at this point some of the technical vocabulary used in this book.

The cataphatic/apophatic distinction

The basic argument of this book turns on the ancient but always useful device of distinguishing between positive, or cataphatic, and negative, or apophatic, predication. The terms *apophatic* and *cataphatic* are derived from Greek terms that date back at least as far as Aristotle, where they are logical terms that mean "affirmation" and "negation."[10] These technical terms in Western theological and philosophical studies of mysticism and philosophical theology name the two most basic ways of talking about being or the divine. The affirmative way (*cataphasis*) approaches the divine through analogy, metaphor, and the attribution of predicates to the sacred, while the negative way (*apophasis*) systematically negates these expressions in order to open the way to an encounter with being, or the divine, free from the limited constructs generated by language, the mind, and culture. This distinction has been expressed in numerous ways in the West, such as the positive and the negative ways, positive and negative theology, the *via eminentiae* and the *via remotionis*, the *via negationis* (or *negativa*) and the *via affirmativa* (or *positiva*), *thesis* and *aphairesis*,[11] as well as *cataphasis* and *apophasis*, from which the adjectives *cataphatic* and *apophatic* are derived.

If, in this book, I use words derived from the Greek *apophasis* and *cataphasis* to describe negative and positive predication, this is not out of any sense that Western philosophy and theology are superior on this topic to Indian notions of negative and positive predication, but rather to the circumstance that these terms have a long history in Western studies of mysticism, theology, and the philosophy of religion. Perhaps, the place of these terms could be complemented by a pair of terms from Indian philosophy, *adhyāropa* (or *adhyāsa*) and *apavāda*, which can be translated as "superimposition" or "wrong attribution," and "de-superimposition" or "the withdrawal of the *adhyāropa* or superimposed attribute."[12] These terms have similar but not identical functions to *cataphasis* and *apophasis*. (One significant difference is that the Greek terms lack the quasicreative and quasidestructive force of the Sanskrit pair, which involves adding to and removing from *nirguṇa brahman* the ultimately false but conventionally real attributes of *saguṇa brahman*.[13]) And, at least for now, to speak in English of *adhyasic* and *apavadic* modes of predication, which might be good candidates to replace or complement the Greek and Latin terms, seems unduly neologistic. This can change, of course, and such a change when dealing with Indian texts in Western languages, might be preferable to current usage.

The tripolar typology: Exclusivism/inclusivism/pluralism

Although the terms of the tripolar typology, exclusivism, inclusivism, and pluralism are now widely familiar and virtually canonical,[14] a few words of definition may still be helpful. *Exclusivism* may be defined as taking one of the many available bodies of religious teachings as final to the exclusion and even negation of other bodies of religious teaching; *inclusivism* may be defined as a weaker or minimal expression of exclusivism that takes terminology in the home tradition as the "final vocabulary"[15] to interpret all religious phenomena; and *pluralism* (as a theological and philosophical stance rather than just as the reality of religious diversity or diverse religious views[16]) may be defined as the view that the limitations of language necessarily imply the ceaseless proliferation of religious languages, none of which can be universally plausible.

Against charges that this familiar typology is inadequate, Perry Schmidt-Leukel offers a plausible and logically precise reinterpretation and reaffirmation of the typology.[17] While I agree with his rejections of dubious views like Gavin D'Costa's claim that "pluralism and inclusivism are subtypes of exclusivism,"[18] I think that the typology can be further refined and simplified in the following ways. First, for the sake of brevity, I often include exclusivism and inclusivism under the term "particularism,"[19] since both can be seen as stronger and weaker versions of the view that one particular body of religious teaching and practice is final and, therefore, exclusively binding on humanity. This leads to a second possible modification: the simplification of the tripolar typology to a binary typology in which particularism is taken as the negation of "nonparticularism" (i.e., pluralism). On this approach, exclusivism and inclusivism can be seen as stronger and weaker expressions of particularism, while nonparticularism (or pluralism) can also be distinguished into a stronger version that tries to construct a universal religious teaching or practice based on the many available religious traditions and a weaker version that holds that no contextually shaped body of religious teachings can justify a claim that it is final, normative, and universally binding.[20]

It is not necessary, however, to completely abandon the tripolar typology, since this last suggested simplification can be achieved by viewing each of the three standard categories as located on a spectrum of positions with weaker and stronger versions of each category that resemble the adjacent categories. Stronger versions of exclusivism may hold militantly to the falsity of all other views than the favored one, a stance that can easily sponsor activities designed to insult, uproot, or replace religious others. Exclusivism can thus move beyond this spectrum of religious views altogether to become a political stance that justifies policies of organized violence against religious others. Weaker versions of exclusivism may look for loopholes such as the mystery of election or degrees of culpability as conditions for the practical waiving of the need for belief in the unquestionable truth of the teaching held to be final and without peer. This kind of exclusivism begins to resemble inclusivism.

Stronger versions of inclusivism may give a provisional value to other bodies of religious teaching by seeing them as deficient or incomplete expressions of the favored teaching. They resemble exclusivism by holding to the finality and normativity of one body of teaching even while inclusivistically granting provisional value to religious teachings and practices other than the favored one. Weaker versions of inclusivism may allow that sincerity of intention without explicit acceptance of the peerless teaching or practice is acceptable, a view that resembles pluralism. Other versions of weaker inclusivism may withhold judgment on other traditions while learning from them, a view that also moves in the direction of pluralism.[21]

Stronger versions of pluralism may be based upon attempts at constructing a universal religious teaching or practice, a strategy that, positively, can suggest the outlines of a general religious view of life, or that, negatively, resembles inclusivism by suggesting that there is one final religious teaching or practice required for all human beings. Weaker versions of pluralism may see the availability of multiple bodies of internally plausible but malleable religious teachings as negating absolute claims for any of them. These weaker versions of pluralism see the existence of multiple self-consistent and comprehensive bodies of religious teachings as a function of the limitations of language and thus as necessitating modesty about claims that any corpus of religious teachings is final and binding upon the whole of humanity. This version of pluralism may move beyond the spectrum of religious views altogether, since it resembles secular, historical, literary, and social-scientific approaches to the study of religion.

Departicularization

I have coined the neologism "departicularization" to express in a single word the process whereby every religious tradition slowly unravels itself as it adapts to cultural change (this process is also commonly called "syncretism"). As I view departicularization, it has two subprocesses, namely: religious hybridity and departicularization. New religious movements arise as innovative syntheses of previously unrelated religious ideas and practices under the impulse of creative innovators. These creative founders and reformers create new ways of being human religiously that blend formerly unrelated religious elements into new, hybrid expressions. Over time, these hybrid forms of religiosity, should they find a niche and survive, continue to change as they adapt to new circumstances. Ultimately, as they die out or morph into their successor(s), the unique forms that they brought to the overall complement of human religious forms fade from the scene, or are departicularized.[22] This process of departicularization is inevitable for every religious tradition, since it is an unavoidable result of the ongoing movement of time and history and of changes in culture. Against the background of a hundred thousand years or more of prerecorded and recorded human history, to claim that any particular religion is the final religion and essential to the spiritual life of humanity is like saying that one particular society is the final society and essential to the social life of humanity. As influential as Rome was, and as important as the USA, the European Union, the Republic of India, etc., may be to many of us today, none of these societies is final nor essential to human well-being. If human life continues for another 100,000 years or more, will any significant trace of any of these societies remain? One can only wonder at what the successor religions to today's religions will look like a dozen or so millennia from now—if humans survive that long. Will any significant trace of today's religions persist in those future religions? Viewed against such a broad vista, departicularization can be seen as the future of each religious tradition, whether it creatively embraces it or whether the passage of time forcibly departicularizes it. Given the realities of syncretism, religious hybridity, and departicularization, an apophatic pluralist stance seems, therefore, to be a more ethical and responsible approach to the global diversity of religion than any form of exclusivism or inclusivism.

Epicycles

Likening to epicycles the *ad hoc* and *ex post facto* interpretive devices created by inclusivist theologians to defend the view that this or that religion is final and normative for humanity is a favorite metaphor of pluralist theologians and philosophers of religions. This theological use of the concept of the epicycle can be credited (as noted earlier) to John Hick, who adapted the notion from Ptolemaic astronomers who wanted to "save the appearances" of geocentricity by postulating epicycles, or smaller orbits, centered on the orbits of the planets around the earth to account for irregularities that would later be better explained by the heliocentric theory. Classic examples of epicycles include notions such as the Christian *praeparatio evangelica*, *logos* christologies, Karl Rahner's concept of anonymous Christians, the Hindu view that the Buddha is the ninth *avatāra* of Viṣṇu, and the Jewish notion of a universal Noahic Covenant (Gen. 9.1-17). Each of these makeshift devices stretches the hermeneutical resources of a home tradition to account for religious others within the framework of the home tradition. Epicycles suffer from two defects, however, which make them ultimately unworkable: they are implausible to the members of the target tradition, and they eventually reveal their implausibility even within the home tradition, if that tradition becomes more open to encountering religious others on their own terms.

Comparative theology and the theology of religions

James Fredericks names himself and Francis X. Clooney as the initiators in the late 1980s of "the new comparative theology."[23] As distinct from the theology of religions, which is concerned with typical patterns of interreligious interactions and their theological significance, comparative theology, in their view,[24] attempts to formulate a common theology through careful comparative and critical reflection on the texts and practices of different religions.[25] In the wake of the neo-Reformation reversion to exclusivism, as expressed in the influential writings of Karl Barth[26] and Hendrick Kraemer,[27] comparative theology fell into disregard in the decades following the 1910 Edinburgh Missionary Conference. The christocentric inclusivism of the older comparative theologies, as symbolized by the efforts of J. N. Farquhar and Nicol Macnicol, also made them suspect both for exclusivists and pluralists. Although Fredericks and Clooney have clearly and correctly distinguished the roles of these two theological disciplines,[28] they slight the fundamental role of the theology of religions as a needed prolegomenon to comparative theology.[29] Thus, Fredericks holds that "comparative theology should be taken up as an alternative to the theology of religions"[30] and Clooney refers to an "allergy to theory."[31]

In opposition to this novel stance, Kristin Beise Kiblinger cogently argues that "theology of religions is properly prior to comparative theology,"[32] since it is evidently the case that a comparative theology is predicated upon a theology of religions. Kiblinger points out that even when their theologies of religions remain unacknowledged or covert, the programs of recent comparative theologians "clearly point to unadmitted theology of religions inclinations."[33] Remarkably, Fredericks admits under her challenge to being an inclusivist, while Clooney comes close to admitting the importance of the theology of religions in his evaluation of her position.[34]

By compelling two of the leading contemporary comparative theologians to come to terms with the theology of religions, Kiblinger has demonstrated that it is naïve, as Fredericks allows,[35] to think that comparative theology can proceed without reference to the theology of religions, even if the relationship remains unthematized. Indeed, as the continual interactions with the theology of religions in this volume suggest, it is impossible to separate the two disciplines,[36] leading this writer to suspect that the desire to suppress the theology of religions in favor of comparative theology is the final strategy of the inclusivist before either retreating into an unargued exclusivism or fully embracing pluralism.

Defining *religion*

There are at least two major problems with using the word *religion*. The first is the notorious and, I think, exaggerated difficulty of defining *religion* as a concept. (Religious studies scholars are familiar with the habit of offering lists of pithy definitions of religion begun by H. J. Leuba in 1912,[37] so I won't offer my own list of definitions here.) The range of definitions is not so wide as to indicate that religion is an utterly equivocal concept, since some indications of the direction we can look for an adequate definition are given in the very limits imposed upon our attempts at defining religion. These limitations on the concept of religion can be illustrated by visualizing the many definitions of the concept of religion as ranging along a number of spectra. One spectrum ranges from realistic to stipulative,[38] and another ranges from restrictive to expansive. One can also distinguish between religious or naturalistic definitions of religion.[39]

On the realistic–stipulative spectrum, realistic definitions stress a particular aspect of one or more religious traditions and value it at the expense of other aspects. A realistic definition might be that religion is a concern for the sacred. Stipulative definitions, at the other end of the spectrum, see the use of the word *religion* as arising from more or less arbitrary social practices and thus as not grounded on one or more typical characteristics of a realistic definition of religion. A stipulative definition might take *religion* as a term of art developed by religious studies scholars that can be applied in various ways according to the needs of the scholar,[40] an approach that reflects the lack of consensus about the meaning of religion among scholars of religion. On the restrictive–expansive spectrum, restrictive definitions narrowly limit religion to only some aspects of religion, thereby failing to encompass all of the phenomena generally associated with religion. A restrictive definition might be that religion is worship of God or *īśvara*, which is too narrow a definition, since it fails to include nontheistic religions within the category of religion. Expansive definitions are overly generous in including phenomena as essential to defining religion, thus rendering the concept vague and ineffective. An expansive definition might be that religion incites intense passion or interest, which is too broad a definition, since it fails to distinguish religion from other basic human activities such as politics, sports, business, entertainment, etc. On the naturalistic–religious spectrum, naturalistic definitions explain religion in nonreligious terms, such as theories grounded in the human and natural sciences. A naturalistic definition might be that religion aids adaptation by building community, which is true as far as it goes, but which fails to capture, similarly to other reductionistic theories, everything that religion means for people. Religious definitions see religion as relating primarily to a realm not discernible to the methods of the natural and social sciences. These kinds of definitions imply the reality of a distinctive, or self-generating, religious aspect of life, which make them generally unacceptable to purely secular approaches to the study of religion. A religious definition might be that religion is oriented to dimensions of reality that, at least in part, escape the purview of the sciences and exceed their powers of explanation.

My own view of religion is that stipulative definitions (and their underlying theories) fail to uncover why human beings refer to some phenomena as religions and not as (or only as) sports, professions, businesses, clubs, associations, corporations, or governments, while naïvely realistic definitions fail to capture the diversity of religious intensions that animate religious people as religious people in their different settings. I also want to frame as expansive a definition as possible for religion without allowing it to fade indistinguishably into other human interests like health, wealth, well-being, truth, social justice, and so forth. And, as will become clear in the following pages, I prefer a religious to a naturalistic definition of religion, since I see religion as irreducibly a part of the human experience as music, poetry, science, and philosophy and, like each of them, concerned with its own proper object.

Thus, I propose as my working definition of religion (and so add my own definition to the inevitable lists of definitions offered in introductory texts and courses): *Religion is the human quest to relate to an immaterial dimension of beatitude and deathlessness.* Clearly a religious definition, this approach avoids the lasting temptation of realism to orient religion toward a singular reality or substance, yet it avoids the failing of stipulative definitions by attempting to say what is unique to religions as distinct from other enterprises such as sports, business, entertainment, or the military (all of which involve ceremonies, values, beliefs, and many other kinds of "religious" activities). My definition avoids restrictiveness by selecting as religious those activities that are oriented to an immaterial order in which beatitude and deathlessness can be discovered (there may or not be such an immaterial order, but the most salient distinction of religions as religions, whether Buddhism, Christianity, Islām, and so on, is that they purport to give us information about an immaterial dimension of beatitude, or blessedness, and to aid us in becoming acquainted with it. This is not done by economics, sports, entertainment, science, etc.). This definition also avoids expansiveness by discovering a characteristic of religions—their concern with beatitude and deathlessness—that is not shared by other activities (with the exception of some aspects of the arts and philosophy, which sometimes orient people to an immaterial order. This points to another topic, one that I will not address here, of the close relationship between art, religion, and philosophy traditionally considered). The focus on the immaterial order of reality, something that necessarily moves beyond the range of any standard definition of modern science, shows that this is a religious and not a naturalistic definition of religion.

I hold this relatively realistic, somewhat restrictive, and forthrightly religious view of religion because I think that, at least at the level of conventional discourse and experience, there is a sortal, that is, a type or category of entities, called "religion", as Paul J. Griffiths claims.[41] (Even as probing a critic of the European academic concept of religion as Tomoko Masuzawa has allowed that "the stubborn facticity" of the categories associated with the concept of religion is "obviously not of the European academy's making."[42]) Against Griffiths, however, I do not think that this sortal is a natural kind, and I reject categorically the privileging by Griffiths of his version of Christianity.[43] Instead, I would hold that all kinds are what he calls "artifactual," since the patterns of order that we create or discern are not ultimate or written into the fabric of being. Indeed, notions like "fabric" and "being" are conventions that finally dissolve or mutate into successor terms and concepts (that is, they are departicularized in the language of this book). From the standpoint of apophatic pluralism, which sees the finitude of language as guaranteeing religious pluralism, Griffiths's beliefs as a Catholic Christian theologian are valid *as far as they go*, which, of course, by definition, is not all the way. For when placed within a large enough temporal frame of multiple thousands of years, the idea that any of the current religions in their evolving forms is the final, normative, and binding religion for all of humanity is untenable. In the end, these beliefs are, like all others, subject to the inevitable transformations and dissolution of departicularization. Although no religious tradition can be final, given the incalculable openness of being, religious traditions can open pathways into deathlessness and beatitude, thereby providing human religiosity in all of its diversity with its irrevocable significance.

The second problem associated with the notion of religion is the often-noted difficulty of using the singular word *religion* to refer to the world's many traditions of spiritual teaching and practice, a criticism that goes back at least as far as W. C. Smith's call to drop the use of the word altogether.[44] As currently used,[45] *religion* has its origins in Latin authors like Cicero, Varro, and early Christian apologists and theologians (most importantly, Augustine) writing in Latin. From these sources, the word, which originally referred to the various cults and sects to which the Romans were quite receptive,[46] developed philosophical overtones through its connection by Cicero to justice and its grounding in philosophical methods of argumentation by the Christian apologists and theologians, with the result that Christianity from almost the beginning began to formulate its teachings in quasiphilosophical form as apparently rational and universally valid propositions.[47] Gradually, Christianity came to see itself as the only true religion, understood as the cult of the one true God, as a way of life oriented to wisdom and justice, and as a quasipropositional body of official teachings, over against the false cults and teachings of the other sects of the Roman world.

The notion of religion as divided between a foundational natural religion accessible apart from special revelation to all reasonable people and a grab bag of less contingent historical, or "positive," expressions of natural religion arose in early modern Europe as it coped with the plurality of Christian sects that arose in the wake of the Reformation and with the deepening encounter with Islām and, later, with the religions and philosophies of China and India. As the distinction between a natural and revealed religion dissolved in the critical acids of later modern thinkers such as Hume, Kant, and Hegel, *religion* becomes, in the words of Peter Henrici, "a catchall term for a great variety of historic phenomena."[48] This view of religion has become a central feature of modern Western thinking about religion, in which the world's spiritual traditions are conceived as discrete entities with distinct doctrinal, legal, and ceremonial boundaries (what John Hick calls "bounded entities"[49]). Although this way of thinking has been mostly discredited in academic circles, it remains as a conceptual centerpiece of thinking about religion in popular apologetics, introductory survey texts, and media analyses of the world's religions.

Numerous Western terminological alternatives to the word *religion* abound, such as the now outmoded *faiths*, the now quasiderogatory *sects* and *cults*, the overused *religious traditions*, and metaphorical expressions like *wisdom traditions*, *paths*, and *ways*. It is also possible to use terms derived from other traditions, a move that has much to recommend it, since they avoid the rigid lines between idealized religious types that form so familiar a part of the Latin Christian West's religious thought (which includes the Catholic Church, the classic Protestant churches, and their successors and dissidents). Thus, we might speak about *dharmas*, *margas*, *jiaos*, *daos*, and *shasanas*. But these still sound odd to the Western ear, especially in the anglicized forms given here with English plural endings, although *dharmas* has as much right as *religions* to global usage, since it is a Sanskrit term used widely in Indian-based religions, including Buddhism, which has spread Indian modes of thinking far beyond India's borders for millennia. In any case, these considerations do nothing to alleviate the difficulty of terminology, even as they indicate the nature of the problem. In the following pages, I will bow to custom and use expressions like *religion*, *religions*, and *religious traditions* because they are familiar, but not yet as outmoded as *faith* or *sects*, nor as neologistic as *dharmas* or *taos*.

A final point about religion relates to the academic discipline of the study of religion rather than to terminological differences. Given the crisis of meaning that the study of religion now experiences because it has renounced the very subject, an immaterial realm of beatitude and deathlessness, that inspired its beginnings, it may be a good time for religious studies to reclaim the idea that, among its many other features, religion is in some degree *sui generis*, or grounded in its own proper awareness of a realm of knowledge and experience that is prior to and more fundamental than the realm of time and space available to the senses. This idea, which was once central to religious studies through the work of Mircea Eliade, Rudolf Otto, and, though seriously limited by his theology, Karl Barth, will be a shockingly religious claim to materialists, naturalists, and others who reduce religion to cultural and biological processes. Without in any way invalidating the role of the social sciences, cultural studies, and the natural sciences in the academic study of religion, it must be said that none of these disciplines can continue to be thought of as capable of exhaustively explaining the immaterial dimension of religion to which all of the traditions, insofar as they are religious traditions, point.[50] As the global return of religion and the rise of the postsecular stance in religious studies indicate, monological explanatory methodologies cannot invalidate the felt sense of people in all religious traditions that in their most profoundly religious activities they encounter a deathless realm that is not exhausted by the historical, cultural, psychological, biological, and material dimensions of life. The proper response to this religious view of religion should not be the doubling down on old hegemonic and reductionistic methodologies such as methodological materialism, but an acknowledgment that materialism is an underdetermined metaphysical view that cannot be made true by fiat. As an account of all of the evidence and insights produced by science, philosophy, and religion, it competes poorly with idealist views of religion, since idealism has the virtue of being able to account not only for the physical world, as shown by the progress of modern physics over the last century, but it can also account in satisfying first-person terms for the mental realms in which our humanity is experienced and actualized.

Only a religious studies that rejects or ignores a sacred dimension of life can argue that religion is merely a product of the scholar's study[51] and that, therefore, religion has no subject matter of its own. This is a *reductio ad absurdum* that is itself absurd if an idealist view of life is true or is at least plausible. If the study of religion can muster the courage to once again range over all of its carefully collected studies of individual traditions to see that, unlike sports or politics, these traditions as religious traditions relate to an immaterial realm of beatitude and deathlessness, it can rediscover the methodology native to religious studies (about which I will have more to say in the concluding chapter to this book). It would be a shame if the study of religion, a discipline whose ethical principles include allowing the world's traditions to speak in their own terms,[52] were to remain dominated by an alien methodological preference for secular, materialist, cultural, and scientific interpretations that are blind to or explain away the ultimate focus of these traditions on dimensions of being that are not limited to biology, culture, history, and the supposedly "real world" of the senses and the unillumined mind.

Notes

1 This much-abused term has a specific usage in American religious history, as the literature on this topic shows. The use of the word was not originally pejorative, since it arose among the early architects of the religious rejection of modernism and the Enlightenment by conservative Protestants in the USA and the UK. Their theological views were summarized in *The Fundamentals* (1910–1915), a series of volumes that became the basis of a theological movement that shaped the rise of separatistic fundamentalism in the 1920s and the New Evangelicalism of the 1940s and that, in muted form, has become the mainstream religion of the contemporary USA. The study of fundamentalism as a serious category of academic research began with the publication of George M. Marsden's groundbreaking *Understanding Fundamentalism and Evangelicalism* (Grand Rapids, MI: Eerdmans, 1991). The use of this rubric as a category of research flourished afterward, culminating in the multivolume, *The Fundamentalism Project* (six volumes, University of Chicago, 1994–2003) under the supervision of Martin E. Marty and R. Scott Appleby. The use of the word *fundamentalism* as a category of academic research seems to have faded since the events of September 11, 2011, as the term has come to be associated with terrorists and has become an imprecise and too widely applied term of abuse among New Atheists such as Richard Dawkins. Reid B. Locklin and Hugh Nicholson replace "fundamentalism" with "maximalism" in an attempt to undercut pejorative usages of this once very useful term. "The Return of Comparative Theology," *Journal of the American Academy of Religion* 78 (June, 2010): 478. Yet, evangelical Protestants who continue to call themselves fundamentalists and are recognized as such by other, nonfundamentalist evangelicals continue to serve as self-appointed guardians of the boundaries of evangelical faith through their articulation and defense of the principle of "secondary separation," which holds that evangelical Christians cannot associate theologically with theological liberals, Catholics, and other Christians whom they see as holding beliefs that are beyond the boundary of orthodoxy. See Kevin T. Bauder, "Fundamentalism," in *The Spectrum of Evangelicalism*, edited by Andrew David Naselli and Collin Hansen (Grand Rapids, MI: Zondervan, 2011), 19–49.

2 As would be the case if what Tomoko Masuzawa sees as pluralistic "world religions discourse" were merely the way in which Eurocentric Christian hegemonism preserved itself over the course of the last century after the decline of the older dogmatic, apologetic, and evangelical discourse about the religious traditions of the world. *The Invention of World Religions: Or, How European Universalism was Preserved in the Language of Pluralism* (Chicago: University of Chicago Press, 2005), xiv, 13, 22, 28–9, 33, 89–90, 97, 103, 259, 265, 267, 310–28. Sharada Sugirtharajah thinks that John Hick, the leading contemporary theorist of religious pluralism, would have rejected this approach by pointing out that the practice of religious pluralism has long been present in India. "Introduction: Religious Pluralism—Some Issues," in *Religious Pluralism and the Modern World: An Ongoing Engagement with John Hick*, ed. Sharada Sugirtharajah (Houndmills: Palgrave Macmillan, 2012), 6. Paul F. Knitter also rejects the notion of pluralism as "a cleverly camouflaged but ultimately exploitative Western imposition" on apophatic and mystical grounds similar to those that I argue for in this book. "Is the Pluralist Model a Western

Imposition? A Response in Five Voices," in *The Myth of Religious Superiority: A Multifaith Exploration*, ed. Paul F. Knitter (Maryknoll, NY: Orbis Books, 2005), 28, 33–6.

3 This is my term for the process whereby a religious tradition is inevitably surpassed by another and fades from the scene or morphs into a new form altogether. I will discuss this term more fully later in this chapter.

4 Kristin Beise Kiblinger, in *The New Comparative Theology: Interreligious Insights from the Next Generation*, ed. Francis Xavier Clooney (New York: T&T Clark, 2010), 35.

5 Nāgārjuna, *Mūlamadhyamakakārikā* 13.8, my translation. David J. Kalupahana translates these lines as: "The Victorious Ones have announced that emptiness is the relinquishing of all views. Those who are possessed of the view of emptiness are said to be incorrigible." *Mūlamadhyamakakārikā of Nāgārjuna: The Philosophy of the Middle Way*, trans. David J. Kalupahana (Albany, NY: State University of New York Press, 1986), 13.8:223. Robert A. F. Thurman translates the second half in this way, "One who adopts emptiness as a view is thereby pronounced incurable." "Introduction," in *The Central Philosophy of Tibet: A Study and Translation of Jey Tsong Khapa's Essence of True Eloquence*, Robert A. F. Thurman, trans. (1991; repr., Princeton, NJ: Princeton University Press, 1984), 53.

6 Plato, *Theatetus*, trans. Francis Macdonald Cornford and Benjamin Jowett, in *The Collected Dialogues of Plato Including the Letters*, eds. Edith Hamilton and Huntington Cairns (Princeton, NJ: Princeton University Press, 1961), 876:171a.

7 The metaphor that likens inclusivistic attempts to universalize old doctrines to the epicycles, or smaller orbits centered on the circle of the main orbit that were employed to make the Ptolemaic geocentric universe conform to emerging data that eventually led to the Copernican heliocentric universe was invented by John Hick. See, e.g., John Hick, "The Copernican Revolution in Theology," in *God and the Universe of Faiths: Essays in the Philosophy of Religion*, ed. John Hick (London: Macmillan, 1973), 123–5; *God Has Many Names* (Philadelphia, PA: Westminster Press, 1982), 32–36; and "Religious Pluralism and Absolute Claims," in *Problems of Religious Pluralism*, ed. John Hick (London: Macmillan Press, 1985), 52–3.

8 Intensions are general notions or ideas that are expressed in concepts and words. Intensions cannot be reduced to their individual instances or expressions. For example, the intension of a tree (i.e., the shared idea of a tree) cannot be reduced to any of the conceptualizations, names, or individual vocalizations that occur in any one language. For a more technical definition of intensions, or "intensional entities," see *Routledge Encyclopedia of Philosophy*, s.v. "Intensional entities," by George Bealar, accessed May 5, 2012, www.rep.routledge.com.read.cnu.edu/article/X019. Intensions must also be distinguished from intentions, as in personal intentions to do something or other, and intentionality, which is a philosophical notion associated with various schools of phenomenology, which see personal intentions as shaping experience. As an example of the use of the latter term, see Steven T. Katz, "Language, Epistemology, and Mysticism," in *Mysticism and Philosophical Analysis*, ed. Steven T. Katz (New York: Oxford University Press, 1978), 63.

9 The recognition of the limits of doctrinal language is indicated in Advaita Vedānta by the term *anirvacanīya*, "inexpressible," an apophatic notion that has a parallel in one of the most apophatic passages in the New Testament, Rom. 11.33–34, where Paul eulogizes his deity's ways as *anexichniastos*, or "untraceable."

10 Aristotle *Nicomachean Ethics* 1.1139a and *Metaphysics* 4.1107b, *The Perseus Digital Library*, accessed September 3, 2010, www.perseus.tufts.edu/hopper/text?doc=Perseus:text:1999.01.0051:book=4:section=1007b&highlight=kata/fasin,kata/fasis and www.perseus.tufts.edu/hopper/text?doc=Perseus:text:1999.01.0053 (). For an English translation of these terms in *Nicomachean Ethics*, see *Introduction to Aristotle*, ed. Richard McKeon (New York: Modern Library, 1947), 425.

11 "*Aphairesis* is opposed to *thesis* as negation is opposed to affirmation," according to the *Encyclopedia of Christian Theology*, s.v. "Negative Theology," by Ysabel de Andia, vol. 1., ed. Jean-Yves Lacoste, trans. Antony Levi (New York: Routledge, 2005), 1109. These terms, which are traceable back to Aristotle and Plato, are found throughout *The Mystical Theology* of Pseudo-Dionysius.

12 *Monier-Williams Sanskrit-English Dictionary* (2008 online revision), s.vv. "*apavāda*," "*adhyāropa*," accessed September 26, 2010, www.sanskrit-lexicon.uni-koeln.de/monier/; *Vedānta-Sāra (The Essence of Vedānta) of Sadānanda Yogīndra*, 2nd edn, trans. Swami Nikhilananda (Kolkata: Advaita Ashrama, 2002; 2nd edn, first published 1974), 2.32; 4.1. The two terms are defined as the "method or theory of prior superimposition and subsequent denial," according to John Grimes, *A Concise Dictionary of Indian Philosophy* (Albany, NY: State University of New York Press, 1996), s.v. "*Adhyāropāpavāda*."

13 See Eliot Deutsch, *Advaita Vedānta: A Philosophical Reconstruction* (Honolulu: The University Press of Hawai'i, 1969), 33, 41–2.

14 The categories of the now canonical tripolar typology can be traced back to Alan Race's *Christians and Religious Pluralism* (Maryknoll, NY: Orbis Books, 1982), 7. The validity of the typology has recently been compellingly reasserted by Perry Schmidt-Leukel in "Exclusivism, Inclusivism, Pluralism: The Tripolar Typology—Clarified and Reaffirmed," in Knitter, *The Myth of Religious Superiority*, 13–27. Alongside the many criticisms of this typology and occasional attempts either to abandon it or replace it altogether, is the reasonable and useful attempt by Paul Knitter to extend it by adding a type to the traditional three, which he calls the "acceptance model." Paul Knitter, *Introducing Theologies of Religions* (Maryknoll, NY: Orbis Books, 2002), 171–237. Summarizing this model, Rita M. Gross writes that "value judgments about the validity of various religions should be suspended in favor of learning more deeply what each of the religions is actually claiming." Rita M. Gross, "Excuse me, But What's the Question? Isn't Religious Diversity Normal?" in Knitter, *The Myth of Religious Superiority*, 76. Gavin D'Costa has produced what he sees as an unprecedentedly "differentiated typology" of pluralisms. "Pluralist Arguments: Prominent Tendencies and Methods," in Karl J. Becker, Ilaria Morali, and Gavin D'Costa, (eds), *Catholic Engagement with World Religions: A Comprehensive Study* (Maryknoll, NY: Orbis Books, 2010), 329. In formulating this new typology, which distinguishes pluralism into four categories and multiple subtypes, he draws upon and modifies earlier attempts at schematizing pluralism by Jacques Dupuis, Alan Race, and Paul Knitter. Becker, Morali, and D'Costa, *Catholic Engagement with World Religions*, 580n1. D'Costa's typology is valuable in indicating the varieties of theory (Marxism, mysticism, feminism, etc.) that animate much contemporary and theological reflection upon religious diversity, yet, in keeping with his own forthright rejection of pluralism as "an orthodox option for a Catholic" (Becker, Morali, and D'Costa, *Catholic Engagement with World Religions*, 329), his new

typology does not come to terms with what I see as the reality of religious pluralism, behind which regress is not possible so long as we retain our current awareness of the historicality of all phenomena. In the typology that I offer here, however, pluralism is an essential feature. For orthodox Christian and genuinely pluralistic theologies of religion, which can withstand the rejection of pluralism by D'Costa (and the Vatican's *Dominus Iesus* declaration against Haight's position), see Roger Haight, "Pluralist Christology as Orthodox," and K. P. Aleaz, "Pluralism Calls for Pluralistic Inclusivism," in Knitter, *The Myth of Religious Superiority*, 151–61; 162–75. For *Dominus Iesus*, see Congregation for the Doctrine of the Faith, Rome, "Declaration "*Dominus Iesus*" on the Unicity and Salvific Universality of Jesus Christ and the Church," accessed December 26, 2011, www.vatican.va/roman_curia/congregations/cfaith/documents/rc_con_cfaith_doc_20000806_dominus-iesus_en.html.

15 An evocative phrase used by Richard Rorty in *Contingency, Irony, and Solidarity* (Cambridge: Cambridge University Press, 1989), 68.

16 Chad Meister helpfully distinguishes between *religious diversity*, which refers merely to the fact that there are significant religious differences among adherents of different religions, and *religious pluralism*, which refers to views that encourage such diversity, see salvation and liberation in all religions, and rejects the idea that belonging to any particular religion is essential to salvation and liberation. "Introduction," in *The Oxford Handbook of Religious Diversity*, ed. Chad Meister (Oxford and New York: Oxford University Press, 2011), 3–4. As used in this book, the phrase *religious pluralism*, or *pluralism* for short, will refer to views similar to those indicated by Meister in his definition of *religious pluralism* or to my own version of pluralism, which I call apophatic pluralism. (My own use of the phrase *religious diversity* appears to conform to Meister's definition of that phrase.) Diana Eck has concisely clarified the difference between the two expressions: ". . . the mere presence of wide-ranging religious diversity is not itself pluralism. Religious pluralism requires active positive engagement with the claims of religion and the facts of religious diversity." *Encountering God*, 192.

17 Schmidt-Leukel, "Exclusivism, Inclusivism, Pluralism," in Knitter, *The Myth of Religious Superiority*, 18–23.

18 Gavin D'Costa, "The Impossibility of a Pluralist View of Religions," *Religious Studies* 32 (1996): 225. Quoted in Schmidt-Leukel, "Exclusivism, Inclusivism, Pluralism," in Knitter, *The Myth of Religious Superiority*, 19.

19 I discuss this usage further in Kenneth Rose, "Doctrine and Tolerance in Theology of Religions: On Avoiding Exclusivist Hegemonism and Pluralist Reductionism," *The Scottish Journal of Religious Studies* 17:2 (Autumn 1996): 119; "Keith Ward's Inclusivist Theology of Revelations," *New Blackfriars* 79 (April 1998): 171.

20 A position that I have called "modest pluralism" in "Toward an Apophatic Pluralism: Beyond Confessionalism, Epicyclism, and Inclusivism in Theology of Religions," *Journal of Ecumenical Studies* 46:1 (Winter 2011): 67–75.

21 Kiblinger, "Relating Theology of Religions and Comparative Theology," in Clooney, *The New Comparative Theology*, 28, where she follows Paul Griffiths in distinguishing between open and closed inclusivisms. See Paul J. Griffiths, *Problems of Religious Diversity* (Malden, MA: Blackwell, 2001) 57, 59–60. Griffiths often refers to other

traditions as "alien religions" (e.g., 59, 129) from which religiously significant truth might nevertheless be learned by the home religion, thus showing that this remains an inclusivistic position.

22 Kenneth Rose, "Interspirituality and Unsaying: Apophatic Strategies for Departicularizing Christ and the Church in Current Roman Catholic Mystical Movements," presented at the 2003 American Academy of Religion's "Mysticism: The Mysticism Group of the American Academy of Religion," accessed May 10, 2012, www.aarmysticism.org/documents/Rose03.pdf. An abridged version appeared as "'Interspirituality': When Interfaith Dialogue Is but a Disguised Monologue," *Hinduism Today* 29 (October/November/December, 2007): 54. See also Kenneth Rose, "Is Christianity the Most Universal Faith? A Response to Robison B. James's *Tillich and the World Religions: Encountering Other Faiths Today*" (Mercer University Press, 2003), *The Bulletin of the North American Paul Tillich Society* 30 (Winter 2004): 15–19.

23 James Fredericks, "Introduction," in *New Comparative Theology: Interreligious Insights from the Next Generation*, ed. Francis X. Clooney (London and New York: T&T Clark International, 2010), ix. Also see Nicholson and Locklin, "The Return of Comparative Theology," 477–514, and Nicholson's "The New Comparative Theology and the Problem of Hegemonism" in Clooney, *The New Comparative Theology*, 43–62.

24 For a review of the meanings associated with what now, after Clooney and Fredericks, might be called the "old comparative theology," see *Encyclopedia of Religion*, ed. Mircea Eliade (New York: Macmillan, 1987), s.v. "Theology: Comparative Theology," by David Tracy, 446–55. The main difference between the new and old approaches is that the newer approach does not divide the concerns of the theology of religions from comparative theology. Although the theology of religions as a distinctive branch of theology had hardly been launched when Tracy's article was written and the new comparative theology had yet to be suggested, it still remains the case that the linkage of these two differentiated disciplines is indissoluble.

25 Fredericks, "Introduction," in Clooney, *New Comparative Theology*, ix.

26 Karl Barth, *Church Dogmatics: the Doctrine of the Word of God*, vol. I.2, trans. G. W. Bromiley, G. T. Thomson, and Harold Knight (London and New York: T&T Clark, 2000), 17:81–163.

27 Hendrik Kraemer, *The Christian Message in a Non-Christian World*, 2nd edn (1947; repr., New York and London: International Missionary Council, 1946).

28 Fredericks, "Introduction," in Clooney, *The New Comparative Theology*, xiii–xiv; Clooney, "Response," in Clooney, *The New Comparative Theology*, 195–6.

29 Fredericks, "Introduction," in Clooney, *The New Comparative Theology*, xiv–xv, and James L. Fredericks, *Buddhist and Christians: Through Comparative Theology to Solidarity* (Maryknoll, NY: Orbis Books, 2004), xiii, where he writes that "the time has come to put aside the quest for an adequate theology of religions." See also Francis X. Clooney, *Comparative Theology: Deep Learning Across Religious Borders* (Malden, MA and Oxford: Wiley-Blackwell), 2010), 15. The fallacy of thinking that one can do comparative theology to the exclusion of the theology of religions has been analyzed by Kristin Beise Kiblinger, "Relating Theology of Religions and Comparative Theology," in Clooney, *The New Comparative Theology*, 21–42.

30 Fredericks, "Introduction," in Clooney, *The New Comparative Theology*, xiv.
31 Clooney, *Comparative Theology*, 42.
32 Kiblinger, "Relating Theology of Religions and Comparative Theology," in Clooney, *The New Comparative Theology*, 29. Earlier than Kiblinger, Peter C. Hodgson described the systematic interrelation of two distinctive tasks in the theology of religions, "one critical and the other constructive." The first, which corresponds to what is generally thought of as the theology of religions, is the critical task of "exposing idolatries," that is, of undercutting inadequate views of the fundamental relationship between the religions. The second, which seems to correspond to comparative theology as conceived by Clooney and Fredericks, is directed toward "drawing out converged truths" from the various religions. "The Spirit and Religious Pluralism," in Knitter, *The Myth of Religious Superiority*, 144.
33 Kiblinger, "Relating Theology of Religions and Comparative Theology," in Clooney, *The New Comparative Theology*, 30. Perry Schmidt-Leukel clearly delineates the logic that underlies the various options in the theology of religions and that implies the priority of the theology of religions to comparative theology as a foundational discipline. "Exclusivism, Inclusivism, Pluralism," in Knitter, *The Myth of Religious Superiority*, 19–21.
34 Fredericks, "Introduction," in Clooney, *The New Comparative Theology*, xiv–xv; Clooney, "Response," in Clooney, *The New Comparative Theology*, 195–6. Clooney affirms a Rahnerian and Dupuisian inclusivism (with perhaps a nod in the direction of the open pluralism of Paul Griffiths) without referencing Kiblinger (Clooney, *Comparative Theology*, 16). Clooney does reference Kiblinger in *The New Comparative Theology*, but, perhaps in line with the tentativeness of his method and perhaps due to a protopluralist aversion to the implications of any sort of inclusivism, he defers reaffirming himself as an inclusivist (195–6), despite the avowal of inclusivism noted above in his *Comparative Theology*, 16.
35 Fredericks, "Introduction," in Clooney, *The New Comparative Theology*, xvi. Kiblinger points out the unacknowledged theology of religions stances that seem to underlie the comparative work of Fredericks and Clooney. "Relating Theology of Religions and Comparative Theology," in Clooney, *The New Comparative Theology*, 31–2.
36 A point cogently argued against Fredericks by Schmidt-Leukel. "Exclusivism, Inclusivism, Pluralism," in Knitter, *The Myth of Religious Superiority*, 24, 27. Jeffrey Long argues similarly in "(Tentatively) Putting the Pieces Together: Comparative Theology in the Tradition of Sri Ramakrishna," in Clooney, *The New Comparative Theology*, 152.
37 H. J. Leuba presented a well-known list of 48 definitions of religion in *The Psychological Study of Religion: Its Origin, Function, and Future* (New York: Macmillan, 1912), as Peter Henrici point outs. "The Concept of Religion from Cicero to Schleiermacher," in Becker, Morali, and D'Costa, *Catholic Engagement with World Religions*, 1. About this whole enterprise of accumulating lists of definitions, Jonathan Z. Smith has notably complained "that there is no more pathetic spectacle in all of academia than the endless citation of the little list of fifty odd definitions of religion from James Leuba's *Psychology of Religion* in introductory textbooks as proof that religion is beyond definition, that it is a *mysterium*." "Religion and Religious Studies: No Difference at All," in *Theory and Method in the Study of Religion: A Selection of Critical Readings*, ed. Carl Olsen (Belmont, CA: Wadsworth/Thomson Learning, 2003), 27–8. Previously published in *Soundings* 51:2–3 (1988): 231–44.

38 Terry F. Godlove, Jr. distinguishes real and nominal (or explicative) definitions from stipulative ones, "in which we simply make-up or fabricate the meaning of a concept." "Religion in General, not in Particular: A Kantian Meditation," *Journal of the American Academy of Religion* 78:4 (2010): 1034. Ann Taves in her AAR Presidential address in 2010 criticized the practice of scholars of religion who only use stipulative, task-related definitions of religion. "'Religion' in the Humanities and the Humanities in the University." *Journal of the American Academy of Religion* 79:2 (June 2011): 291.

39 John Hick distinguished between religious but not confessional and naturalistic approaches to religion without intending to negate the naturalistic approaches and without limiting a religious approach to a single religion, sect, or denomination. See John Hick, *An Interpretation of Religion*, 1.

40 As in the writings of Jonathan Z. Smith. See, e.g., "Tillich['s] Remains . . . " *Journal of the American Academy of Religion* 78:4 (2010): 1139–70, where he stipulatively reduces religion to the labor of religion scholars who work in the very long shadow of Paul Tillich. Smith famously sees religion as "solely the creation of the scholar's study." Smith, *Imagining Religion: From Babylon to Jonestown* (Chicago: University of Chicago Press, 1982), xi. On this issue, I tend to side against Smith with Kevin Schilbrack, who, taking a critical-realist tack, cogently argues that though the concept of religion is a European product that is not ideologically pure, "it does not follow that the word is substantively empty or refers to nothing." "Religions: Are There Any?" *Journal of the American Academy of Religion* 78:4 (2010): 1132, and Terry F. Godlove, Jr., who justifies the methodological use of the concept of religion through a subtle analysis that draws deeply upon Kant to suggest that while concepts do not map out the essence of things, they remain indispensable to thought. Thus, attempts at defining and using the concept of religion do not reflect a supposed real essence of religion, nor are they merely stipulative definitions made up by the scholar or others for some specific purpose. Instead, they can be seen as nominalistic and pragmatic explications of how we use nested sets of more general and more specific concepts to make sense of experience. "Religion in General, not in Particular: A Kantian Meditation," *Journal of the American Academy of Religion* 78:4 (2010): 1025–47.

41 Paul J. Griffiths, "On the Future of the Study of Religion in the Academy." *Journal of the American Academy of Religion* 74:1 (March 2006): 66–74.

42 Masuzawa, *The Invention of World Religions*, xiv.

43 Griffiths, "On the Future of the Study of Religion in the Academy," 69. This view clearly contradicts antiessentialist views such as that articulated by Richard King, *Orientalism and Religion*, 11, 40–1.

44 Wilfred Cantwell Smith, *The Meaning and End of Religion*, 1st pb. edn (San Francisco: Harper & Row, 1978), 12, 13, 17–19, 50, 121, 125, 152, 194.

45 The history of the term *religion* as it developed from the Romans to the early nineteenth century is comprehensively charted by Peter Henrici in "The Concept of Religion from Cicero to Schleiermacher: Origins, History, and Problems with the Term" in Becker, Morali, and D'Costa, *Catholic Engagement with World Religions*, 1–22. See also the pioneering study by Wilfred Cantwell Smith in *The Meaning and End of Religion*, 15–79.

46 Henrici, The Concept of Religion from Cicero to Schleiermacher," 2, 4. According to Henrici, "Arnobius calls the Romans *patres novarum religionum* ("fathers of new religions") because of their assumption of foreign cults, . . ." (4).

47 Henrici, "The Concept of Religion from Cicero to Schleiermacher," 5–6.
48 Henrici, "The Concept of Religion from Cicero to Schleiermacher," 14.
49 John Hick, "The Next Step Beyond Dialogue" in *The Myth of Christian Superiority* (Maryknoll, NY: Orbis Books, 2005), 6. He also refers to them as "mutually exclusive groups, each based on its own proprietary gospel." John Hick, "Foreword by John Hick," in Wilfred Cantwell Smith, *The Meaning and End of Religion*. 1st edn (Minneapolis, MN: Fortress Press, 1991), x.
50 Richard King, *Orientalism and Religion: Postcolonial Theory, India, and the "Mystic East"* (London and New York: Routledge, 1999), 44–61, cogently argues for a middle ground between reductionistic etic approaches and "religionist" emic approaches to the study of religion.
51 Smith, *Imagining Religion*, xi.
52 Ian S. Markham, "A Religious Studies Approach to Questions about Religious Diversity," in Meister, *The Oxford Handbook of Religious Diversity*, 21, cogently expresses this principle: "A central goal of religious studies is to make sure that we are completely fair to the different traditions of the world."

1

Impasse in the Theology of Religions

The inclusivistic caricature of pluralism

The theology of religions, which is an emerging theological subdiscipline addressing issues raised by religious diversity, has reached an impasse.[1] The currently dominant inclusivist theologies of religions, which defend the inclusive finality of specific religions, have calcified and now spin inwardly in self-justificatory spirals—or perhaps epicycles—of increasingly self-consistent but dialogically barren arguments. S. Mark Heim, a leading antipluralist theologian of religions, equates the pluralist stance of liberal Christian theologies with the exclusivist stance of conservative theologies because both supposedly claim exclusive finality for their religious views.[2] Gavin D'Costa[3] and Aimee Upjohn Light[4] view theologies and philosophies of religious pluralism as covertly exclusivistic and triumphalistic because they promote as the one truth of all religions the claim that an essentialistic, universally applicable doctrine is the essence of all religions.[5] Naïve and cognitively imperialistic, pluralists are guilty, claim these antipluralists, of the same kind of exclusivistic thinking that they reject in others.[6] For example, Light characterizes the influential views of the leading pluralist, John Hick, as "a meta-position claiming to represent the world religions [that] actually contradicts them all."[7] In clever moves such as these, antipluralist theologians of religions have, for two decades now, tried to parody pluralist interpretations of the undeniable fact of religious diversity as self-contradictory and religiously imperialistic, or hegemonic, expressions of "liberal universalism."[8] Pluralist interpretations of religious diversity, conclude the antipluralists, should be dismissed as instances of the exclusivistic error that they were designed to counter, and theological inclusivisms centered upon tradition-specific beliefs should become the basis for theological reflection on the reality of religious diversity.

But this specious argument fails for two reasons: first, it relies on a strategic misreading of theories of religious pluralism as reducible either to the crypto-exclusivism ("All religions teach *x* and nothing else") that is the straw-man argument of many particularistic opponents of pluralism or to the crypto-inclusivism ("All religions are true") that defines *true* in generic terms, reflecting the definer's biases. But the theory of religious pluralism that will be outlined in these pages begins from the apophatic insight that human languages are incapable of generating a final and irreplaceable body of teachings about the nature of being, which eludes the power of language to express it exhaustively and definitively (an insight that has been reinforced in many of the world's leading mystical traditions). And given the limitations of language, the plurality of bodies of religious teachings follows as a matter of simple logic as well as a matter of historical fact.

Second, this specious, antipluralist argument can easily be turned against antipluralism itself: Since antipluralists claim that pluralism replaces the particularity of religious teachings with an essentialist doctrine toward which all religions supposedly point, antipluralists claim to know better than pluralists themselves what pluralists believe, which is a situation that, of course, no pluralist would accept. Ironically, this antipluralist claim that pluralism equals exclusivism is itself a form of exclusivism that claims to represent all forms of pluralism while actually contradicting most if not all of them. But an attempt to discredit antipluralism as exclusivism in this way is as sterile a move as the logically identical move of trying to undercut pluralism by calling it a form of exclusivism. *A priori* reasoning of this sort is a kind of intellectual activity at which religious apologists excel, whether in the epicycles of academic antipluralist apologetics or in the exclusivistic antipluralism of popular apologetics.

With the undermining of the claim that pluralism equals exclusivism, antipluralist inclusivism's only defense against pluralism dissolves, and, barring a retreat into exclusivism or obscurantism, the door opens to apophatic pluralism, which sees the rise of the world's many religious traditions and teachings as a logical outcome of the cultural and historical conditions that necessarily limit every form of religious language (appeals to revelation or to divine preservation of tradition are compromised by the fact that these kinds of claims have been made for many traditions). This plurality further implies that there can be no generally accepted, nontradition-specific method of determining which one of humanity's religious traditions, if any, is correct at the expense of the others. Nor can any religious tradition evade the departicularizing changes brought about by converts, heretics, the churning of syncretism, the formation of new religious movements, the development of hybrid religious personalities, and the supersession or annulment of older religious forms by new religious forms. Since no historically arising form of religious practice and conviction can permanently survive these processes intact, apophatic pluralism rules out the possibility that any religious tradition or interpretation of religion can gain universal acceptance or reasonably claim universality and finality for itself. Consequently, apophatic pluralism rules out every form of theological inclusivism as implausible and obscurantistic and asserts that inclusivism cannot be the basis for responsible reflection about the world's religious tradition.

Although inclusivism can be shown to be inadequate to the diversity of the world's religious traditions, the inclusivist parody of pluralism has become an article of common sense among leading inclusivist theologians of religions. This rise to dominance of inclusivism as the default theology of religions for many theologians is an unanticipated and ironic outcome for the theology of religions, which seemed to be boldly moving toward pluralism from its origins over 40 years ago. A glance at the recent history of the theology of religions will show how the field has landed in an inclusivist impasse.

The Copernican revolution in the theology of religions

Early in 1972, a time when virtually no Christian theologians were pluralists[9] and when the inclusivist moves of Vatican II still seemed bold and were at the edge of the conceivable, even in liberal Christian theologies, John Hick, a renowned theologian and philosopher of religion, boldly called for a revolution in theology as radical as Copernicus's revolution in astronomy.[10] Just as Copernicus had displaced the earth from the center of the universe in favor of the sun, Hick boldly removed Christianity from the center of what he called "the universe of faiths" in favor of God.[11] Hick ingeniously assailed stopgap interpretations of doctrine like Karl Rahner's notion of anonymous Christians and Hans Küng's distinction between the Catholic Church as the extraordinary means of salvation and other religions as ordinary means of salvation as theological analogues to the Ptolemaic epicycles that extended with increasing implausibility the explanatory power of geocentrism.[12] Hick pointed out that while these adaptations of doctrine are capable of limitless adaptation, they are ultimately "artificial," "burdensome," "antiquated," and "improbable."[13]

Although Hick's incisive criticism of theological inclusivism will stand the test of time, given the inevitable failure of every inclusivist *ad hoc* and *ex post facto* argument that tries to keep Christianity—or any other tradition—at the center of the universe of faith, it is likely that the call was issued too early for mainstream theology, since the reaction to the Copernican revolution has overall been more negative than positive.[14] And while numerous progressive, revisionist, and radical theologians heeded the call, many other theologians struggled against it, usually by attempting to turn the tables on the Copernican revolution by claiming that it is itself a form of exclusivism,[15] or by claiming that it would be unacceptable to all religious thinkers except for nondualist Vedāntists,[16] or by asserting that it postulates a concept of God that is empty of all content, thus opening the door to skepticism and noncognitivism.[17] So forceful was the counterassault on the Copernican revolution in theology from the middle and right wings of the theological spectrum that just ten years after its declaration, one of its leading foes, Gavin D'Costa, could boast that it is "widely thought that the debate [over the validity of the Copernican revolution] is today a dead one."[18]

While this may have seemed the final word about the Copernican revolution to some in 1983, the refusal to embrace pluralism in favor of renewed attempts to create inclusivist theologies of religions has led to the current impasse in the field in which inclusivist *tu quoque* rejections of pluralism as itself just a veiled and naïvely universalized expression of exclusivism have stalled all efforts to move beyond religious chauvinism. The only way forward for stalled inclusivist theologies of religions that want to avoid fideism or authoritarianism is to recognize the inevitability of pluralism, as Hick did, as well as the process of departicularization through which pluralism is actualized. As can be seen from the history of religions, this process of departicularization has always been at work, as for example in the startling claim of the Upaniṣads that the knower of *brahman* becomes the self (*ātman*) of the Vedic deities, thereby rendering these deities superfluous for the knower of brahman.[19]

Other examples of departicularization include the often ecstatic writings of the highly influential Christian mystical theologian Pseudo-Dionysius in which he calls upon a Trinity beyond being, goodness, and most daringly, beyond God (*hypertheos*), and in which he urges his readers to go beyond all of the seemly and unseemly images of cataphatic religion;[20] scholastic Christian theologian Meister Eckhart's distinction between the god (*got*) of conventional piety and the hidden depths of the godhead (*gotheit*), which led him to "ask God to free us from 'God'"[21]; the negation of conventional religious and philosophical language in the Kena Upaniṣad and the Daodejing; and the apophatic quest for a religious depth or ground beneath the façade of conventional religious imagery in the writings of recent theologians and spiritual writers including Paul Tillich, who wrote about "the God above God,"[22] Gordon Kaufman, who distinguished between "the available God" and "the real God,"[23] and Thomas Merton, who cultivated a protopluralist stance of apophatic openness to an inscrutable reality beyond the machinery of institutional religion and the ordinary economy of theology and Christian redemption.[24] It can also be seen in every movement that attempts to improve upon, supersede, overthrow, reinterpret, fulfill, or replace earlier forms of religion. Every cry of the reformer, heretic, or prophet, and every innovation of the theologian and religious thinker is an instance of departicularization and evidence for pluralism. And in any theological discussion of God conducted in a pluralistic setting, the apophatic pluralist insight will almost inevitably emerge, as when Harvard Indologist and scholar of religious pluralism Diana L. Eck reminds her readers that "the one we Christians call 'God' . . . transcends our imagining and is more mysterious than everything we think we mean."[25]

While all of these examples are controversial, and some of them have been subjected to vigorous attempts by orthodox thinkers to reinscribe the departicularizer within the outmoded system of images and doctrines,[26] the irrepressible energy whereby the new wine of the spirit bursts old wineskins[27] cannot finally be resisted, for it is simply an expression of the vitality and creativity latent within the spiritual intelligence of humanity. Indeed, the acceptance of pluralism and of departicularization can be seen as essential elements in the normal path of spiritual development, in which increasingly inadequate imagery of the spiritual dimension of life is replaced by newer, more vital imagery.

Crossing the theological Rubicon

In 1987, John Hick and Paul Knitter published a collection of essays, *The Myth of Christian Uniqueness: Toward a Pluralistic Theology of Religions*, which has achieved iconic status in the Christian theology of religions. In this book, Hick, Knitter, and their co-contributors boldly pushed the Copernican revolution a step further by taking the momentous step of crossing the "theological Rubicon"[28] through setting aside the "myth" of Christian absoluteness.[29] One consequence of this bold step was that Christian theology began demonstrating the philosophical and theological sensitivities needed to move decisively beyond the sad and morally disturbing legacy of Christian particularism, both exclusivistic and inclusivistic (as evidenced in an essay on the Goan Inquisition by Klaus Klostermaier).[30] Another consequence was a fundamental reorientation of liberal Christian theologies away from particularism toward pluralism, a move, however, that was quickly countered by the reversion of less liberal theologians to the current default position in the theology of religions of inclusivism.

Despite this rejection of pluralism by many theologians of religions and comparative theologians, the enduring strength of *The Myth of Christian Uniqueness* is its uncompromising demand, still relevant today, that absolutist interpretations of Christianity be dismissed as oppressive and unwarranted in light of the world's religious diversity. In brave and clear-eyed essays, leading theologians envisioned a new path for Christian theology in its dealing with the religions of the world. For example, Wilfred Cantwell Smith forcefully rejected the "idolatry" of Christian finality,[31] while Gordon D. Kaufman stressed the inescapably historical character of the many "frame[s] of orientation" that human creativity and imagination have shaped in the face of the mystery of life.[32] And Langdon Gilkey traced a dialectic of the infinite and the particular in which "no cultural logos is final and therefore universal (even one based on science); no one revelation is or can be the universal criterion for all the others (even, so we are now seeing, Christian revelation)."[33]

Besides generating widespread rejection from exclusivists and inclusivists, this book also inspired successor volumes such as Gavin D'Costa's edited volume, *Christian Uniqueness Reconsidered: The Myth of a Pluralistic Theology of Religions*,[34] which resisted the movement toward pluralism, and Knitter's later edited volume, *The Myth of Religious Superiority: A Multifaith Exploration*,[35] which views the quest for pluralism from the perspective of the world's leading religions. But because *The Myth of Christian Uniqueness* is a collection of essays offering a set of creative but diverse proposals for overcoming particularism, it lacked the unity of a single pluralist proposal that could chart a clear path across the theological Rubicon toward a widely accepted and workable theory of religious pluralism.

John Hick's pluralistic hypothesis

The most influential proposal for a way forward across the theological Rubicon was subsequently developed by John Hick in *An Interpretation of Religion: Human Responses to the Transcendent*,[36] which is based on his 1986–87 Gifford Lectures in which he systematized the philosophical views on religious pluralism that he had worked out in a series of influential essays and books published since his first call for a Copernican revolution in 1972. In this, the most significant work to date by a Christian philosopher on religious pluralism, Hick comprehensively laid out a new philosophical interpretation of religious pluralism, which he calls the "pluralistic hypothesis." Taking his cue from the critical philosophy of Kant, Hick sees humanity's many religious traditions as phenomenal expressions of the noumenal Real. Shifting his emphasis in earlier works from ascertaining the meaningfulness of religious beliefs and myths to ethical considerations, Hick now proposed to judge the worth of religious traditions through the "soteriological criterion," which measures a tradition's capacity for actualizing "saintliness."[37] Although the pluralistic hypothesis was forcefully, if wrongly, rejected by particularistic theologians as an instance of the very exclusivism it rejected and was also challenged on philosophical grounds for its interpretation of Kant,[38] the pluralistic hypothesis will likely long remain the most influential Western attempt to make philosophical sense of humanity's religious diversity. It makes no compromises with halfway, *ad hoc*, *ex post facto* attempts to preserve a special place for Jesus, the Bible, or Christianity at the table of the world's religion—or what Knitter calls the religious "community of communities."[39] Because it stresses the conceptual unknowability of the noumenal Real along with its effectiveness as productive of saintliness, Hick's pluralistic hypothesis is an essential foundation for the apophatic pluralism proposed in these pages. My version of pluralism, in common cause with Hick and apophatic philosophers, theologians, and mystics of numerous traditions, recognizes the variability and thus the impermanence of humanity's many poetic attempts to name the unnamable, which is nevertheless felt as a power of spiritual illumination and sanctification in human life.

Coming to terms with the pluralist revolution

In the wake of the theistic Copernican revolution in theology and the posttheistic pluralist hypothesis in philosophy of religions, a flood tide of mostly theological proposals attempted to accommodate or, more usually, to reject the versions of pluralism outlined by John Hick, whose name seems to have become synonymous with pluralism, and by Paul Knitter, the leading Catholic pluralist (or "mutualist"[40]) who has moved further along the path of pluralism into experiences of hybrid religious identities blending Christianity and Buddhism.[41] These proposals have mostly resisted the implications of pluralism, as will be seen from the following examples.

Post-Copernican Protestant exclusivisms

The rise of pluralistic philosophies and theologies of religions has inspired fundamentalist and traditionalistic rejections of pluralism. Sadly, but predictably, an uncompromising exclusivism continues at the level of popular evangelicalism in the USA (and wherever this religious tradition is influential). These fundamentalistic forms of Protestant orthodoxy, aided by apologetic strategies developed in early classical Protestantism, continue to promote the absolute rejection of the value of other religions as well as most other variants of Christianity. It is not uncommon in the USA to encounter evangelical Protestants who are convinced that nonevangelical Christians are *ipso facto* doomed to eternal damnation. Even trained theologians and philosophers among evangelicals in the USA rarely stray from the position of what I call "unreformed exclusivism" because it steadfastly maintains the exclusive truth of specific forms of Christianity. This position is typified by figures such as Ronald Nash,[42] Albert Mohler,[43] William Lane Craig,[44] and Alvin Plantinga. Plantinga, the most well-known unreformed exclusivist, is inalterably opposed to pluralism and sees it as "a manifestation of our miserable condition" caused by cognitive dimming due to sin and the fact that Christians and non-Christians are not "epistemic peers."[45] Plantinga's arguments for exclusivism and against Hick's pluralist hypothesis are grounded in attempts to begin from what he defines as a "properly basic belief" about the God of Christian doctrine and tradition "that just arises within us"[46] and whose truth or "warrant" is apparent only to those holding it.[47] As pointed out by Peter Byrne, such an antieveidentialist approach to questions of religious truth certainly relieves the Reformed philosopher of having to engage in apologetic strife with atheists, agnostics, and theorists of other religions and allows those taking this approach to rest assured in the internal certainty that their beliefs provide.[48] But Plantinga's argument gives away as much as it gets from this strategy, since antievidentialism can also justify the properly basic beliefs that arise in other traditions as well as in the home tradition. Thus, in strict agreement with its own grounding principle, an argument such as this will be persuasive only to those who are inclined to be persuaded by it.

Another learned figure who fits into the unreformed exclusivist category is evangelical theologian Ronald Nash, who articulated what he thought of as a biblically mandated exclusivism[49] (a stance, however, that doesn't seem mandated by the Hebrew Bible, when read through the lenses of the Noahic code, the stories about Ruth and the prophet Jonah, as well as the theistic universalism of Isaiah and other prophets. Biblical exclusivism can be justified only on the basis of a few overinterpreted passages in the New Testament, which will be considered in Chapter 6). Because of his narrow reading of the Bible, Nash thinks that the only biblically acceptable stance for orthodox Christians is an exclusivism that sees all alternatives such as pluralism and inclusivism and all religions other than orthodox Christianity as categorically false.[50]

An academic evangelical apologist who must be placed almost in a category of his own is Steven Tsoukalas,[51] who is the rare exclusivist who has scholarly competence in a religion other than the home tradition. Although Tsoukalas compares Christian patristic writings and Hindu *śāstra* in the original languages, he nevertheless subjects Hinduism one-sidedly to criticism from the standpoint of classical Protestant apologetics without a corresponding consideration of the possibility that Hinduism can offer a cogent critique of Christianity. This approach, which combines a technical knowledge of another tradition with traditional Christian exclusivism, is a position that I call "renewed exclusivism," because it is offered by a scholar who has scholarly competence in a tradition other than the home tradition.

In contrast, then, to these expressions of exclusivism, it is encouraging to see tentative moves toward inclusivism among a few of the more daring evangelical theologians, an event that is as notable in the evangelical world as was the earlier emergence of inclusivism among Catholics during Vatican II. Evangelical Protestant theologians of religions whose thought is trending in this direction include the late

Clark H. Pinnock[52] Terrance L. Tiessen,[53] and Hendrik Vroom.[54] Also, it seems appropriate to place the analytical Christian philosopher Paul K. Moser in this group.[55] While retaining a bedrock commitment to the ultimacy of Christ, these approaches strain toward inclusivism as far as a strictly christocentric position will allow. I call this position "chastened exclusivism" because these theorists display an inclusivist or even pluralistic sensitivity to the people, teachings, and practices of religious traditions other than their own, even while maintaining the normativity and finality of Christ.

Post-Copernican pluralisms

Roger Haight

While pluralism is no longer a controversial position among progressive Protestant theologians, it remains a challenge for Catholic theologians, who have mostly remained inclusivists. One Catholic figure who has boldly moved into pluralism is Roger Haight, who has charted a daring course for a Jesuit theologian. After rejecting in *Jesus: Symbol of God* the beliefs that Christianity is "the superior religion" that inhabits "the center into which all others are to be drawn" and that Christ is "the absolute center to which all other historical mediations are relative,"[56] claims for which he was censured by the Vatican,[57] in *The Future of Christology*, Haight lays out the logic of an orthodox christology that is also pluralist, since, as he holds, "what God has done in Jesus, God can do in other religious mediations and does."[58] Although his retention of theistic language may seem to require placing Haight in the ranks of the inclusivists, this would be a mistake, since his intention is thoroughly apophatic and pluralistic, even if he, as a Christian pluralist, retains a theistic and Christian language in his own formulations of a religious truth that must remain mysterious and ineffable. This pluralist view is entailed by the belief that God has willed the salvation of all people (1 Tim. 2.4). But if this salvation is not merely eschatological, then this divine intention must take the social form of a multiplicity of religions.[59] Indeed, were there not a plurality of religions, God's will could not be effective in history, since, clearly, Christianity is neither absolute nor exhaustive.[60] Furthermore, Christianity requires the other religions, since, taken as a whole, they together mediate more of the divine than any one religion, including Christianity, can do on its own.[61] Yet, this remains a *Christian* pluralism, since, in Haight's view, each religion, including Christianity, makes universal and normative claims that, to the degree that they are true, are "relevant to all" people.[62]

Consistent with this stance, Haight makes a claim that is virtually identical with the apophatic pluralism outlined in this book: "From the transcendence of ultimate reality, or God, it follows that no religion in the sense of a set of religious truths can adequately portray its object."[63] In Haight's view, religious knowledge (and so, necessarily, religious language) is "mysterious, mediated, and dialogical" because it has to do with a transcendent mystery that is incomprehensible and unfathomable. Thus, rather than holding up any one version of religious knowledge as final and absolute, Haight sees all expressions of religious knowledge as mystagogical and dialectical. Such a stance implies the pluralistic claim that "no single salvific mediation can encompass God's reality or human understanding of it."[64] By his own example, then, Haight shows that it is possible to adopt an apophatic pluralist view of religious diversity while continuing to use the traditional language of the tradition within which one remains as a committed practitioner. Whether one will be accepted as such by fellow practitioners is a separate question, one that, at least officially, has been answered in the negative in the case of Haight.

S. Mark Heim

One of the most forceful criticisms of the pluralisms of Hick, Knitter, and Cantwell Smith is S. Mark Heim's charge that they are covert exclusivists who propose to replace the distinctive objects, or "salvations," of the many religions with their own particular plans or themes.[65] They are thus exclusivists in spite of themselves.[66] Heim rejects Hick's pluralism as a pseudopluralism covertly promoting a nonpluralistic reliance on a singular, absolute reality, the Real in itself, a stance that contradicts the self-understanding of virtually all specific religious traditions.[67] In opposition to this covertly exclusivistic pluralism, Heim argues for "a true religious pluralism" that rejects a single soteriological intension as the aim of the different religions.[68] This "orientational pluralism,"[69] as he calls it, is, essentially, a form of inclusivism, for, as he insists, "all theories of religion are either exclusivist or inclusivist in nature."[70] Since every pluralism, on this view, is actually the perspective of an individual, no pluralism can be taken as the position of the sighted person among the blind people in the ancient elephant parable.[71] Although orientational pluralists will continue to see "their tradition's religious ultimate at the center," they will hold open the possibility that the religious goods of people of other religions could, though seen as penultimate, still somehow "endure as the religious fulfillments of those who pursue various religious ends."[72] Out of respect for the particularistic integrity and finality of individual religious traditions, Heim lays aside attempts to generalize over these traditions to a common soteriological intension,[73] and he calls for a pluralism of diverse religious ends, or "salvations," in which each religion lays out its own incommensurate vision of the end of the religious life.[74] In this way, writing as a Christian theologian of religions, Heim attempts simultaneously to recognize "the decisive and universal significance of Christ" as well as the "particularistic integrity" of other religious traditions.[75] He thinks that he can do this since, in his view, Christian finality and the validity of other ways are not "mutually exclusive."[76]

The strength of Heim's proposal is its stressing, against overly generalized theories of religious similarity, the irreducible particularity of religious traditions, movements, and bodies of teaching and practices (similarly to contextualist or constructivist philosophers of mysticism such as Steven T. Katz and Robert M. Gimello). Its weakness, however, is that it fails to resolve the question of how religions relate to one another, which is the most fundamental question motivating the theology of religions. Were we to follow Heim in merely leaving the traditions in unresolved tension with each other, we would find ourselves in a situation worse than that of traditional exclusivism, since we would now find ourselves surrounded on all sides by religious traditions promoting irresolvable final religious ends. This seems as unworkable and as unjustifiable as a relativism that simply allows all claims about theoretical questions to stand as they are in their own self-presentation as final and absolute, a situation that leaves the question of truth unmet and unanswered. But if, as Heim seems to allow, the diverse ultimate goods of the different traditions are grounded in the noumenal realm,[77] then the question about which of these "salvations" is closer to the truth will remain an open one. Heim seems to acknowledge this problem, since he steps back from the idea that reality might finally support multiple ultimate, but utterly discrepant, solipsistic salvations when he allows that some of the currently distinctive traditions may "collapse together in some further state."[78]

Jeffery D. Long

Taking his stand in the highly influential but often maligned (at least by academic religion scholars and particularist theologians of religions) Neo-Vedānta tradition of Sri Ramakrishna, Jeffery D. Long persuasively argues for a broadly conceived form of Neo-Vedāntic pluralism that does not presuppose the truth or falsity of any position while holding to the integrity, if incompleteness, of particular visions of truth.[79] In a vision of pluralism that is also indebted to India's ancient self-conscious pluralists, the Jains, as well as to various process philosophers and theologians, Long sees each tradition as offering a piece of a puzzle that is in the process of being worked (my own completion of his metaphor). This philosophically astute theology of religions attempts to blunt any tendency to relativism in pluralism by retaining the inclusivist insistence that, despite their inevitable limitations, each tradition should honor others as a piece of the puzzle while firmly holding onto its own puzzle piece.[80]

This is not a pluralism that can be dismissed as just the idiosyncratic musings of a creative yet unaffiliated individual. On the contrary, Long takes his stand on the tradition of Neo-Vedānta, as powerfully envisioned by Sri Ramakrishna, as proclaimed by Swami Vivekananda, and as faithfully pursued and maintained by the monks and nuns of the Ramakrishna Order and the Vedanta Society for over a century. This is a pluralistic synthesis that is unparalleled in its influence, especially in the West, but also in India, as testified not only by resistance to it by constructivist and particularistic religious academicians and theologians of religions,[81] but also by its influence upon mainstream religious life in the West, which, especially in the USA, has moved decisively in the last 50 years toward universalism and pluralism (trends detectable even within evangelicalism, the most pluralistically resistant area of American religious life, which has responded by criticizing and sometimes condemning yoga and Neo-Vedāntic pluralism and by retreating into self-consciously particularistic theologies of religions).

The strengths of Long's position are its insistence that pluralism does not imply relativism, its respect for diverse bodies of religious teaching as offering truth-claims worthy of consideration, and its finding a model for a significant form of pluralism in the venerable Neo-Vedānta of Sri Ramakrishna. A weakness is its insistence, even if tentatively, that one's own piece of the puzzle is true, which brings a needlessly inclusivistic element into this attempt to do pluralism. Essential to a philosophically viable version of pluralism is the recognition that even one's most deeply held conviction may, despite the best efforts of apologetics, turn out to be unfounded. It could, after all be the case that materialism is correct despite all the arguments, experiences, and realizations that religious people produce as evidence to the contrary. To put this in terms of the famous Jain and Buddhist parable of the blind people and the elephant, there may not actually be an elephant there for the blind people to touch, since even the people telling them that they are touching an elephant may also be mistaken, deceived, or subject to an illusion.[82]

The dead-end of inclusivism

As a position in the theology of religions, pluralism seems, for now at least, to have peaked with the work of Hick in philosophy, and Hick and Knitter in the theology of religions. Subsequent pluralist proposals have been few, and even these have been marked by compromises with inclusivism, as is clear in the proposals of Heim and Long. It seems, then, that the massive rejection of pluralism in mainstream theology of religions has been effective, although the price of this victory has been stalemate and impasse. For now at least, and perhaps for a while longer, D'Costa's boast in 1984 that the Copernican revolution is over appears to be justified. But this will be a short-lived victory, since the flow of history and change will undercut the basis of all current inclusivisms as surely as mountains erode under the steady pressure of the elements.

That this gradual displacement of current inclusivisms is underway is evidenced by the reality that in the wider stream of liberal Christian theologies, pluralism has become the uncontroversial default theology-of-religions position, thus rendering obsolete the question of the validity of religions other than the home tradition.[83] And because popular exclusivism, which has virtually no audience among academic theologians, has been forcefully reasserting exclusivism in the face of an ever more religiously pluralistic global culture by the use of threadbare apologetic arguments, no respectable path to a real exclusivism remains open for mainstream theology of religions (as was still on the edge of plausibility for Hendrik Kraemer at the International Missionary Council conference in Tambaram in 1938). Thus, the imagination of contemporary theology of religions has come to be dominated and limited by inclusivist positions, even to the point of reaching an impasse in which regression to exclusivism is clearly impossible on ethical, theological, historical, and philosophical grounds and the path to a genuine pluralism seems closed.[84] Because inclusivism is the dominant stance of the field and because numerous leading figures have sponsored some version of inclusivism, a survey of inclusivism's varieties, proponents, and weaknesses deserves a chapter of its own.

Notes

1 Catherine Cornille also speaks about an impasse in the theology of religions. "Introduction," in Catherine Cornille, ed. *Many Mansions? Multiple Religious Belonging and Christian Identity* (Maryknoll, NY: Orbis Books, 2002), 5. Earlier, James L. Fredericks noted that the theology of religions had reached an impasse because the critics of pluralist theologies of religion had, in his view, successfully exposed the inadequacies of pluralism, just as the pluralists had previously been successful in pointing out the inadequacies of exclusivism and inclusivism. *Faith Among the Faiths: Christian Theology and Non-Christian Religions* (New York/ Mahwah, NJ: Paulist Press, 1999), 8.

2 S. Mark Heim, *The Depth of the Riches: A Trinitarian Theology of Religious Ends* (Grand Rapids, MI: Eerdmans, 2001), 17. A less stringent variant of antipluralism identifies pluralism with inclusivism, apparently because it is assumed that pluralist stances always embody a substantive claim that reflects the covert religious biases of the pluralist (see, e.g., Kiblinger, "Relating Theology of Religions and Comparative Theology," in Clooney, *The New Comparative Theology*, 27). As will become clear in these pages, apophatic pluralism makes no such claim.

3 Gavin D'Costa appears to have pioneered the claim that pluralists are anonymous exclusivists. "The Impossibility of a Pluralist View of Religions," *Religious Studies* 32 (June 1996): 223–32; see also D'Costa, *The Meeting of Religions and the Trinity* (Maryknoll, NY: Orbis Books, 2000), 3, 19–20, and 22; and D'Costa, *Christianity and World Religions: Disputed Questions in the Theology of Religions* (Oxford, Chichester, UK, and Malden, MA: Wiley-Blackwell, 2009), 10–12, 18.

4 Aimee Upjohn Light, "Harris, Hick, and the Demise of the Pluralistic Hypothesis," *Journal of Ecumenical Studies* 44 (Summer, 2009): 467–70.

5 The increasingly common rejection of such pluralist approaches as Hick's as a form of the "liberal universalism" that grounds twentieth-century comparative religion and the older comparative theology is expressed in Reid B. Locklin and Hugh Nicholson, "The Return of Comparative Theology," *Journal of the American Academy of Religion* 78(2): 480, 482. See also Gavin D'Costa, "Christ, Revelation and the World Religions," in T. W. Bartel, ed. *Comparative Theology: Essays for Keith Ward* (London: SPCK, 2003), 35.

6 As in the increasingly common rejection by postmodernist particularists of pluralist approaches like Hick's as a form of the "liberal universalism" that grounds twentieth-century comparative religion and the older comparative theology. This view is expressed, for example, by Reid B. Locklin and Hugh Nicholson in "The Return of Comparative Theology," 480, 482.

7 Light, "Harris, Hick," p. 468. This seems to be an instance of what S. Wesley Ariarajah calls "ritual Hick-bashing" (S. Wesley Ariarajah in "Power, Politics, and Plurality," in *The Myth of Religious Superiority*, 191), which are all too common in writings in the theology of religions, perhaps because Hick's Copernican revolution in theology is a view that likely will be perceived as the default position in responsible theologies of religions in the future, should human societies in continuity with ours continue, and as Christianity inevitably loses its central religious position in its traditional cultural homes (which may be delayed a millennium or so due to the spread of Christianity outside its traditional borders).

8 Reid B. Locklin and Hugh Nicholson, "The Return of Comparative Theology," 480, 482. Paul Knitter offers a cogent critique of the postmodernist rejection of pluralism as just another particularism in "Is the Pluralist Model a Western Imposition? A Response in Five Voices," in Paul Knitter, ed. *The Myth of Religious Superiority* (Maryknoll, NY: Orbis Books, 2005), 29, 33. An example of a fallacious *tu quoque* argument of this type that can easily be turned on itself is found in Hugh Nicholson's *Comparative Theology and the Problem of Religious Rivalry* (New York: Oxford University Press, 2011), where Nicholson rejects Wilfred Cantwell Smith's pluralism, as well as the "cognate" pluralism of John Hick, by accusing them of negating exclusivism through an unacknowledged act of exclusion, thereby contradicting themselves by failing to acknowledge their own particularity. It would almost be too tedious to point out that making general claims about "liberal universalism" is itself a general critique of essentialized positions, one that makes an exclusive claim, which, in this case, is the view that everything is fundamentally political. Of course, many religionists might resist a hegemonic and "exclusory" discourse cloaked in the expert language of political theorists that claims that the political is as fundamental an aspect of human life as the spiritual (5–8). (As an aside, it seems extremely odd to characterize exclusivistic positions as merely "polemical," but the views of courageous and pioneering pluralists such as Cantwell Smith and Hick as "hegemonic" [8].)

9 Anticipation of the full-blown pluralism advocated by John Hick can be seen in the historicism of Troeltsch, which sadly lurches back into a fitful inclusivism after carefully decoupling religious normativity from the traditional orthodox apologetic of revelation and historical miracles and from any specific historical expression of the concept of religion as articulated in their different ways by Schleiermacher and Hegel. Ernst Troeltsch, *The Absoluteness of Christianity and the History of Religions*, trans. David Reid (Richmond, VA: John Knox Press, 1971), 57, 158–63. This early and subtle move toward pluralism, which had numerous counterparts in the liberal Protestant theologies of a century ago, was inaugurated by Schleiermacher in 1799 when, in a move of extraordinary prescience and boldness for the time, he implicitly affirmed a pluralism grounded in the historical character of all forms of religiosity. Consistent with the pluralist claim that humanity is finite while religion is infinite, Schleiermacher, as far as a Christian inclusivism pressed to its absolute limit will allow him, grants that there can be other mediators of salvation besides Jesus Christ and asserts that the historical process that sponsored the rise of the Christian Bible cannot rule out the rise of other Bibles, or bodies of sacred scriptures. Friedrich Schleiermacher, *On Religion: Speeches to its Cultured Despisers*, trans. Richard Crouter (Cambridge: Cambridge University Press, 1988), 191, 220. Whatever he may have thought of this bold view later in life, and neglected as it has been by mainstream theologians (though similar ideas were taken in a more radical and consistent direction by Ralph Waldo Emerson in his "An Address" at Harvard Divinity School in 1838), it remains as a clear recognition of the pluralism that is inherent in human religiosity as expressed in varied human historical and cultural forms. Echoing both Schleiermacher and his own teacher Troeltsch, Paul Tillich in a lecture given at the end of his career affirmed that particular religions lose their own importance when one penetrates to their depths, where they are seen as pointers to the "spiritual presence" that he eloquently and in complete accord with

patristic theology names the "God above God." *Christianity and the Encounter of the World Religions* (New York; Columbia University Press, 1961), 97, 91. And, most importantly for Hick, Wilfred Cantwell Smith's now canonical distinction between faith and cumulative tradition, which he articulated in *The Meaning and End of Religion* (156), led Hick to question the idea that there is one true religion. *God Has Many Names* (Philadelphia, PA: The Westminster Press, 1982), 18.

10 Hick first issued his call for a Copernican revolution in theology in his Carrs Lane Church Centre public lectures in February and March 1972 in Birmingham, England. The following year, these lectures were published in *God and the Universe of Faiths: Essays in the Philosophy of Religion* (London: Macmillan, 1973), 120–32.

11 John Hick, "The Copernican Revolution in Theology," in *God and the Universe of Faiths: Essays in the Philosophy of Religion* (London: Macmillan, 1973), 8, 125–30; I summarize this move in *Knowing the Real*, 66–9.

12 Hick, "The Copernican Revolution in Theology," 129.

13 Hick, "The Copernican Revolution in Theology," 125. He later referred to them as "palliatives." "Foreword by John Hick," in Wilfred Cantwell Smith, *The Meaning and End of Religion*, 1991 ed., vi.

14 As shown in the almost comical situation that essays and books in the theology of religions often begin with a repudiation of Hick's work in this area. Not only are these instances of the "ritual Hick-bashing" mentioned in an earlier footnote, but they are clear evidence that religious pluralism poses, alongside materialist rejections of religion altogether, the gravest threat to the self-confidence of particularist interpreters of religion.

15 As argued, for example, by Julius Lipner, who claims that Hick rejects Christ's irreducibility "as emphatically as the absolutist" requires the avowal of Christ. "Does Copernicus Help? Reflections for a Christian Theology of Religions," *Religious Studies* 13 (1977): 252. But the pluralist can respond that while it is absolutistic to claim that any one religious vision is final for all human beings, it is not absolutistic to point out—even if stated forcefully—that such claims cannot secure assent for themselves beyond the circle of those inclined to agree with them.

16 As argued by Duncan B. Forrester, who fails to distinguish between theistic and nondualist Vedāntists in his claim that Hick's approach is "unlikely to be acceptable to committed believers except for Vedantic Hindus." "Professor Hick and the Universe of Faiths," *Scottish Journal of Theology* 29 (1976): 69.

17 As claimed by Gavin D'Costa, *John Hick's Theology of Religions: A Critical Evaluation* (Lanham, MD: University Press or America, 1987), 170, 184. I also made this claim in *Knowing the Real* (112, 117) when I claimed that Hick's reliance on what he calls the noumenal Real leads to theological noncognitivism, a position that I now see as inadequate, since Hick, as I also noted in *Knowing the Real* (117), appealed ultimately to what he calls the soteriological criterion to distinguish between more or less true religious views. While, at that time, I characterized this as a "thin ethical assertion" (117), I now see it as a far more reliable indicator of the worthiness of a religious tradition than bodies of variable and irreconcilable quasispeculative, cataphatic doctrinal teachings, since the saintlier a person is, the less likely she or he is to have religious enemies or to divide humanity along sectarian lines. The saints of all traditions will be more like each other in this respect and less likely to be guardians of dogma who reject or patronize others for merely doctrinal reasons.

18 Gavin D'Costa, "John Hick's Copernican Revolution: Ten Years After," *New Blackfriars* 65 (July 1984): 323–31.
19 Bṛhadāraṇyaka Upaniṣad 1.4.10.
20 *Pseudo-Dionysius. The Mystical Theology*, in *The Complete Works*, trans. Colm Luibheid (Mahwah, NJ: Paulist Press, 1987), 997A–1000A; 1032D–1048B. For *hypertheos*, see Dionysius Areopagita, *De Mystica theologia*, 1048B. This radically nonsubstantive view of how things are beyond the mediating and limiting powers of language verges on the ontological openness of Buddhist *prajñāpāramitā* literature. As Kevin Hart writes, "Dionysius does not think of God as a being: it is just that image which his negative theology is concerned to deconstruct." Since "the mystic does not deny reason, memory, or the will; he or she situates them with respect to a far wider configuration." *The Trespass of the Sign: Deconstruction, Theology, and Philosophy* (Cambridge: Cambridge University Press, 1989), 267.
21 *Meister Eckhart: Selected Writings*, trans. Oliver Davies (New York: Penguin Books, 1994), Sermon 22 (DW 52, W87), 205. Oliver Davies, *The God Within: The Mystical Tradition of Northern Europe* (revised edn). (Hyde Park, NY: New City Press, 2006), 45–6.
22 Paul Tillich, *The Courage to Be* (2nd edn). (New Haven, CT: Yale University Press, 2000) 15, 187.
23 Gordon D. Kaufman, *God the Problem* (Cambridge, MA: Harvard University Press, 1972), 86.
24 See, for example, *Contemplative Prayer* (New York: Doubleday, 1971), 24–5, 76–8, 81–2, 85, 92–3, 98–116.
25 Diana L. Eck, *Encountering God: A Spiritual Journey from Bozeman to Banaras* (Boston, MA: Beacon Press: 2003; originally published 1993), xv.
26 As can be seen in the case of Eckhart in Oliver Davies, *Meister Eckhart: Selected Writings*, xvii; *God Within*, 39–40, 71–2. Despite belated and unconvincing attempts to render Eckhart a misunderstood orthodox theologian, Eckhart's near nondualism, as evident particularly in his German sermons, supports an essentializing (or Platonizing) and dehistoricizing reinterpretation of Christian doctrine that has affinities to the approaches of Hegel, Schopenhauer, Schleiermacher, Heidegger, and Bultmann. The parallels with the teaching of the Upaniṣadic Yājñavalkya are also striking (BU 2.4 and 4.5; see also 1.4.10 for a similarly radical apophatic teaching). Even though Davies's translation in the Penguin Classics series attempts to render Eckhart orthodox, the strong tendency of Eckhart's sermons and mystical thought to divest the mystical experience of reliance upon created things like doctrine, concepts, and institutions is there for all to see. This can also be seen in Davies's discussion of *Wesenmystik* (*God Within*, 3–4, 192–3), which, along with Advaita Vedānta and Buddhism's *prajñāpāramitā* literature, boldly contravenes the received imagery of the home tradition. This leads to Luther, of course, but more radically, it moves beyond him toward D. T. Suzuki and the later writings of Thomas Merton (a latent aspect of Eckhart's thought that Davies acknowledges, *God Within*, 72). The attempt to reinscribe Eckhart within orthodoxy is an approach that is unduly deferential to traditional authorities and is an interpretative holding pattern, for Eckhart, following the more radical apophatic mystics, is a doorway—or "a bridge figure" in the words of Davies (*God Within*, 72)—that leads out of external, exclusive, doctrinaire religiosity into the universality of the pluralistic, apophatic

mystical experience that has no native land, language, or era. That Eckhart affirmed his orthodoxy after being accused of heresy was to be expected in the climate of totalitarian religious oppression that prevailed in thirteenth-century Europe. What is more astonishing is the boldness, whose price we can barely imagine today in religiously free societies, that allowed Eckhart to draw close to the views of the Brethren of the Free Spirit and of Marguerite de Porete, who was burned along with her book, *Le mirouer des simples âmes et anéanties*, at the command of Eckhart's onetime neighbor in Paris, as noted by Davies, *God Within*, 69.

27 See Mk 2.22; Mt. 9.17; Lk. 5.37-38.

28 John Hick, "The Non-Absoluteness of Christianity," in John Hick and Paul F. Knitter, *The Myth of Christian Uniqueness*, 22. Knitter referred to "the somewhat labored image of the Rubicon" in the preface to this volume (ix). Knitter more recently has characterized this step as a "religious Rubicon" in *The Myth of Religious Superiority*, ii.

29 Hick and Knitter, *The Myth of Christian Uniqueness*, vii.

30 Klaus K. Klostermaier, "Facing Hindu Critique of Christianity," *Journal of Ecumenical Studies* 44 (Summer 2009): 461–6.

31 Wilfred Cantwell Smith, "Idolatry: In Comparative Perspective," in Hick and Knitter, *Myth of Christian Uniqueness*, 61.

32 Gordon D. Kaufman, "Religious Diversity, Historical Consciousness, and Christian Theology," in Hick and Knitter, *The Myth of Christian Uniqueness*, 8, 9.

33 Langdon Gilkey, "Plurality and its Theological Implications," in Hick and Knitter, *The Myth of Christian Uniqueness*, 48.

34 Maryknoll, NY: Orbis Books, 1990.

35 Maryknoll, NY: Orbis Books, 2005.

36 New Haven, CT: Yale University Press, 1989; 2nd edn. 2004.

37 For more detail on these claims about Hick, see Kenneth Rose, *Knowing the Real: John Hick on the Cognitivity of Religions and Religious Pluralism* (New York: Peter Lang Publishing, 1996).

38 Alvin Plantinga, for example, tries to exploit differences on the noumenal-phenomenal distinction between Kant, whom he sees as more favorably disposed to traditional god-talk, and Hick, whom he sees as allowing only formal and negative properties to the Real *an sich*. *Warranted Christian Belief* (New York: Oxford University Press, 2000), 47. Plantinga finds this position incoherent, but that seems to be due to his consistently misunderstanding the Real *an sich* as similar in kind, if of greater magnitude, to finite entities, such as tricycles and a mendacious letter-writer comparing herself to a world-class tennis star and a tenor like Pavarotti (45, 50). This invalid move seems to be identical to Guanilo's attempt to undermine Anselm's ontological argument by likening the reality than which nothing greater can be thought to an island, a move that Plantinga has elsewhere rejected. *God, Freedom, and Evil* (Grand Rapids, MI: Eerdmans, 1974), 90. I take up Hick's use of Kant in *Knowing the Real*, 10–12, 42, 72–80, 110–14.

39 Paul F. Knitter "My God is Bigger than Your God! Time for Another Axial Shift in the History of Religions," *Studies in Interreligious Dialogue* 17: 1 (2007): 101. Knitter also makes use of the table metaphor for interreligious dialogue in "Is the Pluralist Model a Western Imposition?" Knitter, *The Myth of Religious Superiority*, 35.

40 Paul F. Knitter, "My God is Bigger than Your God!" 100.

41 Knitter writes about his fundamental indebtedness as a Catholic to Buddhism in *Without Buddha I Could Not Be a Christian* (Oxford: One World, 2009). This is part of a trend in which Christian dogmatic and spiritual theologians, including Knitter, Thomas Merton, Henri Le Saux (as Swami Abhishiktananda), and numerous Catholic Zen masters present themselves as beginners to leading figures in other religions like Hinduism and Buddhism and take initiation into sacred traditions completely different from their home traditions.
42 *Is Jesus the Only Savior?* (Grand Rapids, MI: Zondervan, 1994).
43 See, for example, the controversial post on his blog, "The Subtle Body — Should Christians Practice Yoga?" accessed May 19, 2012, www.albertmohler.com/2010/09/20/the-subtle-body-should-christians-practice-yoga/.
44 William Lane Craig, "No Other Name: A Middle Knowledge Perspective on the Exclusivity of Salvation through Christ," in *The Philosophical Challenge of Religious Diversity*, eds. Phillip L. Quinn and Kevin Meeker (New York, Oxford: Oxford University Press, 2000), 38–53.
45 Plantinga, *Warranted Christian Belief*, 438, 443–4 (quoted words from 456, 455). The weakness of this ad hominem argument is that, in different words, it can be applied to religious others by adherents of any doctrine that requires a special illumination in order to be comprehended.
46 Plantinga, *Warranted Christian Belief*, 175.
47 Plantinga, *Warranted Christian Belief*, xi, 136, 153, 455–6.
48 Peter Byrne, "A Philosophical Approach to Questions About Religious Diversity," in Meister, *The Oxford Handbook of Religious Diversity*, 32–5.
49 Nash, *Is Jesus the Only Savior?* 12–17.
50 Nash, *Is Jesus the Only Savior?* 19, 21, 24–5, 99–100, 117–36, 106, 149, 169–72.
51 *Kṛṣṇa and Christ: Body-Divine Relation in the Thought of Śaṅkara, Rāmānuja, and Classical Christian Orthodoxy* (Milton Keynes: Paternoster, 2006).
52 Clark H. Pinnock, *A Wideness in God's Mercy: The Finality of Jesus Christ in a World of Religions* (Grand Rapids, MI: Zondervan, 1992), 35–43, 93, 101, 146–7, 157.
53 Terrance L. Tiessen, *Who Can be Saved? Reassessing Salvation in Christ* (Downers Grove, IL: Inter-Varsity Press, 2004), 365–404.
54 Hendrik Vroom, *No Other Gods: Christian Belief in Dialogue with Buddhism, Hinduism, and Islam*, trans. Lucy Jansen (Grand Rapids, MI: Zondervan, 1996), 152–8, 174.
55 Paul K. Moser, "Religious Exclusivism," in Meister, *The Oxford Handbook of Religious Diversity*, 85–6, where Moser allows for an "inclusive exclusivism" that relies upon a distinction between christological salvation *de re* and *de dicto*. That is, all salvation is through Christ, though clearly not all of the redeemed ". . . will acknowledge Jesus as Lord in their earthly lives."
56 Roger Haight, *Jesus: Symbol of God* (Maryknoll, NY: Orbis Books, 1999), 333.
57 Joseph Cardinal Ratzinger, "Notification on the book 'Jesus Symbol of God' by Father Roger Haight S. J." (Rome: The Congregation for the Doctrine of the Faith, December 13, 2004), section 1, accessed October 7, 2011, www.vatican.va/roman_curia/congregations/cfaith/documents/rc_con_cfaith_doc_20041213_notification-fr-haight_en.html. See also David Gibson, "The Vatican levies further penalties on Roger Haight, S. J," accessed January 2, 2009, *dotCommonweal*, www.commonwealmagazine.org/blog/?p=2644.

58 Roger Haight, *The Future of Christology* (New York: Continuum, 2005), 164.
59 Haight, *The Future of Christology*, 157, 159.
60 Haight, *The Future of Christology*, 157–9.
61 Haight, *The Future of Christology*, 158. David M. Elcott expresses a Jewish version of this kind of theistic pluralism, where he characterizes Jewish pluralism "not as a concession but as part of the divine plan . . . ." "Meeting the Other: Judaism, Pluralism, and Truth," in *Criteria of Discernment in Interreligious Dialogue*, ed. Catherine Cornille (Eugene, OR: Cascade Books, 2009), 27.
62 Haight, *The Future of Christology*, 158. This is a position that Paul Knitter approvingly amplifies upon in *Introducing Theologies of Religions* (Maryknoll, NY: Orbis Books, 2002), 155–6.
63 Haight, *The Future of Christology*, 158.
64 Roger Haight, "Pluralist Christology as Orthodox," in Knitter, *The Myth of Religious Superiority*, 157.
65 S. Mark Heim, *Salvations: Truth and Difference in Religion* (Maryknoll, NY: Orbis Books, 1995), 3, 5, 7, 102, 157.
66 Heim, *Salvations*, 102.
67 Heim, *Salvations*, 29–30, 123, 130, 140.
68 Heim, *Salvations*, 7.
69 Heim adopts this term from Nicholas Rescher, *The Strife of Systems* (Pittsburgh, PA: Pittsburgh University Press, 1985); see Heim, *Salvations*, 133–43, 152–3, 219.
70 Heim, *Salvations*, 152.
71 Heim, *Salvations*, 225.
72 Heim, *Salvations*, 152.
73 Heim, *Salvations*, 125–6.
74 Heim, *Salvations*, 5, 7, 146.
75 Heim, *Salvations*, 229.
76 Heim, *Salvations*, 3.
77 Heim, *Salvations*, 146.
78 Heim, *Salvations*, 147.
79 Long, "(Tentatively) Putting the Pieces Together," in Clooney, *The New Comparative Theology*, 151–70.
80 Long, "(Tentatively) Putting the Pieces Together," in Clooney, *The New Comparative Theology*, 160–1.
81 As typified by Paul Griffith's characterization of Neo-Vedanta as "pallid, platitudinous, and degutted." Quoted in Long, "(Tentatively) Putting the Pieces Together," in Clooney, *The New Comparative Theology*, 152.
82 Long, "(Tentatively) Putting the Pieces Together," in Clooney, *The New Comparative Theology*, 167. Long's discussion of the parable does not come to terms with the disanalogy between the situation of the blind people and the religions of the world. While people who aren't blind can tell the blind people that they are touching an elephant, no human being can stand apart from the religions of the world and from an absolute standpoint indicate which one, if any, is true. Self-proclamations by the religions do not escape this difficulty, nor do appeals to revelation, since in both cases, we must judge appeals to absolute authority from a limited perspective in which many claimants struggle to make good on their contrary claims.

83 As seen in the list of contributors to the volume, *The Myth of Christian Uniqueness*: John Hick, Paul Knitter, Wilfred Cantwell Smith, Gordon D. Kaufman, Stanley J. Samartha, Tom F. Driver, Langdon Gilkey, Raimon Panikkar, Rosemary Radford Reuther, Marjorie Hewitt Suchocki, and Aloysius Pieris. To this list can be added numerous other contemporary theologians, including Reinhold Bernhardt, Roger Haight, Peter C. Hodgson, K. P. Aleaz, and S. Wesley Ariarajah, all of whom were contributors to *The Myth of Religious Superiority*, and the pluralistic, liberal Protestant theologian John Thatamanil, who offers a nondual interpretation of Tillich in light of Śaṅkara. *The Immanent Divine: God, Creation, and the Human Predicament* (Minneapolis, MN: Fortress Press, 2006).

84 As is evinced in the case of Daniel Strange, whose epicyclic attempt at resurrecting a Kraemerian exclusivism in a dialogue with Gavin D'Costa and Paul Knitter involves starting history with a real Adam in the Near East and leads to ad hominem negations of religions other than his own. "Perilous Exchange, Precious Good News: A Reformed 'Subversive Fulfillment' Interpretation of Other Religions," 91–136 and "Daniel Strange Re-Responds to Gavin D'Costa and Paul Knitter," 213–28, in *Only One Way? Three Christian Responses on the Uniqueness of Christ in a Religiously Plural World*, Gavin D'Costa, Paul Knitter, and Daniel Strange (London: SCM Press, 2011). Such views, if widely adopted by Catholic and mainline Protestants would lead to the end of dialogue and, perhaps, even of discussion.

2

The Inclusivist Counterrevolution

Retreating behind the theological Rubicon

Despite the clarity of Hick's pluralistic hypothesis, which highlighted the implausibility of any form of inclusivism and the inadequacy of the various *ad hoc* and *ex post facto* arguments upon which theological inclusivisms are based, the theology of religions has, as noted in the preceding chapter, become stalled over the past 20 years in the impasse of inclusivist epicyclical theorizing about the salvific value of religions other than Christianity, with the result that inclusivism has entrenched itself as the default position in the theology of religions. Beginning in the mid 1990s, inclusivist theologians of religions, with the help of George Lindbeck's postliberal, regulative theological methodology,[1] began to retreat from the edge of pluralism toward doctrinally centered inclusivisms. As indicated in Chapter 1, the progress of this reversal can be traced in the rise of revisionist interpretations of John Hick's paradigm-breaking pluralistic hypothesis[2] as itself just another version of particularism (i.e., inclusivism or exclusivism).[3]

This ironic reversal appears to have neutered pluralism and given cover to the rise of antipluralist theologies of religions. Thus, inclusivist theologians of religions have blocked the inevitable movement of Christianity and Christian theologies toward embracing as a settled truth the nonabsoluteness of Christianity and of all other religions. Rather than moving forward kenotically, prophetically, and mystically as witnesses to nonabsolutism, leading theologians of religions have doubled back into renewed inclusivisms that are dependent upon ever more labored and sometimes offensive epicycles. Rejecting both exclusivism and pluralism in favor of an imagined middle ground, an influential group of theologians has attempted to roll back the pluralist revolution, to blunt it through parody and failed reductio ad absurdum arguments, to evade it by reasserting universal Christian normativity as a matter of faith, preference, or missionary imperative, or to temporize by avoiding foundational theological issues while formally remaining inclusivist. In these ways, inclusivistic theologies have succeeded in blunting the move toward pluralism in many sectors of Christian theology.

But these often ingenious and often sympathetic approaches to religions other than Christianity are undercut by three interrelated limitations: (1) they are defenses of bodies of doctrine that are finite and cannot, therefore, claim to be final and normative for all human beings; (2) this finitude and nonuniversalizability require the invention of theological epicycles, or *ex post facto* and *ad hoc* adaptations of the original body of teachings, in order to accommodate them to the undeniable reality of other religions; (3) these epicyclic adaptations, as finite and nonuniversal, inevitably fail to persuade the unpersuaded and will without exception eventually be set aside as implausible by later representatives of the communities they were designed to serve.

My claim that no inclusivist approach to theology can survive scrutiny in light of these limitations stems not from a personal animus against inclusivism but from the logic of the proposals themselves. Since it is impossible to generate an inclusivistic proposal that will persuade everyone everywhere of the universal normativity of a particular religious tradition, all inclusivist proposals will fail to provide adequate grounding for their claims to universal normativity. Indeed, such proposals are self-refuting, for in the very act of arguing for them, they collapse through the internal contradiction of trying to universalize a particular (which, ironically, is the often-repeated criticism of pluralism offered by numerous inclusivists). It turns out, then, that particularist criticisms of pluralism as particularistic and hegemonic are themselves universalized and hegemonic particulars.

Given the massive and undeniable reality of religious diversity on our currently thoroughly interconnected planet, it would seem as if the days of self-preserving inclusivist orthodoxies should be over. Living side by side with people from all religious traditions, religious people should now be in an ideal position to learn from one another about their diverse religions and to lay aside as unworthy the idea that any one of the currently available religions is final and normative for all human beings.[4] Sadly, however, as shown in the return over the last 30 years of particularistic, fundamentalistic, and extremist forms of religion as powerful and often disruptive forces in the global public square, antipluralist religious views seem to be prevailing over liberal, progressive, and pluralist religious views, a change of mood that is reflected in the dominant inclusivism in recent theologies of religions.[5]

Inching toward the Rubicon: Pluralistic inclusivism

Yet, even as inclusivism has fortified itself against pluralistic (and exclusivistic) criticism, much progress has occurred even among inclusivists. Under the pressure of religious diversity as experienced in the intensive interreligious dialogues of the last half-century, leading inclusivistic Christian theologians have increasingly acknowledged the independent vitality of religions other than Christianity. As may be seen from the survey of recent inclusivisms in the next section, current inclusivisms are more pluralistic than the inclusivisms of the comparative theologies of a century ago, which firmly placed Christ at the center of the world of faiths, as in all but forgotten fulfillment-theory classics such as Frederick Denison Maurice's *The Religions of the World and their Relations to Christianity* (1847), Charles Hardwick's two-volume *Christ and Other Masters* (1863), Nicol Macnicol's *Indian Theism: From the Vedic to the Muhammadan Period* (1915), J. N. Farquhar's *The Crown of Hinduism* (1913),[6] and James Clarke Freeman's *Ten Great Religions* (1883).[7] Newer inclusivisms have also moved beyond the ecclesiastical scope of the Second Vatican Council's *Nostra Aetate* by conceding more independent validity to other traditions. Some of these inclusivist approaches persist in implying that the outcome of dialogue and comparison will be to show the ultimate adequacy of the inclusivist's favored tradition, while others seek to defer the question of truth while remaining inclusivist. Because many recent inclusivists remain profoundly open to the reality of religions other than their own, whether as scholars of other traditions, as ecumenical religious leaders, or as hybrid spiritual practitioners, their inclusivisms are marked by varying degrees of pluralism. It may well be the case that the more pluralistic formulations of recent inclusivisms will one day be seen as steps that led to true pluralism.

Francis X. Clooney and the new comparative theology

Francis X. Clooney is a central figure in the development of more pluralistic inclusivisms that try to avoid reliance on implausible epicycles. Clooney has written numerous methodologically innovative and influential books and articles in which he reads Hindu and Christian texts side by side in what he calls "a reflexive back-and-forth reading process,"[8] thereby creating an open space in which the mutual attractions and claims of the compared traditions affect the reader and the traditions themselves in novel, theologically significant ways. Deferring the task of making theological claims,[9] Clooney allows the worlds of formerly unrelated texts to speak together in such a way as to create new religious realities. He likens this process to the *maṇipravāla* texts of Śrīvaiṣṇava scholars, which blend the *maṇi* ("ruby") of Sanskrit words with the *pravāla* ("coral") of Tamil words to create an even richer language[10] (this process is an instance of syncretism, about which I will have more to say in Chapter 4). This interactive rather than monological approach distinguishes Clooney's understanding of comparative theology, which he characterizes as "a mode of interreligious learning,"[11] from the older comparative theologies of a century ago, which were intent on using other religions to demonstrate the finality of Jesus. This innovative and sensible approach is virtually pluralistic, since through it Clooney formulates what he sees as a number of basic theological claims that might be agreed upon as "normative" by Christian, Hindu, and other theologians,[12] a quasipluralistic stance that tarries at the boundary that divides comparative theologies that are tradition-specific from those that are not.[13]

Clooney also comes close to pluralism when, immediately after admitting that if he were to do theology of religions, it would be inclusivist along the lines of Rahner and Dupuis, he blunts the edge of this inclusivism by refusing to see Christianity as including other religions within itself. Instead, he views these religions as illumining and enriching his own tradition.[14] Instead, then, of an inclusivism in which "Christianity subsumes all else," Clooney subscribes to a kind of reverse inclusivism that he calls "including theology" in which he seeks to supplement his Christian faith with what he learns in other traditions[15] (a move that might be seen as a kind of personal syncretism by traditionalists). Clooney models a quasi pluralism that really wants (rightly, I think) to dispense with the unpleasant business of making judgments about the truth of other religions or seeing them as leading up to one's own. (Yet, despite this quasi pluralism, there remains a potentially exclusivistic side to Clooney's approach, which can be seen in his theological insistence that certain theological truths, such as the view that "Christ founded the one universal religion and that Jesus is the universal savior,"[16] might be true to the exclusion of others. And while it is clear where Clooney's sympathies as a Christian lie, he pluralistically points out that other theological traditions beside Christianity make universal—and thus normative—claims.[17])

One consequence of Clooney's quasi pluralism is his surprising (for an orthodox Christian theologian) openness to his chosen "other" tradition, Hinduism, especially in its theistic forms. There are moments in reading Clooney's works when one senses that, like many people who develop hybrid religious personalities as a consequence of belonging to multiple religious communities, Clooney might have become a convert to theistic Hinduism instead of remaining a Jesuit. Indeed, like many other Christians and people of other religions who have come into deep contact with Hinduism, Clooney faced a boundary (in his case during a winter festival honoring a south Indian Hindu saint) when he realized that he could not "go forward" into Hinduism from Catholicism.[18] That going forward into Hinduism could have been felt by him as a real choice indicates how deeply he has been shaped by his scholarly study of and personal connections to Hinduism, as is clear when he suggests that at some moments it might be difficult to choose Christ over Kṛṣṇa.[19]

Because of his real openness to Hinduism as an independent set of religious traditions (seen especially in his near-reverence for Hindu goddesses[20]), despite his own formal inclusivist loyalties, it is possible that in the writings of Clooney, in the last writings of Henry Le Saux (better known as Abhishiktananda),[21] in the hybrid speculations of Raimon Panikkar,[22] and in the pluralist Christology of Roger Haight, we are seeing the beginnings of a future Catholicism in which Catholicism pluralistically allows its own insights to be enriched, modified, and sometimes negated by the world's religions, which it has for too long tried to rebrand as Christian truth.

It is clear, however, that traditionalists in Clooney's tradition will likely view him as a theologian who, in his own words, is "seeing beyond the expectations of her tradition."[23] And while Clooney is an adventurous religious visionary, and thus to be applauded for his forays into religious hybridity, a caution is in order here, for while this may be a promising way forward in Christian comparative theology, it can easily lay the ground for more vigorously Christian-centric inclusivist theologies of religions and missiologies based on them. It would be a baleful result if the fruit of the new comparative theology was to give more and better tools to apologists and missionaries. So, real care needs to be taken here, and the place to start may be to ask why Christian theologians are generally far more interested in these kinds of comparisons than thinkers from the compared traditions. One hopes that the answer is simply that their study of other religions serves to illumine their own Christianity,[24] a relatively harmless interest, although it raises the issue of what possible deficits in the home tradition drive this ceaseless comparative activity.

Kenneth Cracknell's Word/Spirit/Logos Christology

Kenneth Cracknell, a widely respected voice in interfaith circles and an innovative theologian of religions, moves in a recent masterful book toward an almost pluralistic inclusivism,[25] which attempts to be faithful both to Christian and biblical traditions and to the undeniable and independent spiritual worth of other religious traditions.[26] Reminiscent of the logos christology of the early Christian apologists and the more generous Protestant theologies of religions of a century ago that were sidelined by the more influential voices of Karl Barth and Hendrik Kraemer,[27] Cracknell argues for a "Word/Spirit/Logos Christology" that holds that "God has moved and still moves among the nations in self-revelation."[28] This places Cracknell on the verge of a pluralistic theology of religions. Here, where *mārga*, *magga*, *sharīʿa*, *halakhah*, and *dao* meet the Christian *hodos* as compelling alternatives,[29] the last obstacle to pluralism should dissolve. Indeed, Cracknell moves into pluralism when he writes that Christians "ought to be more conscious of talking about the Christian path as but one way among many ways,"[30] but he then immediately reverts to inclusivism when he claims that the "Way of God has been most clearly discerned in the way that Jesus followed,"[31] which is a way of love and suffering.

Attractive as this genial approach is for people who still retain the idea that one of humanity's many religions must be final and normative, it remains within the self-reflecting house of mirrors of Christian inclusivism. Consequently, Cracknell feels compelled to affirm, in the end, the supreme clarity of the way of the divine in Jesus's way. Instead of placing the reality variously thematized in the religions of the world at the center of the universe of faiths (to borrow John Hick's memorable phrase and conception), Cracknell resorts, arbitrarily it seems to me, to seeing Jesus at the center, even if this would require inclusivistic reinterpretations of other religions that would render them unrecognizable to their followers. This insistence on placing Jesus at the center of humanity's religious life, despite the massive evidence to the contrary demonstrated by the whole religious history of humanity, is expressive of the epicyclic inventiveness of inclusivism. But this inclusivist claim will be no less plausible to the unpersuaded than will the inclusivist remark of Jotiya Dhirasekera that Cracknell himself quotes: "the future Buddha on whom the salvation of this present world is said to be hinged is named Maitreya."[32]

Just a step beyond the final epicycle of this inclusivism is the entrance to a genuine pluralism, which begins when religious adherents recognize that there is no universally agreed-upon method of choosing decisively between the different available religious traditions. One may continue to give primacy to one's own tradition out of devotion, faith, or traditionalism, but it remains, nevertheless, a personal or communal choice and cannot be universalized. Accepting this and not regressing back to inclusivism is thus the first requirement of a pluralistic theology of religions. In an age of renewed religious tribalism and popular revivals of crude scientistic atheisms, the acceptance of all authentic religions as fellow pilgrims rather than as preparations and backdrops for one's own tradition must become the starting point for responsible religious thought about religious diversity.

Catherine Cornille and doctrinal humility

Other leading theologians of religions seem, like Clooney and Cracknell, to straddle the fence between inclusivism and pluralism and to be moving toward pluralism without finally affirming it. The result is a kind of quasi pluralism that seems to be the last stage before genuine pluralism erupts out of inclusivisms that have been pushed beyond their limits. This is to be expected, and in fact can be predicted on the basis of the theory of apophatic pluralism, since it is not possible for an inclusivism to be elaborated indefinitely without the laboriousness of its increasingly ornate equivocations becoming apparent and onerous to the honest and religiously sensitive inclusivist. Even in cases where the inclusivist is less generous and more attached to the conceit of the finality of the home tradition, the time will inevitably arrive when no amount of *ad hoc* patching up of an old inclusivism can continue to render it plausible. At that point, so long as the religion being defended has not disappeared from the scene or morphed into its successor, the inclusivist must either go forward into a genuinely pluralist admission of the nonfinality of the home religion or retreat into an absolutism that no longer allows the home religion to be challenged, questioned, or justified.

Thus, as the case of Belgian theologian of religions Catherine Cornille shows, a realistic, hospitable, and religiously modest theologian of religions will inevitably approach the shore of pluralism. Because of the genuine sensitivity to religions other than one's own that arises among people who live and work on the boundary between more than one tradition, they will likely be receptive to Cornille's call for a "doctrinal or epistemic humility" in interreligious dialogue that "entails a certain degree of admission of the finite and limited ways in which the ultimate truth has been grasped and expressed within one's own religious teachings, practices, and/or institutional forms."[33] As a person involved in the study of religious hybridity, Cornille moves toward a view virtually identical to the apophatic pluralism[34] for which I am arguing in this book, when she claims that doctrinal humility, when "thought through to the end . . . is the very realization of the ineffability of the ultimate reality that brings into perspective the contingency of all finite expressions of that reality."[35] Yet, tantalizingly, just when she seems to be approaching a clearly pluralist position, she throws a backward glance toward muted forms of inclusivism, thus making it hard to discern her own view on this significant issue.[36] Similarly to Clooney, she defers the making of a direct declaration of a pluralist stance and so remains on the outer edge of an inclusivism that is rightly allergic to epicycles and sensitive to the demands of genuine pluralism. Yet, even when she regresses behind the Rubicon by asserting that "Christians may or must believe that they have a privileged understanding of the will of God in Jesus Christ" or that "Christians may not be able to recognize complete equality between religions,"[37] her genuine openness to other religions and her apophatic sense of epistemological and theological modesty in the theology of religions represents the beginning of an eventual step forward beyond implausible and unwelcome attempts at the incorporation of people of other traditions within one's own tradition, as in the *ad hoc* and *ex post facto* epicyclic doctrinal modifications of the inclusivists to be discussed in the next sections.

Tarrying by the rubicon: The postpluralist reassertion of inclusivism

Gavin D'Costa and the limbo of the just

Gavin D'Costa, the Catholic theologian who, as noted earlier, pioneered the claim that pluralists are anonymous exclusivists, has in a series of influential articles and books articulated a muscular reversion to inclusivism in which the Trinity serves as the matrix within which the particularity and normativity of Christ is reconciled with the universality of God's grace. This negation of both exclusivism and pluralism allows for the emergence of an inclusivism that, in a nod to pluralism, recognizes God as active in religions other than Christianity.[38] Yet, unlike the approaches discussed in the previous section, D'Costa's approach is a classical inclusivism that deploys *ex post facto* and *ad hoc* theological epicycles that are certain to be plausible only to those inclined to be persuaded by them. (Curiously, D'Costa seems to have moved away from pluralism toward exclusivism in his later writings, perhaps in order to prevent the flowering into a real pluralism that the opening to religious others through inclusivism seems to foreordain.[39])

For example, D'Costa innovatively, but unpersuasively and irrelevantly to people outside his theological circle, tries to find a way for people who are not Christians to share in the Christian version of a heavenly afterlife.[40] D'Costa considers but rejects an epicycle proposed by Joseph DiNoia, who opens purgatory to "righteous non-Christians" who die in a state of grace. D'Costa rejects this approach not because it is an epicycle that will be implausible to people outside the Catholic Church, but because D'Costa is looking for a solution that "keeps purgatory Christian."[41] This leads him to rehabilitate the ancient Christian teaching of the limbo of the just (the *limbus patrum* as opposed to the better-known *limbus infantium* for infants who die without being baptized). As conceived by D'Costa, limbo is not, as in popular imagination, an actual "celestial waiting room under the earth"[42] but a theological conception that allows him to provide "righteous non-Christians" a postmortem opportunity to respond to the gospel.[43] Then—and only then—as new Christians, they may be allowed to enter the purificatory fire of purgatory in order to continue "their pilgrimage into the community of the saints and the blessed."[44] D'Costa's generosity even extends to the "difficult . . . to imagine"[45] possibility that non-Christians possessed of "startling righteousness" will go to heaven immediately without having to undergo purging in the fire of purgatory.[46]

The rehabilitation of the doctrine of the limbo of the just is an epicycle of venerable if dubious pedigree[47] that originally arose as a way of including the patriarchs and prophets of the Hebrew Bible in the economy of Christian salvation, as well as figures of classical antiquity whom no learned person, including Christians, could in the late classical world imagine as being subject to eternal damnation. Then, as now, this theological epicycle is inadequate to the realities of other religious traditions. While this strategy may seem to solve the problem for people who think that the contingent teachings of orthodox Christianity are final and normative for all of humanity, it remains an *ad hoc* and *ex post facto* solution to what remains for inclusivist Christians the embarrassing and insoluble problem of trying to account for the saints of other traditions without recourse to pluralism. People of other religious traditions are less likely to be persuaded by the ingenuity of this epicycle than to be amused or appalled by its implausibility.[48] At best, this implausible, clearly *ad hoc* teaching can be seen as a stopgap measure that is the last but weakest defense against the inevitability of pluralism. At worst, it subjects to rejection and perhaps ridicule from pluralists the tradition that epicycles like this are meant to defend.

Rowan Williams and the radical singleness of Jesus Christ

In a plenary address to the delegates of the World Council of Churches at Porto Alegre in 2006, Rowan Williams, then the Archbishop of Canterbury, argued for what can only be seen as a qualified reversion to an "anonymous Christianity" type of inclusivist theology of religions. In a gesture of critical embrace of this epicyclic innovation associated with Karl Rahner and the Second Vatican Council, Williams reminds his hearers of the value of this approach even as he concedes that it is problematic.[49] Taking a position that is consonant with Vatican II and subsequent Vatican documents, Williams reminds his Christian hearers, many of whom were involved in interfaith activities, that they may often have had a "sense of an echo, a reflection, of the kind of life Christians seek to live"[50] when engaged in dialogue with people of other traditions. Williams suggests that if the values of adoption and forgiveness, which derive from "the history of Israel and Jesus," are found to be present in some degree in other traditions, then "God has found a path for himself"[51] in those other traditions where these values are not otherwise known.[52] Even if they do not have the words that Christians have for these experiences, it is still possible, Williams offers, "to see in their eyes a reflection of what we see."[53] This appears to be possible, because, citing the apostle Paul, Williams claims that God has not left himself without a witness. Thus, even in those places where the name of the Messiah has not been explicitly named, Williams trusts that "God may yet give himself to be seen."[54]

In line with his more conservative hearers and reflecting the move of the theology of religions away from liberal, progressive views in the last two decades toward epicyclic and self-cherishingly Christian stances, Williams cautions against identifying interfaith sensitivity with the "modern liberal" attempt to relativize "the radical singleness of Jesus Christ."[55] Sensitivity to religious others doesn't mean relativizing Israel and Jesus to the status of "one way among others"[56] because these other traditions, even if they sometimes sense the values of adoption and forgiveness, do not have these values at their center—a stance that he admits "will never be obvious to those others."[57] Since they thus "leave out what matters most in human struggle," there remains a vital role for Christian witness to Jesus.

Yet, as even Williams himself admits, this stance is implausible to all but those committed to this way of seeing the world. His central conceit is the epicyclic notion that, despite all evidence to the contrary, the human experience of forgiveness is always somehow bound up with biblical notions of adoption by the God of Israel as mediated by Jesus, as if the experience of forgiveness were unavailable in any other tradition except as an echo or reflection of the experience that Christians characterize as adoption by the father of Jesus. (The magnificent story of Buddha's forgiveness of King Ajātasattu in the Sāmaññaphala Sutta seems in no need of Christian theological supplementation.) As a strategy in a confessional setting this may work, for a long time perhaps, as a coping strategy within a community bound by a comfortingly familiar religious identity, but as a way of thinking about people of other religions, it is not different from other fulfillment theologies in seeing Jesus as the truth behind the truths of other traditions, a stance that can never persuade the unpersuaded.

In the end, however, as time passes and changes accumulate, this locally familiar identity will have varied to the point where it will either disappear or become unrecognizable to its successors. The experience of forgiveness will continue to be a part of human religious experience, whether mediated by divinities or religious teachers, while the ideology of adoption as articulated in the New Testament will slowly (if we survive on this planet for multiple millennia) be superseded by the novel theologies and religious philosophies of the future.

Wayne Teasdale and interspirituality

Wayne Teasdale was a popular interfaith activist who is better known to the general public than leading academic inclusivists such as Gavin D'Costa, and Jacques Dupuis. Teasdale founded a movement of religious rapprochement that he called "Interspirituality." He was also an early voice seeking to make sense of the phenomenon of what Catherine Cornille and others call "multiple religious belonging."[58] Teasdale called attention to what he characterized as an "already existing and thriving community" of interspiritual pioneers in the world's religions who are trying to "evolve a higher view" of the religions and humanity by stressing the spiritual interdependence of the religions of the world.[59] As Teasdale describes it, Interspirituality is a fertile and synthetic movement that is bringing together people who simultaneously follow one or more of the spiritual practices of the many religions of the world. Teasdale's ecumenism includes interspiritual pioneers outside of the Catholic tradition, such as the fourteenth Dalai Lama, Masao Abe, and unnamed Hindus who are "passionately committed to the Sacred Heart of Jesus."[60] More central to Teasdale's Interspirituality and giving it its Christian theological character is a core group of Catholics from the last four centuries who shared the common vision of the Christianization of Hinduism and India. This group includes the seventeenth-century Jesuit missionary and self-proclaimed *sannyāsin* Roberto de Nobili, the nineteenth-century convert to Catholicism Brahmabandhab Upadhyay, the twentieth-century French priest Jules Monchanin, the Benedictine monk Henri Le Saux (or Abhishiktananda), and Teasdale's Catholic "guru," the Benedictine Bede Griffiths, who initiated him in India as a "Christian *sannyāsin*," a title that is as odd perhaps as "Hindu cardinal."[61]

Teasdale portrays this lineage of indigenizing and contextualizing Catholics as visionaries looking for a way to bring about the "convergence"[62] of Hinduism and

Christianity—a hope dramatically expressed in Bede Griffith's exclamation when he left England for the subcontinent: "I'm going out to India to seek the other half of my soul."[63] Unlike other Christian inclusivistic theologies of religion that merely want to account for the existence of other religions in the economy of salvation, Interspirituality sees itself and Catholicism as midwives to what it views as the *Christian* potential of other traditions. Teasdale's Interspirituality thus sees Hinduism as a provisional version of Catholic Christianity and a child of the Church. Instead of an exclusivistic rejection of Hinduism, Teasdale inclusivistically thinks that the Catholic Church "has decided to offer itself as a bridge that allows other religions to discover the source of their common identity in community."[64] Thanks to this bridging function, Teasdale claims that "the Church also becomes a matrix of intermysticism and the spiritual life as all forms of the inner experience take root in its being, and the universal elements shine forth in all its sons and daughters."[65]

It does not take much probing, however, to see how Interspirituality is undercut by the limitations inherent in all inclusivistic theologies of religions. The belief that the Catholic Church is the parent of other religions and the view of Interspirituality as a bridge to fulfillment for religions other than Catholicism are epicyclic variations on the ancient Christian contention that Christian revelation is the final revelation for all of humanity. While measures like this may make sense to theologians adhering to the basic premises of traditional Christianity,[66] they can continue to do so only by ignoring the fact that other global traditions are as self-sufficient and self-contained as Christianity and stand no more in need of external supplement than Christianity does. Further attempts to claim that other religions can only be understood in light of another religion—a claim that initiates a potentially never-ending regression of claims of supremacy—can only further obscure the reality that the world's religious traditions are only contingently related to each other and internally are aware of no need of external and extrinsic supplements from other religions. Since every religious tradition has able and fully persuaded apologists, it is more likely that any offer by one tradition to fulfill another will be met with a similar counteroffer. Consequently, the epicyclic inventiveness of Interspirituality, which is necessitated by the nonuniversalizability of Christian doctrine, will only be persuasive to those who are already persuaded of its truth.

Jacques Dupuis on the unity of salvation and distinct regimes of salvation

The inclusivist musings of Jacques Dupuis, the Jesuit theologian of religions who was censured by the Vatican shortly before his death, are in the same family of views as that of Teasdale, Griffith, and others who envision Christ as what Dupuis calls "the obligatory Savior of all men and women"[67] who is necessarily latent[68] in other religions. Even in Dupuis's most mature thoughts on the theology of religions, he held to a clearly inclusivist position, one that maintains that "God's saving action . . . never prescinds from the Christ-event, in which it finds its highest historical density."[69] Since for Dupuis, the mystery of Christ is "the center of history"[70] it follows that if God is merciful and will not leave himself without a witness, then this mystery must be present in varying degrees in other religions. To justify this claim, Dupuis introduces the *ad hoc* device of "distinct regimes of Christian salvation."[71] The idea here is that all authentic religious experience is, in fact, an experience of the Christic mystery, though this is portrayed in its fullness only in Christianity.[72] Yet, because this mystery is inexhaustible, it will be present to a lesser degree in other traditions, which are "in a certain manner 'channels' of Christ's saving power."[73] Thus, a truly Christocentric theology of religions, which is grounded in the mystery of Christ, will be able to integrate "all religious experiences into a truly catholic—inclusive and universal—theology."[74] This will necessarily be a hierarchical theology, with other religions "obviously in an inferior position as mediators of Christian salvation."[75] One should not thus minimize the differences between Christianity and other religions on this point, in Dupuis's view, since there is a real difference of natures between them,[76] as shown in the circumstance that those who explicitly become Christian, as opposed to those who remain in their original traditions, "must undergo an intrinsic transformation consisting of entering into a new order of the mediation of the grace of Christ."[77] Yet, even if the "sacramental realism" of Christianity evinces the nonequality and noninterchangeability of the world's religions,[78] the other religions do possess salvific value as "incomplete signs" of the mystery of Christ, who remains the *Ursakrament*, or "primordial sacrament" behind the religions.[79] Thus, even though "the mystery of salvation remains one" as the mystery of Christ explicitly revealed in Christianity, it is present "beyond the boundaries of Christianity," even if imperfectly and in a manner distinctly inferior to that of Christianity.[80] For all their limitations, these "subjectively implicit"[81] forms of Christianity are "actual ways of salvation"[82] that "mediate salvation for their followers."[83] Moving toward the majestic conclusion of this ultimately implausible inclusivist theology of religions, Dupuis contends that when "the believers of other traditions perceive God's call through their own traditions . . . they find salvation and become members of the Reign of God in history."[84]

Had this theology of religions appeared in 1970, before the outbreak of Hick's Copernican revolution in theology, it might have appeared as a bold and innovative Christian attempt to make sense of other religions. (It is difficult to imagine the reception it would have received ten years earlier, in 1960, when it would likely have been seen as a step too far for the Catholicism of that period.[85]) But by the late 1980s and 1990s, when Dupuis's major work in this area was published, his theology of religions already seemed anachronistically patronizing in its explicit relegation of the world's religions to subordinate and intermediate roles in relation to Christ and Christianity. Even so, Dupuis went too far for the Vatican, for rather than merely seeing the other religions as children of the church, like Teasdale, or as reflecting "a ray of that Truth which enlightens all men," as in *Nostra Aetate*,[86] Dupuis characterized other religions as vehicles, if imperfect, of what he calls "the mystery of salvation."[87] By granting that the mystery of Christ, and thus of salvation, is present beyond the boundaries of Christianity, Dupuis undercut the necessity of the Catholic Church, its sacraments, and the Christian economy of salvation. By seeing other religions as "actual ways of salvation,"[88] he called into question the unique salvific role of Christianity, thereby calling down censure upon himself. As the Vatican stated in a notification that refuted some of Dupuis's views, which he expressed in a later book, "It must be firmly believed that the Church is sign and instrument of salvation for all people. It is contrary to the Catholic faith to consider the different religions of the world as ways of salvation complementary to the Church."[89]

Dupuis thus embodies the dangers of inclusivistic theologies, which are invariably suspect to more orthodox believers while remaining implausible to the outsiders for whom they are meant to serve as doorways into the inclusivists' traditions. Unless inclusivists finally accept the ultimate logical implication of their own endless *ad hoc* concessions to the independent reality of religious traditions other their own and embrace pluralism, they will find themselves endlessly caught in an impassable frontier where the way back to exclusivism remains barred while all promising inclusivistic trails fade away long before the frontier of pluralism is reached.

The need for an apophatic pluralist theology of religions

Just as each of these inclusivist theologies of religions is incapable of overcoming the inherent limitations of inclusivism, so all future attempts to articulate an inclusivist theology of religions will necessarily suffer the same fate, which is an outcome that shows the need for a more adequate starting point for theologies of religions. I will take it as a general rule, then, and one justified by these failed attempts at inclusivism, that an adequate theology of religious pluralism must from the beginning be both apophatic and pluralistic. That is, it must take as an axiom that the necessary nonfinality of every body of religious teachings implies religious pluralism. Because none of the theologies of religions considered in this chapter begins with this axiom, none of them can be the view of just one pilgrim among many others who are searching together for truth, an intellectual and spiritual stance that must inform a religiously responsible and spiritually fit version of pluralism. On the contrary, these inclusivist theologies of religions are the stances of people who seem to know something about other people's religions that the followers of those religions don't yet know, but who may one day be privileged to arrive at this understanding. There is always a degree of certitude in inclusivist theologies that is not justified by the partiality and finitude of every human vantage point. An apophatic and pluralistic theology of religions, on the contrary, respects the sovereignty of each religion and rejects the a priori, self-serving, and unverifiable belief that one's own religion is the culmination of other people's religions. Apophatic pluralism is, therefore, a more adequate basis than any form of inclusivism for responsible reflection on the world's spiritual heritage.

Taken together, these lines of argument converge upon the conclusion that no inclusivist theology of religions can finally evade its unraveling as inadequate as an account of the religious life of humanity. Inclusivisms are doomed from the start by their reliance upon historically contingent, *ad hoc*, and finally implausible doctrinal devices designed to help the original theology remain relevant in a changed context, one that either no longer senses a need for the original theology or that finds it irrelevant and alien because it is a product of a different time and place. If this failure is acknowledged (as it inevitably will be through the sheer passage of time and cultural change) without bitterness or rejection of religion altogether, then it will open the door to an apophatic and pluralist theology of religions that is better able to account for the whole of humanity's religious and spiritual experience than any particularist approach.

Notes

1 George A. Lindbeck, *The Nature of Doctrine: Religion and Theology in a Postliberal Age* (Philadelphia, PA: The Westminster Press, 1984), 46–69.

2 Hick's most detailed exposition of his position is in *An Interpretation of Religion: Human Responses to the Transcendent* (New Haven, CT: Yale University Press, 1989), 233–96 (especially 239–40, 244–5, 249). He continued to refine this philosophical hypothesis over the years in light of continual and intense criticism. See, in particular, "The Possibility of Religious Pluralism: A Reply to Gavin D'Costa," *Religious Studies* 33:2 (June 1997): 161–6; "The Next Step Beyond Dialogue in Knitter," *The Myth of Religious Superiority*, 3–12; "Exclusivism versus Pluralism in Religion: A Response to Kevin Meeker," *Religious Studies* 42 (2006): 207–8; "A Brief Response to Aimee Upjohn Light," *Journal of Ecumenical Studies* 44:4 (2009): 691; and personal correspondence with the author.

3 Gavin D'Costa appears to have pioneered the claim that pluralists are anonymous exclusivists in "The Impossibility of a Pluralist View of Religions," *Religious Studies* 32:2 (June 1996): 223–32; see also Gavin D'Costa, *The Meeting of Religions and the Trinity* (Maryknoll, NY: Orbis Books, 2000), 3, 19–20, 22, and Gavin D'Costa, *Christianity and World Religions: Disputed Questions in the Theology of Religions* (Oxford: Wiley-Blackwell, 2009), 10–12, 18. In this muscular reversion to inclusivism, D'Costa has been seconded by S. Mark Heim in *Salvations: Truth and Difference in Religions* (Maryknoll, NY: Orbis Books, 1995), 29–30, and *The Depth of the Riches: A Trinitarian Theology of Religious Ends* (Grand Rapids, MI: Eerdmans, 2001), 17. More recently, Aimee Upjohn Light has taken up the antipluralist criticism of Hick in "Harris, Hick, and the Demise of the Pluralistic Hypothesis," *Journal of Ecumenical Studies* 44:3 (Summer 2009), 467–70.

4 As seems to be the conclusion of many of the contributors in Cornille, *Criteria of Interreligious Discernment*, and in all of the essays in Knitter, *The Myth of Religious Superiority*.

5 The rightward turn in the theology of religions has happened even though most progressive theologians working outside the subfield of the theology of religions accept pluralism as a matter of course, even as axiomatic. Thus, Peter C. Hodgson rejects postliberal theologies of Christian inclusivism and, in the spirit of a radical liberal theology "committed to religious pluralism," has declared that "now is the time to acknowledge that [claims about Christ as the only source of salvation for all humanity] are incompatible with a genuinely comparative theology, which brings

with it the recognition that the revelation of salvific wisdom transcends and enriches Christ." Peter C. Hodgson, *Liberal Theology: A Radical Vision* (Minneapolis, MN: Fortress Press, 2007), 88–9.

6 For a short evaluation of Farquhar's fulfillment-theory approach, see Howard A. Netland, *Encountering Religious Pluralism: The Challenge to Christian Faith and Mission* (Downers Grove, IL: InterVarsity Press, 2001), 33–5. See also *An Introduction to the Theology of Religions: Biblical, Historical, and Contemporary* by Veli-Matti Kärkkäinen (Downers Grove, IL: InterVarsity Press, 2003), 103–5.

7 A fluent and insightful survey of the until recently neglected Anglophone comparative theologians of the later nineteenth century and early twentieth century has been charted by Tomoko Masuzawa in *The Invention of World Religions*, 72–104. See also Francis X. Clooney for a brief evaluation of the older comparative theologies, *Comparative Theology*, 24–40.

8 Francis X. Clooney, *Divine Mother, Blessed Mother: Hindu Goddesses and the Virgin Mary* (Oxford and New York: Oxford University Press, 2005), 23. See also Clooney's, *Hindu God, Christian God: How Reason Helps Break Down the Boundaries Between Religions* (Oxford: Oxford University Press, 2001), 10, where he says "the back-and-forth dynamic of a theological conversation across religious boundaries" is a practical requirement of comparative theology. See also Clooney, *Comparative Theology*, 1.

9 Clooney, *Comparative Theology*, 42.

10 Clooney, *Comparative Theology*, 85.

11 Clooney, *Comparative Theology*, 3. In the spirit of the new comparative theology, Clooney says that "there is nothing essentially Christian about comparative theology." Clooney, *Comparative Theology*, 11, 80.

12 Clooney, *Hindu God, Christian God*, 13. He repeats this list of general areas of agreement between theistic Hindu and Christian theologies in *Comparative Theology*, 116.

13 Examples of comparative theologies that seek to articulate theological ideas beyond the limits of specific traditions include the "whit more" generic comparative theology of Wilfred Cantwell Smith, which suggests the rethinking of traditional terms like *God*, *salvation*, *faith*, and *theology*. *Towards a World Theology: Faith and the Comparative History of Religion* (Philadelphia, PA: Westminster Press, 1981), 181–5, and the project of John J. Thatamanil, a comparative theologian who brings Śaṅkara and Tillich together in conversation in order to discover a "deeper truth" than that currently known in any contemporary tradition. Thatamanil, *The Immanent Divine*, 25. To make this pluralistic point, Thatamanil quotes Gordon D. Kaufman on the result of interreligious conversation that "deeper truth than that presently known in any of our traditions will in due course emerge." Gordon D. Kaufman, *God, Mystery, Diversity: Christian Theology in a Pluralistic World* (Minneapolis, MN: Fortress Press, 1996), 199–200.

14 Clooney, *Comparative Theology*, 16.

15 Clooney, *Comparative Theology*, 16. Later in *Comparative Theology*, Clooney defers the making of any final claim for Christian teaching. He rejects the view that "comparative theological work necessarily vindicates particular Christian doctrines or necessarily leads to Christian conclusions" (107). He makes this claim after a section in this book in which he tries to see various religious phenomena from other religious traditions as part of what it means to say that one is "going deep in Christ" without "going blind" (105).

16 Clooney, *Comparative Theology*, 12.
17 Clooney, *Comparative Theology*, 12–13.
18 Clooney, *Hindu God, Christian God*, v. Other places where one senses his deep appreciation, which sometimes verges on conversion or at least to a momentary crossing over from his Catholicism into his preferred Hindu traditions, include *Comparative Theology*, 16–19, 89, 91, 93–4, 122, 139; Clooney, "Surrender to God Alone: the Meaning of *Bhagavad Gītā* 18:16 in Light of Śrīvaiṣṅava and Christian Tradition," in *Song Divine: Christian Commentaries on the* Bhagavad Gītā, ed. Catherine Cornille (Leuven: Peeters/Grand Rapids, MI: W.B. Eerdmans, 2006), 207. At one point, Clooney virtually identifies the Christian deity and Nārāyaṇa and suggests that Christians can pray to Nārāyaṇa when it is seen that these deities share numerous perfections. *Comparative Theology*, 122.
19 Clooney, *Hindu God, Christian God*, v.
20 Clooney has written that ". . . by an intuitive move that I cannot fully justify, I have felt a connection between reflection on Laksmi and Devi and renewed attention to the Virgin Mary." Clooney, *Comparative Theology*, 93–4.
21 See "The Experience of God in Eastern Religions," *Cistercian Studies* 9: nos. 2 and 3 (1974). Cited by Wayne Teasdale, *Bede Griffiths: An Introduction to His Interspiritual Thought* (Woodstock, VT: SkyLight Paths Publishing, 2003), 111.
22 Clooney sees Panikkar's clearly comparativist model of "mutual inhabitation" as "a worthy goal," though he does have some stylistic differences with Panikkar. Clooney, *Comparative Theology*, 50.
23 Clooney, *Comparative Theology*, 45.
24 Paul F. Knitter, *Introducing Theologies of Religions*, 237, criticizes Fredericks and, to a lesser extent, Clooney for engaging in often insightful dialogue with other religions in order only to create "new ways to come to a deeper understanding of what they already have and implicitly know [as Christians]." Thus, their bold comparative experiments are not keeping pace with the needs of comparative theology, since a bold theology of religions will call into question the singular normativity of Jesus.
25 Kenneth Cracknell, *In Good and Generous Faith: Christian Responses to Religious Pluralism* (Peterborough: Epworth, 2005), xix, 96.
26 Cracknell, *In Good and Generous Faith*, 64.
27 See Diana L. Eck, "The Religions and Tambaram," *International Review of Mission* 77 (July 1988): 379, 381; Wesley Ariarajah, *Hindus and Christians: A Century of Protestant Ecumenical Thought* (Amsterdam: Editions Rodopi/Grand Rapids, MI: Eerdmans, 1991), 17–31, 52–88.
28 Cracknell, *In Good and Generous Faith*, 40.
29 Cracknell, *In Good and Generous Faith*, 63–71.
30 Cracknell, *In Good and Generous Faith*, 70.
31 Cracknell, *In Good and Generous Faith*, 71.
32 Cracknell, *In Good and Generous Faith*, 68.
33 See Catherine Cornille, *The Im-Possibility of Interreligious Dialogue* (New York: Crossroad, 2008), 4, 9–58, 211. See also the reviews of this book by Paul F. Knitter, *Theological Studies* 70:4 (December 2009): 952–4, and Freek L. Bakker, *Exchange: Journal of Missiological and Ecumenical Research* 39 (January 2010): 199–201.
34 Cornille, *The Im-Possibility of Interreligious Dialogue*, 26, where she claims that spiritual humility should lead the Christian back to "the long tradition of apophatic theology, which emphasizes the ineffability of ultimate reality." See also 31, 55, 58.

35 Cornille, *The Im-Possibility of Interreligious Dialogue*, 213.
36 See, for example, *The Im-Possibility of Interreligious Dialogue*, 79, 84–9, 202–5.
37 Cornille, *Many Mansions?* 6.
38 D'Costa, "Preface," in Gavin D'Costa, ed. *Christian Uniqueness Reconsidered: The Myth of Pluralistic Theology of Religions* (Maryknoll, NY: Orbis Books, 1990b), xii; "Christ, the Trinity, and Religious Pluralism," in D'Costa, *Christian Uniqueness Reconsidered*, 16–18, a stance that skirts close to what he later denies, i.e., that religions other than Christianity have "salvific status." *Christianity and World Religions: Disputed Questions in the Theology of Religions* (Malden, MA and Oxford: Wiley-Blackwell, 2009), xiii.
39 Contrast *Christianity and World Religions*, 25, 31, 174, 161, where he seems to associate himself with an open form of exclusivism that avoids giving salvific status to religions other than Christianity by rehabilitating the doctrine of the limbo of the just, with his earlier claim to be an inclusivist in "Christ, the Trinity, and Religious Pluralism," in D'Costa, *Christian Uniqueness Reconsidered*, 16.
40 D'Costa, *Christianity and World Religions*, xii.
41 D'Costa, *Christianity and World Religions*, 191.
42 D'Costa, *Christianity and World Religions*, 174, 187. Yet he does succumb to less abstract language in D'Costa, "Theology Amid Religious Diversity," in Meister, *The Oxford Handbook of Religious Diversity*, 143, where he refers to the *limbus patrum* "as a kind of holding tank for the righteous who died before Christ."
43 D'Costa, *Christianity and World Religions*, 174–5, 177. See also Gavin D'Costa, "Christianity and the World Religions: A Theological Appraisal," in *Only One Way?* Gavin D'Costa, Paul Knitter, and Daniel Strange, 20–1, 148.
44 D'Costa, *Christianity and World Religions*, 177, 191.
45 D'Costa, *Christianity and World Religions*, 177.
46 D'Costa, *Christianity and World Religions*, 175, 190–1, 167, 177.
47 For a full discussion of the pre-Vatican II teaching about the two limbos, see *The Catholic Encyclopedia* Vol. 9, s.v. "Limbo," by Patrick Toner, 1910, New York: Robert Appleton Company, accessed April 27, 2011, www.newadvent.org/cathen/09256a.htm. The currently official *Catechism of the Catholic Church* (New York: Doubleday, 1995), does not mention either of these two limbos, and the International Theological Commission of the Roman Curia's Pontifical Commission, after an exhaustive study of the *limbo infantium*, dismissed it merely as "a possible theological opinion" that "has never entered into the dogmatic definitions of the Magisterium." "The Hope of Salvation for Infants Who Die Without Being Baptised," section 1.7.41 and the preamble. April 19, 2007, accessed April 27, 2011, www.vatican.va/roman_curia/congregations/cfaith/cti_documents/rc_con_cfaith_doc_20070419_un-baptised-infants_en.html. There appears to be no mention in this Vatican document of the limbo of the fathers, though the issue of the just of faiths other than Christianity seems to be settled in the same way as that which makes the limbo of infants unnecessary: hope in the universal salvific will of God.
48 The same might be said of D'Costa's attempt to discern "an *inchoate* presence of the Christ and his church" in the now mostly discredited practice of *sati* in Hinduism, a move that he admits is terrifying, "Roman Catholic Reflections on Discerning God in Interreligious Dialogue," in Cornille, *Criteria of Discernment in Interreligious Dialogue*, 85, 82.

49 Rowan Williams, "Christian Identity and Religious Plurality," in *God, in your Grace . . . : Official Report of the Ninth Assembly of the World Council of Churches* (Geneva: WCC Publications, World Council of Churches, 2007), 183.
50 Williams, "Christian Identity and Religious Plurality," 183.
51 Ibid.
52 Williams expressed a similarly inclusivist idea, when, following Raimon Panikkar, he spoke of a "christic fact" that emerges as "the Christian goal" in interfaith encounters that brings about for these communities "the formation of children of God after the likeness of Christ." "Trinity and Pluralism," in D'Costa, *Christian Uniqueness Reconsidered*, 5, 9. Needless to say, this move can be reversed and used on Christianity by any of the other participants in the dialogue who might be inclined to make inclusivist claims for their own traditions.
53 Williams, "Christian Identity and Religious Plurality," 183.
54 Ibid.
55 Williams, "Christian Identity and Religious Plurality," 184.
56 Williams, "Christian Identity and Religious Plurality," 183.
57 Ibid.
58 Cornille, *Many Mansions?* 6.
59 Wayne Teasdale, *The Mystic Heart: Discovering a Universal Spirituality in the World's Religions* (Novato, CA: New World Library, 1999), 27–8.
60 Teasdale, *The Mystic Heart*, 32.
61 Wayne Teasdale, *A Monk in the World: Cultivating a Spiritual Life* (Novato, CA: New World Library, 2002), xvii–xx. Although he is best known as a semipopular comparative mystical theologian, Teasdale was a trained theologian and academic who did more than anyone else to make the inculturationist legacy of Monchanin and Griffiths better known (Le Saux seems to have gone further in crossing a personal boundary into the heart of Hinduism than the other two, as noted in an earlier chapter in this book). Despite the possible objection that a popular theologian like Teasdale does not belong in a volume like this, he is part of the company of contextualizing "spiritual theologians," such as Le Saux and Griffiths, who, according to Clooney,

> "all studied Hinduism with more consciously configured combinations of scholarship and spiritual commitment. Their work was detailed and respectful, and intellectually and spiritually open to the project of rethinking the Christian tradition through seriously earning from Hinduism. . . . Even if comparative theology will usually be more academic than the writings of Griffiths, Le Saux [and, I would add, their disciple Teasdale] . . . , it ideally shares their attentiveness to the particularities of other religious traditions."

Clooney, *Comparative Theology*, 38–9. This approach is more consistent with what Clooney calls his own "including theology" (*Comparative Theology*, 16) than with typical inclusivisms, which would complete the other religions through Christianity. Yet, by seeking to supplement Christianity through the study of other religions, both Interspirituality and Clooney's project will appear as either syncretistic to the hostile traditionalist or as parasitic on the host religions by an outside observer.
62 Teasdale, *The Mystic Heart*, 34.

63 Quoted in Wayne Teasdale, "Bede Griffiths as Mystic and Icon of Reversal," *America*, September 30, 1995, 22.
64 Teasdale, *The Mystic Heart*, 248.
65 Ibid.
66 D'Costa assumes that denying the Apostle's Creed is "inadmissible "for a Catholic theologian. *Christianity and World Religions*, 4. Yet, he holds this not merely as a confessional or cultural-linguistic point along Lindbeckian lines, but as one who also holds to the necessity of Christ for human salvation (x, xiii), a teaching that cannot be held literally by adherents of other religions.
67 Jacques Dupuis, *Jesus Christ at the Encounter of World Religions* (Maryknoll, NY: Orbis Books, 1991), 150.
68 Dupuis, *Jesus Christ at the Encounter of World Religions*, 149.
69 Dupuis, *Toward a Christian Theology of Pluralism* (Maryknoll, NY: Orbis Books, 2001; originally published in 1997), 316.
70 Dupuis, *Jesus Christ at the Encounter of World Religions*, 244.
71 Dupuis, *Jesus Christ at the Encounter of World Religions*, 148.
72 Dupuis, *Jesus Christ at the Encounter of World Religions*, 243, 247; *Toward a Theology of Christian Pluralism*, 319.
73 Dupuis, *Toward a Theology of Christian Pluralism*, 317.
74 Dupuis, *Jesus Christ at the Encounter of World Religions*, 247.
75 Dupuis, *Jesus Christ at the Encounter of World Religions*, 148.
76 Ibid.
77 Dupuis, *Jesus Christ at the Encounter of World Religions*, 149; *Toward a Theology of Christian Pluralism*, 319.
78 Dupuis, *Jesus Christ at the Encounter of World Religions*, 151.
79 Dupuis, *Jesus Christ at the Encounter of World Religions*, 145.
80 Dupuis, *Jesus Christ at the Encounter of World Religions*, 148, *Toward a Theology of Christian Pluralism*, 319.
81 Dupuis, *Jesus Christ at the Encounter of World Religions*, 149.
82 Dupuis, *Jesus Christ at the Encounter of World Religions*, 5.
83 Dupuis, *Toward a Theology of Christian Pluralism*, 315, 318.
84 Dupuis, *Toward a Theology of Christian Pluralism*, 347, 390.
85 Before the Second Vatican Council, Catholicism was exclusivistic and, as Douglas Pratt claims, "the notion of establishing any kind of dialogical relationship with any other religion was an idea on the fringes." Douglas Pratt, "The Dance of Dialogue: Ecumenical Interreligious Engagement," *The Ecumenical Review* 51 (July 1999): 279. This attitude changed dramatically when Vatican II issued the "Declaration on the Relationship of the Church to Non-Christian Religions," October 26, 1965, accessed December 26, 2011, www.vatican.va/archive/hist_councils/ii_vatican_council/documents/vat-ii_decl_19651028_nostra-aetate_en.html. From the perspective of the older, insular Catholicism, this is an extraordinary document, for it may well mark the first time in the history of the orthodox branches of Christianity that the spiritual values of other religions were explicitly affirmed. This trend within Catholicism was further strengthened in other Vatican documents, such as Pope Paul VI's *Lumen Gentium*, November 21, 1964, accessed May 19, 2012, www.vatican.va/archive/hist_councils/ii_vatican_council/documents/vat-ii_const_19641121_lumen-gentium_en.html, which included other religions in the "plan of salvation" (Pratt,

"Dance of Dialogue," 280); Pope Paul VI's *Ecclesiam Suam*, August 6, 1964, accessed May 19, 2011, www.vatican.va/holy_father/paul_vi/encyclicals/documents/hf_p-vi_enc_06081964_ecclesiam_en.html, which places the Catholic Church directly at the center of what John Hick was later to call the universe of faiths (Pratt, "Dance of Dialogue," 280); and "Dialogue and Proclamation" (1991), in which the Vatican attempts to parse the difference between preaching to members of other religions and talking to them about their religions. Veli-Matti Kärkkäinen, *An Introduction to the Theology of Religions: Biblical, Historical, and Contemporary Perspectives* (Downers Grove, IL: InterVarsity Press, 2003), 119–22, and the Congregation for the Doctrine of the Faith's "Declaration *Dominus Iesus* On The Unicity And Salvific Universality of Jesus Christ and the Church," August 6, 2000, accessed May 19, 2012, www.vatican.va/roman_curia/congregations/cfaith/documents/rc_con_cfaith_doc_20000806_dominus-iesus_en.html, which acknowledged the presence of grace in other traditions, despite their being in a "gravely deficient situation" in comparison to those who receive "the fullness of the means of salvation" in the Catholic Church, VI.22.

86 *Nostra Aetate*, or "Declaration on the Relationship of the Church to Non-Christian Religions," section 2.

87 Dupuis, *Jesus Christ at the Encounter of World Religions*, 147.

88 Dupuis, *Jesus Christ at the Encounter of World Religions*, 5.

89 Congregation for the Doctrine of the Faith, "Notification on the book *Toward a Christian Theology of Religious Pluralism* (Orbis Books: Maryknoll, New York 1997) by Father Jacques Dupuis, S. J.," January 24, 2001, accessed December 26, 2011, www.va/roman_curia/congregations/cfaith/documents/rc_con_cfaith_doc_20010124_dupuis_en.html, Section IV.6; see also V.8.

3

The Impossibility of an Inclusivist Theology of Religions

An inclusivist returns: A thought experiment

The lessons taught by the overreach and inevitable failure of each of the examples of theological inclusivism discussed in Chapter 2 can be portrayed in the following thought experiment. An inclusivistic Christian theologian of religions attains celebrity for proposing a novel interpretation of religious others: religious others will be considered as virtual participants in the one, final, and normative religious community just so long as they express care as appropriate in the various dimensions of their personal, familial, social, and planetary life. God, on this generous and irenic view, sees action oriented to care as evincing the goodness of heart that is formally if unknowingly acquired by people outside the normative tradition by the action of Christ. In the eschaton, when time has played itself out, and the divine will realizes itself in a redeemed cosmos and a community of the blessed, the virtual participants in the ultimate community will learn that their goodness of heart was a foretaste of the fullness of life to be found in Christ. This widely admired and genial theologian of religion dies in due course; however, in a scenario that can exist only in the imagination of the author of this thought experiment, she returns after three millennia to survey the religious scene. To her astonishment, she discovers that the inclusivism that she had proposed is now completely forgotten as a relic of a surpassed and forgotten religious tradition. Historical and archeological research have recently revealed tantalizing fragments of the religious tradition that she served, but the ravages of war, countless natural disasters, and the rise of multiple compelling new religious movements and charismatic founders have thrust her beloved religion into a past that is virtually unrecoverable.

Thinking this thought experiment through should turn every inclusivist into a pluralist, for just as the dominant religions of today were all new religious movements at one time, and the symbols of authority that they deploy have not always existed, so these religions will either die out or morph into their successors over the long stretches of time that we human beings potentially have ahead of us before we evolve into the species that may replace us. If one book or city is held today to be at the center of the religious universe by a religious movement, it is certain that with the passage of enough time, these symbols will change and be surpassed. To think otherwise is, as John Hick has pointed out, a "historically short-sighted position,"[1] for they will be undone by the sheer passage of time and change. Inevitably, then, with the passage of time, one body of religious knowledge will give place to another, and the process of departicularization will demonstrate that an apophatic pluralist approach to religious teachings is the only sound basis for a responsible theology of religions. (For a religious tradition that bases it claims on apparent historical events, it would be better if history were short, since the longer the span of time in which humanity is active, the less significant becomes any one historical event, actual or imagined, and the less likely it is to be remembered by descendents in the far future, should there be one for humanity.) While no religious absolutist will likely accept the implications of this insight (despite the fact that the religious ground upon which they stand is slowly shifting), it has wider explanatory power than tradition-specific inclusivisms or exclusivisms and it will, unlike them, survive the disappearance of particular religious traditions. One can confidently proclaim, therefore, that apophatic pluralism, whether recognized by particularists or not, is the future of religion.

The pathos of overextended inclusivist theologies of religions

While the claim that apophatic pluralism is the only responsible basis for responsible reflection about the world's religions may seem impossible, irreverent, heretical, or even preposterous to people committed in advance, for logical or nonlogical reasons, to the finality of one religious tradition, it will become clear to anyone who has seriously considered the difficulty of finding a doctrinal resolution to the contrary claims of competing religious traditions that make absolute claims for themselves. Philosophical reflection on the conflict of absolutized views of life, in contrast to scriptural and theological arguments for these views, will inevitably acknowledge the impossibility of demonstrating such claims to the satisfaction of the unpersuaded without detours into fundamentalism and religious absolutism. The cure for these religious pathologies is to recognize that religious absolutism is always a kind of hope or demand that is self-evident to the persuaded but implausible to the unpersuaded. This situation, when multiplied beyond one absolutist religious movement, results in an unavoidable stalemate where apologists for competing absolutes meet in conflict and contradiction. Here is where particularisms and other forms of religious absolutism are forced to take their stand on inadequate or indefensible measures, including custom, nostalgia, narrowly interpreted religious experience, fideism, authority, fundamentalism, or, in the worst instances, force.

Since none of these practices can permanently secure religious absolutism by persuading the unpersuaded of the plausibility of *ad hoc* and *ex post facto* adaptations of originally foreign and unacceptable religious teachings, an apophatic pluralism that sees the plurality of religions as a consequence of the finitude of religious language, becomes a practical necessity for an ethical and reasonable religious life. People who, nevertheless, steadfastly believe in the final normative truth of their religious traditions will find themselves inevitably overcome by the mounting sum of disproofs brought on by the passage of time and the inevitability of change.

A case in point is Hendrik Kraemer's attempt in 1937 to define an exclusive status[2] for his theocentric "Biblical realism,"[3] which was an application of neo-Reformation theology to the data of comparative religion and the missiological issues of his time. The irony here is that the more absolute the divide between his supposedly realistic and uniquely revealed doctrine[4] and other religions, which he called "naturalist non-Christian religions,"[5] the more desperate appeared his attempt to delineate authentic Christian faith from close competitors such as "empirical Christianity,"[6] Catholicism,[7] Protestant Pietism,[8] mysticism,[9] post-Reformation Protestantism,[10] American-style fundamentalism and literalism,[11] and even, in the end, the theology of Karl Barth.[12] In one breath, he negates a natural theology like that of Thomas Aquinas,[13] but in another he sides with Emil Brunner[14] against Barth. It seems as if the one true revelation is, for Kraemer, a vanishing point on the horizon that is ever receding from view. But so subtle a teaching, which depends only upon the gracious initiative of a sovereign deity who has no commerce with the easy relativism and divinizing monism of anthropocentric and naturalistic religions,[15] raises the thorny issue of "the point of contact" between the sovereign theocentric revelation[16] and the defective thinking of self-assertive sinners addicted to distorting the natural recognition of God into self-serving idols.[17] While Kraemer rejects Barth's stern declaration that "there is no point of contact" as sterile and doctrinaire intellectualism[18] and moves in the direction of Brunner,[19] he yields no ground to religions other than his own favored tradition by allowing only two points of contact: the gospel as an antithesis to natural religious consciousness and the missionary as a religious artist.[20] That is, human religiosity is, for Kraemer, an expression of self-will that can lead only to failure and brokenness, which is an acceptable point of contact for the creative missionary, who, nurtured as much on the data of comparative religion as on the Bible and correct theology, is thus equipped to lead the way from natural religions to the revelation of the sovereign deity.[21]

It is a mark of how far we have traveled since 1937 that such sentiments today could not flow from an academic practitioner of comparative religion or the history of religions. Such sentiments linger today only at the far margins of academic theology, for apart from fundamentalists and many conservative evangelicals, academic theology, when it is not pluralistic, embraces some form of inclusivism as its default position. Also, comparative religion has left behind appeals to *sui generis* religious truths, whether articulated by Barth[22] or Eliade. Kraemer's book now reads like the desperate appeal of one who senses perhaps the coming negation of his stance,[23] except among the very literalists and fundamentalists that he decried.[24] Even in its title, one senses that the largeness of the world and its immense religious diversity had finally begun to dawn upon missiologists by 1938, along with a sense of the impossibility or even illegitimacy of the project of insisting upon the finality and normativity for all human beings of the Christian faith.[25] One feels the pathos of Kraemer's situation when one reads him today, and one is bemused by the certainty with which a professor of the history of religions declares only one version of only one of humanity's many religions as true and as necessary for all human beings.[26] Even odder and less reasonable is the hegemonism that one hears behind his repeated characterization as "obstinate" the people in India, China, Japan, and elsewhere who have failed to accept the truth of his variety of Christianity.[27]

Just as Kraemer's last ditch epicycle of singular revelation is no longer plausible except at the farthest margins of academic theology (while remaining the default stance in popular apologetics), so the antipluralistic sophistry that pluralism is merely a veiled expression of particularism fails as a criticism of pluralism. It is nothing more than a dodge and holding maneuver without any logical or philosophical substance. It cannot stand, since the pressing issues about the ultimate significance of life that are raised by the existence of multiple, competing religious visions can better be resolved by an appeal to apophatic pluralism than by retreating into exclusivism, inclusivism, confessionalism, fideism, or apologetics. Inevitably, then, a nonuniversalizing and nonsubstantive apophatic pluralistic interpretation of religions must remain as the only final truth in the theology of religions for the simple reason that no religious community can preserve its language against change and decay forever.

Toward an apophatic pluralist theory of religion

This claim, however, is not just another theological claim in competition with other theological claims. Insisting on the necessity of an apophatic pluralistic stance in the theology of religions is not the same as, for example, proclaiming universalism to proponents of a limited atonement. The claim that apophatic pluralism is a necessary principle of the theology of religions is more like a grammatical rule. To state the grammatical rule that substantives in the accusative case can be objects but generally not subjects of sentences is not the same as forming a sentence with an accusative noun. Similarly, to make a general claim about the nature of religious language is not the same as articulating a theological doctrine. To say that no doctrine is final, given the limits of human cognition and language, is not the same as claiming that all religions are true or that all religions point to the Absolute. The first statement is a regulative claim and is thus a second-order observation about the strengths and weaknesses of first-order substantive claims about the nature of reality, while the latter statements are speculative claims. At its most modest, an apophatic theory of religious pluralism involves the recognition of the limits of language and culture. While this approach can threaten absolutistic religious views, it is consistent with the nonabsolutistic practice of any religious tradition.

Given the sensitivity of religious faith, which is often inextricably rooted in the particular language, customs, and practices of specific communities, it is understandable that making a clean break with inclusivism and the renunciation of ever less plausible epicycles will be difficult for many inclusivists. Yet, if inclusivists move no further than accepting this first, apophatic stage of pluralism, they will have freed themselves, in principle at least, of the need to continue to construct ever more implausible epicycles to save the appearances of an overextended worldview. Only the most determined particularists will continue to reject this basic insight, while the inevitability of accepting it confirms it as a kind of law of religious history. This claim is not merely a Western, Enlightenment imposition on humanity's religious heritage,[28] for it is an insight that was already ancient for the author of the Kena Upaniṣad, who proclaimed: "It is different from the known;/it is different, too from the unknown;/So have we heard from those of old/Who have revealed it to us."[29] In the New Testament, this mystical unknowing also has its occasional witness: "For now we see in a mirror dimly" (1 Cor. 13.12 NRSV).[30] It would be tedious and superfluous in an academic essay on religious studies to enumerate multiple instances of the apophatic/cataphatic dialectic, for it is precisely the universality of this distinction in modes of religious discourse (even the silence of the Buddha on metaphysical and theological questions is itself a skillful deployment of apophatic discourse) that foretells the nonfinality of every religious orthodoxy.

Yet, nonfinality does not mean insignificance, since a world of machines, decorated surfaces, and surface identities, as in modern, post-Enlightenment, hypercapitalist contexts, cannot provide as much meaning for people as lives embedded in the great sacred narratives that humanity has devotedly told and retold over the millennia. Many people want to live in the light of the Trinity, the Trimūrti, the Trikāya, or some other stirring religious metaphor and not merely in the light of the Internet or a reductionistic science. Our full humanity requires sacred sustenance as much as technological and scientific support—perhaps even more. As long as this remains true of human beings, people will go on telling stories about the sacred and will make them the ultimate point of reference for their lives. But, what must always be part of this storytelling is the insight that our story can at any time be supplemented by a new episode, one as yet unimagined by us, as it has in the past, since no religion is without its revered or dishonored predecessors (and is it not the case that yesterday's heretics are often today's revered founders?). So long as at least some of us remember this necessary condition of every religious narrative while we continue to tell our sacred stories, we may soften for our religious descendents the disillusionment and sense of loss that religious movements go through when they die out or morph into their successors.

Contrary to those who might see theologies of religious pluralism as symptoms of decadence in the late stages of liberal Christianity, pluralism is the application of a historically sensitive philosophy of religions to the specific cases of individual religious movements. Thus, pluralism is the only responsible basis for global theologies and for religious studies. This may be rejected by people whose beliefs are based on authority, narrowly interpreted personal experiences, or tradition and by those who do not generalize from religious change in the past to religious change in the future. Yet, change is inevitable, and the dominant religious particularisms of today can no more avoid the changes, negations, and departicularizations of the future than those of the past could. If this insight were generally accepted and acknowledged by inclusivists, it would spell the end of inclusivistic interpretations of other religious movements as unaware beneficiaries of the fulfillments offered in one's own movement. (The ease with which people from competing inclusivisms can use this argument against each other shows that this sort of argument is invalid.) Working through the implications of the incapacity of religious absolutisms to secure themselves against change and the indifference of the unpersuaded should serve as the first step beyond the current impasse in the theology of religions.

Notes

1 John Hick, *An Interpretation of Religion: Human Responses to the Transcendent* (2nd edn). (New Haven, CT: Yale University Press, 2004), xxxix.
2 Kraemer, *The Christian Message in a Non-Christian World*, 9, 23, 45, 83, 88, 110, 122, 162, 167, 168.
3 Kraemer, *The Christian Message in a Non-Christian World*, 72, 82–3.
4 Kraemer, *The Christian Message in a Non-Christian World*, 62, 65.
5 Kraemer, *The Christian Message in a Non-Christian World*, 200.
6 Kraemer, *The Christian Message in a Non-Christian World*, 110, 145.
7 Kraemer, *The Christian Message in a Non-Christian World*, 10, 71, 114–15.
8 Kraemer, *The Christian Message in a Non-Christian World*, 169.
9 Kraemer, *The Christian Message in a Non-Christian World*, 113.
10 Kraemer, *The Christian Message in a Non-Christian World*, 10.
11 Kraemer, *The Christian Message in a Non-Christian World*, v.
12 Kraemer, *The Christian Message in a Non-Christian World*, 120.
13 Kraemer, *The Christian Message in a Non-Christian World*, 114–15.
14 Kraemer, *The Christian Message in a Non-Christian World*, 121, 133.
15 Kraemer, *The Christian Message in a Non-Christian World*, 111–12, 142, 165, 210.
16 Kraemer, *The Christian Message in a Non-Christian World*, 70, 103–4, 106.
17 Kraemer, *The Christian Message in a Non-Christian World*, vi, 124–9.
18 Kraemer, *The Christian Message in a Non-Christian World*, 131–3, 120.
19 Kraemer, *The Christian Message in a Non-Christian World*, 133. Karl Barth forcefully denounced Emil Brunner's attempts to discover a "point of contact" between the divine and the human, and he declares that "there is no point of contact for the redeeming action of God." Karl Barth, "No! Answer to Emil Brunner," in Karl Barth and Emil Brunner, *Natural Theology*, trans. Peter Fraenkel (London: Geoffrey Bles: The Centenary Press, 1946), 71, 74.
20 Kraemer, *The Christian Message in a Non-Christian World*, 139–40.
21 Kraemer, *The Christian Message in a Non-Christian World*, 46, 108.
22 Kraemer, *The Christian Message in a Non-Christian World*, 115–16.
23 Kraemer, *The Christian Message in a Non-Christian World*, 38, where he presciently senses the global appeal of Indian thought and yoga.
24 Kraemer, *The Christian Message in a Non-Christian World*, v.
25 Kraemer, *The Christian Message in a Non-Christian World*, 36, where he linked "the unequivocal disavowal at Jerusalem [i.e., the second international missionary conference, held in Jerusalem in 1928] of all spiritual imperialism" to what he saw as the conference's "very weak sense of apostolic consciousness."
26 Kraemer, *The Christian Message in a Non-Christian World*, 1, 45.
27 Kraemer, *The Christian Message in a Non-Christian World*, 57.
28 As summarized and rebutted in Paul F. Knitter, "Is the Pluralist Model a Western Imposition?" in Knitter, *Myth of Religious Superiority*, 33–4.

29 Kena Upaniṣad 1.4, *The Upaniṣads*. trans. Valerie Roebuck (New York: Penguin Books, 2003), 263.

30 A verse that Kevin Hart calls "the single most influential remark on signs and faith." *The Trespass of the Sign*, 7.

4

The Syncretistic Basis of the Theory of Apophatic Pluralism

Pluralism and the churning of religious traditions

Inclusivist theologies of religions are, at best, rearguard attempts to come to terms with religious pluralism and, at worst, futile attempts to blunt its force. However, at this point in the book, if nothing else has become clear, it should be that the churning of religious traditions in the thoroughly interconnected globalized society of the early twenty-first century demonstrates the undeniably pluralistic character of religion as a whole. Pluralism, in turn, implies the eventual departicularization of all religious traditions as the unique elements that they have syncretistically harmonized undergo change, decay, and eventual disappearance or mutation into their successors. But departicularization is not the whole story of pluralism, for it should be seen as the end of a process that begins with the phenomenon of religious hybridity, or multiple religious belonging.[1] Both of these processes of religious change can be seen as parts of the larger process of syncretism. Through religious hybridity, syncretism generates novel religious identities, while through departicularization, syncretism dismantles old identities in favor of novel ones. Rather than something lamentable, as in popular religious and even in learned theological discourses, syncretism is, in fact, the most basic process through which religion regenerates itself from one generation to the next. No understanding of the inevitability of pluralism as the future of religion would be complete without a clear grasp of the role that syncretism plays in the rise and fall of religious teachings and identities.

Syncretism: Hodgepodge or general feature of all religions?

Orthodox religious apologists often disparage syncretism as "cafeteria religion," or what Gavin D'Costa calls "a pick and mix divine."[2] The Christian missiologist Hendrik Kraemer defined syncretism more formally as denoting for Christian theologians "the *illegitimate* mingling of different religious elements."[3] Elizabeth Koepping deftly and critically captures the negative connotations of *syncretism* by characterizing it as "that useful slander for whatever is unclear, new, confused or merged."[4] As far back as the rancorous disputes among Christian theologians in Europe in the sixteenth and seventeenth centuries, the idea of syncretism has denoted a negative blending of religious ideas and practices. Despite the syncretistic elements that can be found in every religious tradition, religious traditionalists generally view syncretism with suspicion as a sign of faithlessness, shallowness, decadence, lack of commitment, inauthenticity, and contamination.[5]

For example, Catherine Cornille, a quasipluralist theologian of religions, expresses, like many orthodox theologians, an ambivalent view of syncretism. She holds that interreligious interactions where the participants are not or do not "remain rooted in the particular religious community from which and for which they speak" is a form of "New Age syncretism."[6] Judging people who "pick and choose"[7] elements from different religious traditions as lacking commitment, she sees them as engaging in more of a "strictly interpersonal" than "genuinely interreligious" dialogue.[8] She thus dismisses the products of their activities as a "hodgepodge"[9] and a "mishmash of ideas."[10]

Yet, this stance is at odds with her own central interest in the syncretistic phenomenon of multiple religious belonging, since encounters with other traditions inevitably involve syncretistic blendings that, to an outsider or to an orthodox critic, can seem like conversions or half-conversions to the religious other. This is the case with the notable religiously hybrid figures whom Cornille praises as courageous religious experimenters and pioneers: Louis Massignon, Henri Le Saux, Bede Griffiths, and Raimon Panikkar, all of whom were religiously hybrid Catholics living on the edges of multiple traditions and who engaged in creative efforts of religious fusion.[11] The activity of these religiously hybrid Catholics, who were inspired by the exigencies of their own personal situations and religious interests, is no less syncretistic than other contemporary syncretisms, which Cornille derides as "New Age." Nor are Cornille's preferred figures any less likely than other syncretists to be viewed favorably by orthodox defenders of their respective religious traditions.

As the examples of these Catholic figures show, syncretism plays an often unacknowledged role in the activity of even traditional theologians. Other fruitful expressions of syncretism include the Cambridge theologian Sarah Coakley, who recounts that her practice as a young Christian theologian of Vedāntic meditation, as presented in Transcendental Meditation, led her to a startlingly rich and fruitful awakening to contemplative silence.[12] Wendy Farley, a noted Protestant theologian, tells how her life was transformed by Tibetan Buddhism and yoga.[13] Other examples of syncretism include Thomas Merton and his famous explorations of Buddhism, Taoism, and Hinduism, which culminated in his meeting with the Dalai Lama, and Paul Knitter, who finds it impossible to be a Christian without also being a Buddhist.[14]

Thus, while some theologians may try to negate syncretism through rejection and denial, others may affirm syncretism as formative in their own theological formulations. This is especially the case for comparative theologians, who, in the view of John Thatamanil, "run the risk of becoming hyphenated, of becoming Hindu-Christian or Buddhist Christians"[15] (or hybrid participants in whatever other traditions they may be mediating). To counter the explicit recognition of the syncretistic elements within even apparently orthodox traditions and to avoid the danger of becoming religious hybrids themselves, particularist theologians may try to evade the pluralistic implications of syncretism by doubling down on their supposedly pristine original religious identities in ways that distort the actual syncretistic origins of these identities.

It seems to be the case then that syncretism is not merely an occasional expression of caprice or misunderstanding by new or forced converts. On the contrary, syncretism should be seen as the basic process of religious change through which new religious identities arise (i.e., hybridity) and are slowly dismantled as they mutate into successor identities (i.e., departicularization). That is, syncretism should be seen as the constitutive element in the formation and dismantling of religious identities. As Adelin Jørgensen writes, "In the field of history of religions, 'syncretism,' is, in the widest sense, defined as the general fact that religions change over time . . . . Therefore syncretism might initially be defined as *change of religions over time through mixture*."[16] So, instead of rejecting syncretism as merely a form of "spiritual shopping"[17] in which atomized modern selves capriciously pick and choose among elements of religious traditions for themselves (instead, that is, of letting others do the picking and choosing for them on the authority of multiple transitory but supposedly heteronomous religious authorities), syncretism should be seen as the fundamental way in which religion renews, recreates, and reproduces itself.[18] Since "syncretism follows syncretism in cultures,"[19] as Jørgensen argues, syncretism should be seen as the matrix out of which new religions arise. This includes the currently dominant religions, which, when they were new religions, were themselves products of syncretism (though this fact is often denied or obscured by their adherents).

The systematic role played by syncretism in the constitution of religions, and of cultures in general, is recognized by anthropologists Rosalind Shaw and Charles Stewart, who write that "an optimistic view has arisen in post-modern anthropology in which syncretic processes are considered basic not only to religion and ritual but to 'the predicament of culture' in general."[20] (New as this idea is among anthropologists, it was already the view of pioneering historians of religions, Gerardus van der Leeuw and Joachim Wach, who, in the words of Kurt Rudolph, held that "every religion is a syncretism when viewed from its own prehistory."[21])

These changed fortunes for syncretism have come about as anthropology in the last decades has stopped focusing on "stable or original form of cultures" and has become more interested in showing "how local communities respond to historical change and global influences."[22] As a consequence, social theory has begun to employ notions such as syncretism, hybridization, and creolization to analyze "globalization, transnational nationalism, and the situation of diaspora communities,"[23] thus weakening the plausibility among anthropologists of the notion of cultural purity.[24] The implications of the changing views of syncretism among anthropologists is clear for religious studies, for as Stewart argues, following van der Leeuw and Andre Droogers, "If we grant the premise that there are no pure cultures, then we are led to suppose that there are no pure religious traditions either."[25]

So, instead of seeing syncretism as a threat to supposedly fixed traditional identities, it should be seen as "a process in which the organizing principle for a religious identity establishes itself . . . ."[26] Thus, the stock dismissal of syncretism as contrary to the maintenance of religious identity should now give way to the recognition of syncretism as the process through which religious identities are formed.[27]

Given these developments, the term *syncretism* can now be reclaimed for positive use in religious studies, theology, and anthropology. It need no longer remain as a term of disapprobation used by missionaries and particularist theologians in quest of an illusory religious purity. For example, despite hesitations about the word, Eliza F. Kent uses it because it would otherwise be "difficult to talk meaningfully about the varieties of religious change without it,"[28] while Anita Maria Leopold argues that the concept is useful for understanding "what happens when religions travel" in order "to obtain an image of how changing contexts influence religious meaning in the minds of people."[29] Indeed, the term has been rehabilitated to such an extent that Charles Stewart advocates an "anthropology of syncretism"[30] because, as he writes, following in the wake of Edward Said and James Clifford, "syncretism describes the process by which cultures constitute themselves at any given point in time."[31]

Syncretism and religious change

When taken in a positive sense as a constitutive expression of the change that generates, transforms, and dismantles religious movements, syncretism becomes a helpful analytical tool for making sense of the constant and sometimes bewildering changes and fusions that characterize the actual, as opposed to the ideal, religious life of humanity. Before applying the concept to some recent expressions of religious change, however, syncretism needs to be distinguished from the related concepts of acculturation and inculturation.

Syncretism, acculturation, and inculturation

Until recently, syncretism had generally been subsumed by anthropologists under the notion of acculturation,[32] a process of synthesis that occurs when two previously unrelated cultures begin to interact with each other.[33] Acculturation must, however, be carefully distinguished from the missionary strategies of "inculturation," "contextualization," "accommodation," and "indigenization."[34] These latter terms name varying aspects of the process of attempting to express one set of supposedly normative religious ideas in the idioms of another, apparently deficient religious tradition.[35] While contextualization has been defined by Elizabeth Koepping as "the minimal accommodation necessary to enable communications" between a local group and missionaries, inculturation is, in her view, "the near-revolutionary challenge posed by the Christian faith to the underlying structure" of "unreflectingly enculturated" persons and groups.[36] The first strategy is more a matter of newcomers adapting to a local context, as the Thomas Christians did quite harmoniously in South India for centuries until the arrival of Portuguese missionaries in the sixteenth century,[37] while the second strategy is clearly part of an inclusivist and even exclusivist missionary program of displacement or replacement of local traditions.[38] Questions about contextualization and inculturation are thus more a theme in missiology, the inclusivist theology of religions, and comparative theologies, which are predisposed to credit the claims to the universal normativity of a specific religious tradition, than in anthropology or in pluralistic theological and philosophical approaches to religions.

Although inculturation must be seen as an attempt to shape acculturation to the advantage of a tradition claiming finality for itself,[39] it nevertheless remains a syncretistic process of acculturation, which will inevitably lead to a pluralist conclusion, since the result of syncretism or acculturation can only be more syncretism. So when Cornille, an almost pluralistic inclusivist theologian of religions, claims that "interreligious dialogue is one of the main components of inculturation,"[40] she is acknowledging that interreligious dialogue is a form of syncretism. Thus, missiological concepts like inculturation (as well as theological stances like exclusivism and inclusivism) must be seen as mystified, reflectively opaque instances of syncretism, which will inevitably be undone by that aspect of syncretism that I call departicularization.

Syncretism and new religious movements

Examples of syncretism at work in generating new religious traditions (hybridity) from old ones (departicularization) are not hard to find. One example is early Christianity, which innovatively blended and reinterpreted Judaism, Zoroastrianism, and Greek and Roman philosophies and religions, influenced perhaps by an undercurrent of ideas and practices from India communicated by wandering yogis and Buddhist monks. The new religious identity that emerged from this syncretistic churn was also part of a process that departicularized the other traditions in the mix. Other examples include the many varieties of contemporary Christianities in the USA that blend European Christianities, early modern, modern, and postmodernist philosophical ideas, Asian religious teachings and practices (as in the various Christian practices based on yoga, mindfulness, and meditation), and indigenous worldviews (as in the intercourse with spirits and the spirit world in Pentecostalism). Another example of syncretism is the ancient and ongoing pluralism of Japanese religion, which synthesizes shamanism, folk religion, Shinto, Buddhism, Taoism, Confucianism, and, in recent centuries, new religions.[41] In South Korea, some Pentecostal groups syncretistically display "shamanic tendencies" by developing a practical, this-worldly spirituality that focuses on salvation, prosperity, and health.[42] In Africa, syncretisms of missionary Christianity, independent churches, and African traditional religions have produced a profusion of new religious forms.[43] In India, the interaction with Christianity has produced many syncretistic movements in which Hinduism has been either simplified or Westernized and in which Christianity has been pushed toward nonexclusivism and a focus on spiritual realization instead of only on doctrine and proclamation.

While the syncretistic effects of Christianity and Hinduism upon each other in India since the days of Rammohan Roy have been well documented,[44] the syncretistic influence of Hinduism on popular religion in the USA has only recently begun to merit serious scholarly and journalistic attention.[45] Even less studied has been the role played in the syncretistic mixing of these once unrelated religious traditions in the writings and examples of countless Western Christian theologians, missionaries, and historians of religions who have been deeply shaped by Hinduism and India. Even when they retain an inclusivist stance, these writings are often suffused with Hindu ideas and its ethos of religious pluralism and tolerance. Leading figures who have been part of this process of mediating Hinduism and Christianity include Rudolf Otto, Thomas Merton, Mircea Eliade, Carl Jung, Francis Clooney, John Carman, Lesslie Newbigin, Ninian Smart, Diana Eck, Raimon Panikkar, Catherine Cornille, Bede Griffiths, Wayne Teasdale, Jacques Dupuis, Henri Le Saux, Felix Willard, John Thatamanil, Anthony de Mello, and countless others. So numerous are the Christian (particularly Catholic) writers who have deeply taken on board Hindu teachings that one wonders if the effect of centuries of missionary activity in India has not actually been the reverse of its original intention as these figures have served as syncretistic bridges to Western societies, many of which have almost effortlessly adopted central Indian ideas like meditation, yoga, rebirth, and karma as part of mainstream religious practice and identities. In any case, it seems that an attraction to Hinduism by Christian thinkers, ostensibly motivated by various theoretical issues and social concerns, has often served to supplement deficits in their home traditions.

Syncretism and global Christianities

The concept of syncretism is increasingly applied to forms of global Christianity, thus bringing Christianity within the scope of the study of religion and the social sciences rather than leaving it as a topic only for theologians, missiologists, and church historians. Chad M. Bauman has developed a theoretically sophisticated historical ethnography[46] that stands at the intersection of religious studies, history, and anthropology (although Bauman's conclusions can be used missiologically, he never breaks his stance in this ethnography as a religious-studies scholar or enters into explicit theological and missiological reflections). In an absorbing account of how some members of the Chamar-Satnami *jāti* in nineteenth-century India sought social uplift through Christianization rather than the traditional Hindu process of Sanskritization, Bauman situates his study of these converts to American Protestantism between truimphalist missionary accounts and the emerging tendency to view Christianities outside the West as religious movements not unlike others (as in the approaches of Devaka Premawardhana,[47] Joel Robbins,[48] Eliza F. Kent,[49] and Jenny Daggers.[50]).

A valuable feature of Bauman's approach is his recognition of religious syncretism as a fact of religious life and not merely as the corruption of a supposedly timeless teaching or revelation. Thus, Bauman shows how Christianity affected Chhattisgarh culture and how this culture, in turn, affected the Christianity of the missionaries, thereby supporting his claim that religious identity is a "process" that is "contested, protean, emerging, and fluid."[51] That is, syncretism is the condition out of which new religious identities emerge and by which they are eventually absorbed. Consequently, Bauman argues that Christian missionary activity in Chhattisgarh cannot be seen simply as the imposition of a foreign system upon a purely indigenous population (i.e., people possessed of a timeless, pure, almost archetypal cultural identity), which had been induced to convert to Christianity because of the potential material and cultural benefits. He further argues that religions are not merely imposed but adopted and adapted to context, that conversions always involve the satisfaction of ideal as well as material interests, that no religion is purely indigenous, and that no religion is purely foreign.[52] (Bauman tries to find support for his position in the phenomenon of the conversion of many Westerners to Hinduism, although the rewards here were invariably less materially and culturally tangible for Western converts.[53])

Similarly, but taking an explicitly theological and missiological stance that seems at odds with his otherwise sophisticated understanding of the pluralistically creative and destructive forces of syncretism, Jonas Adelin Jørgensen draws upon the methodologies of religious studies, anthropology, missiology, the theology of religions, and the philosophy of religions in an attempt to develop an "interreligious hermeneutics" that can support a "Christocentric pluralism."[54] Like Bauman, Jørgensen positively values syncretism and hybrid religious identities as productive of religious differentiation and novelty,[55] yet he wants to make use of these processes for theological purposes.[56] Starting from the "social fact"[57] of syncretism, Jørgensen sees God as issuing a "universal calling" that animates these processes and generates the "luxurious plurality of Christianities."[58] He rejects the pluralism of theologians such as John Hick, but veers away from the inclusivism of what he calls the "neo-classical tripartite division"[59] of paradigms in the theology of religions. Instead, he focuses on novel Christian identities in global Christianity, which are shaped by syncretism and religious hybridity. (One novelty he detects in emergent global Christianities is their innovative shifting from traditional institutional forms toward a sect-based ecclesiology grounded in interiority and intimacy.[60])

Jørgensen thus attempts to place syncretism in the service of Christian theology and missiology, as if syncretism were an as yet unacknowledged mode of Christian revelation,[61] but the creative adaptivity of syncretism is not limited to Christianity, since the process of syncretism has thrown up a luxurious plurality of Buddhist, Mormon, Zoroastrian, Hindu, and other identities over the millennia. Thus, an inclusivist view that this or that deity is uniquely behind the process of syncretism will, if given enough time, be relativized by newly emerging religious identities that no longer recognize the putatively originative deity. Fundamentalisms[62] and inclusivisms, which can be seen as syncretistic adaptations of traditions to newer or alternative ideologies that challenge or undercut them, can, for a time, retard this natural process of new-religion formation. Indeed, Jørgensen seems intent on maintaining the normativity of Jesus in a Christ-centered inclusivism that tries to absorb the lesson of syncretism rather than rejecting it, but, as we have seen in earlier portions of this book, no inclusivism can hold out forever against the syncretistic formation of new religious movements and identities. Just as Christianity arose as a syncretism of Jewish, Greco-Roman, and Zoroastrian religious ideas, so new religious identities with Christianity as a central ingredient are now proliferating on all sides.

Ironically, Jørgensen takes the opposite, positive view of syncretism in contrast to an earlier, influential missiologist, Hendrik Kraemer, who saw syncretism as one of the characteristic marks of "naturalist non-Christian religions" and their "primitive apprehension of existence."[63] Kraemer included all religions except the orthodox Protestant Christian faith and, in a restrictive and conditional manner, Judaism, and Islām within this realm of "naturalist religions."[64] In Christianity alone, what he called, "*the* religion of revelation," he saw an exclusive, theocentric truth flowing in a Barthian manner directly in its purity from God.[65] Because of its uniquely divine provenance, the biblical revelation is, in his view, free of syncretistic admixtures. In contrast to biblical religion, a "spirit" of syncretism, in his view, "runs through the veins of the naturalist religions."[66] This is reflected in "the amiable suavity" of natural religionists, who proclaim that "all religions are ultimately one."[67] Kraemer quotes Sarvepalli Radhakrishnan to the effect that there is not much difference in salvific means between Hinduism and Christianity.[68] He also cited the view of a Japanese Buddhist organization that held that soteriologically, if not doctrinally, Mahāyāna Buddhism and Christianity are essentially the same.[69] With a note of incredulity, Kraemer rejects both claims from the standpoint of a "Biblical realism" (in contrast to his "naturalistic monism"), which is supposedly grounded on the sovereign, creative activity of the Christian God who created the only way of salvation through a real atonement and act of reconciliation.[70] Thus, contrary to Jørgensen, Kraemer saw syncretism as a sign of fallenness and religious lostness rather than as a means for promoting the gospel.

The irony here, however, is that Kraemer's exclusivism is impossible to maintain today, except among the more extreme Protestant fundamentalists, simply because the idea of a pristine Christian revelation is impossible to maintain in light of the increasing awareness of the fundamentally Jewish character of Jesus's teaching and the fundamentally syncretistic context in which Jesus, his teachings, the Jesus movement, and Hellenistic Christianities arose. And trying to use syncretism as a tool of mission, as in current strategies encoded under phrases like "inculturation" and "contextualization," is as much an admission of the syncretistic character of religion as was Kraemer's desperate, last-ditch effort of limiting syncretism to his religious foes while isolating his preferred tradition within an ahistorical realm of religious immutability and purity.

Moving a step further in the study of Christianity along the pluralistic path under the ineluctable pressure of syncretism, Devaka Premawardhana argues for the porosity of even the most rigid and exclusivistic of traditions, such as global Pentecostalism. The "creative bricolage" (i.e., syncretism) of even this kind of Christianity as it draws upon and creatively integrates to or refers to pre-Christian traditions shows, in his view, that Christianity should be no less an object of study than other religious movements.[71] The academic study of religion over the last century typically viewed Christianity in its traditional Western form as either "in opposition to, or as prototype for world religions,"[72] which led to the formal exclusion of the Western version of Christianity from the study of the world's religions (as expressed, for example, in the founding deed of Harvard University's Center for the Study of World Religions[73]). But now that the syncretistic churn that is generating a bewildering variety of Christianities across the planet has focused new attention on Christianity as "one *among* world religions," global Christianity is emerging as a legitimate topic of academic instead of merely theological or missiological study.[74] Yet, the important point here is not so much the return of Christianity as an object of academic study nor the rise of new and often novel and unfamiliar forms of global Christianity, but the inevitable departicularization of Christianity as it modulates itself into countless new dialects.

Thus, the real lesson here, as clearly evidenced in the field studies presented in the work of Bauman, Jørgensen, and many others, is that syncretism lies at the beginning and end of all self-cherishing religious identities. Beginning with the generation of hybrid religious identities, syncretism fosters the rise of novel religious movements; later, through the subprocess of departicularization, syncretism undercuts old identities in favor of novel religious forms. In both cases, syncretism implies pluralism. Indeed, syncretism can be seen as pluralism in action as it inexorably demonstrates through historical and cultural changes that no finite, historically conditioned set of beliefs or practices can preserve itself from inevitable supersession by the unpredictable religious forms arising now and in the future.

Syncretism and apophatic pluralism

These diverse and sometimes bewildering movements and countermovements in humanity's ever-changing, irrepressible religious activity confirm the basic principle of apophatic pluralism that the limitations of religious language necessarily imply religious pluralism. This principle is expressed positively in the abundance of syncretistic religious movements and in the development of often highly original and distinctive religious hybrid personalities that are the seedbed of humanity's new religious movements. Negatively, this is expressed in rearguard attempts by once new religious movements to preserve themselves against change and replacement through often ingenious but always doomed epicyclic reinterpretations of themselves.

Attempts at mastering, restraining, or controlling the fluidic process of spontaneous, syncretistic creativity that is the natural state of human religiosity will inevitably fail. Like detritus left by a receding wave, they will be washed away by the next wave. Instead of continuing to build houses from sand, particularists might learn to see this syncretistic process of creativity and destruction as a natural dialectical process of cataphatic creativity and apophatic purification through which religions, like everything else, rise and fall. Instead of clinging to favored and familiar forms, even as they vanish from our grasp, we might begin to see this process as itself the primary form of religious and spiritual life—as symbolized by the images of hunger and death in the Upaniṣads, in the self-sacrificial cultus of Hegel, and the interplay of negation and manifestation in Mādhyamika and Hua-yen Buddhism. Just as prophets, mystics, and pioneering religious teachers strain every nerve of aspiration and creativity to bring new, life-giving forms of religion to life, so might particularists follow them into the loss of their religious selves that is implied by the supersession of beloved religious forms and emerge, like the seed dropped into the earth, in a new and more luxuriant form. By entering into this creative and destructive process with mindfulness and reverence rather than with fear and *ad hoc* arguments, one may discover that apophatic pluralism is not merely a theory about religious language, but also a spiritual discipline. For those who take an apophatic and pluralistic approach to human religiosity, the Copernican revolution in theology, the pluralistic hypothesis, and apophatic pluralism itself will be recognized as calls to overthrow falsely universalized moments in religious history rather than as apostasy, triumphalism, or hegemonism. In this way, particularism can be liberated by releasing itself into the organic and natural flow of the untamably creative, destructive, and spontaneous life of the spirit.

Notes

1 Cornille, "Introduction," *Many Mansions?* 2.

2 Gavin D. Costa, "Pluralist Arguments," in Becker, Morali, and D'Costa, *Catholic Engagement with World Religions*, 334. Here, D'Costa is arguing against John Hick, who he sees as failing to acknowledge "the epistemic control of any authoritative revelation."

3 Kraemer, *The Christian Message in a Non-Christian World*, 203, italics in the original.

4 Elizabeth Koepping, "India, Pakistan, Bangladesh, Burma/Myanmar," in *Christianities in Asia*, ed. Peter C. Phan (Malden, MA and Oxford: Wiley-Blackwell, 2011), 28.

5 Charles Stewart and Rosalind Shaw, "Introduction: Problematizing Syncretism," in *Syncretism/Anti-Syncretism*, eds. Charles Stewart and Rosalind Shaw (London and New York: Routledge, 1994), 1, 4, 7–8, 14; Anita Maria Leopold and Jeppe Sinding Jensen, "Introduction to Part II," in eds. Anita Maria Leopold and Jeppe Sinding Jensen, *Syncretism in Religion: A Reader* (New York: Routledge, 2005; originally published 2004), 16; Kurt Rudolph, "Syncretism: From Theological Invective to a Concept in the Study of Religion," in Leopold and Jensen, *Syncretism in Religion*, 68–9.

6 Cornille, *The Im-Possibility of Interreligious Dialogue*, 4. See also Cornille, "Introduction," *Many Mansions?* 3–4. Cornille's clichéd dismissal of these emergent spiritualities, which are inspired by the encounters between many of the world's traditions, makes use of the term, "New Age," which is an overly generic characterization of these creative synthesizing movements. This term has now become more of a historical designation or apologetic insult than a term of trade used in alternative spiritual circles themselves, which have moved since the 1990s beyond referring to themselves as "New Age."

7 Cornille, *The Im-Possibility of Interreligious Dialogue*, 64.

8 Cornille, *The Im-Possibility of Interreligious Dialogue*, 60.

9 Cornille, *The Im-Possibility of Interreligious Dialogue*, 64. She quotes this expression from Lowell Streiker, *New Age Comes to Main Street* (Nashville, TN: Abingdon Press, 1990), 46.

10 Cornille, *The Im-Possibility of Interreligious Dialogue*, 64. She quotes the last of these expressions from Peter Lemesurier, *This New Age Business* (Forres: Findhorn Press, 1990), 185.

11 Cornille, *The Im-Possibility of Interreligious Dialogue*, 73–8.

12 Sarah Coakley, "Prayer as Crucible: How My Mind Has Changed." *The Christian Century*, March 22, 2011, 32–3.

13 Wendy Farley, *The Wounding and Healing of Desire: Weaving Heaven and Earth* (Louisville, KY: Westminster John Knox Press, 2005), x, xvi.

14 Paul F. Knitter, *Without Buddha I Could Not Be a Christian* (Oxford: Oneworld, 2009).

15 Thatamanil, *The Immanent Divine*, xiii.

16 Adelin Jørgensen, *Jesus Imandars and Christ Bhaktas: Two Case Studies of Interreligious Hermeneutics and Identity in Global Christianity* (Frankfurt am Main: Peter Lang, 2008), 35. For this definition, Jørgensen relies upon Fritz Stolz, who writes: "In religionswissenschaftlicher Präzisierung ist Synkretismus zunächst ganz generell als spezifische Form des Religionswandels auzufassen. Tatsächlich is kein religiöses Symbolsystem völlig statisch; Veränderungen gehen langasamer oder schneller vor sich." "Synkretismus, I Religionsgeschichtlich." *Theologische Realenzyklopädie*. Vol. 32, edited by Gerhard Müller (Berlin and New York: Walter de Gruyter, 2001), 528.

17 Robert Wuthnow reductionistically characterizes contemporary religious pluralists in the USA as engaging in "spiritual shopping." *America and the Challenges of Religious Diversity* (Princeton, NJ and Oxford: Princeton University Press, 2005), 106–29.

18 Thus, a more positive view of the syncretistic phenomenon of people professing to be spiritual without being religious is emerging in sociology. Omar M. McRoberts, a sociologist at the University of Chicago, argues that "the number of people identifying as 'spiritual, but not religious' has been growing perhaps for three decades. This of course has implications for traditional religious institutions, which may feel pressure to revitalize or altogether repackage their spiritual offerings. We should not assume, however, that 'spiritual' people are individualists who avoid participation in general. Rather we should look carefully for new forms of spiritual sociability emerging in the religious field, and new ways of expressing spiritual values in the public realm." "Growth in secular attitudes leaves Americans room for belief in God," *UChicago News*, accessed October 24, 2011, news.uchicago.edu/article/2009/10/23/growth-secular-attitudes-leaves-americans-room-belief-god.

19 Jørgensen, *Jesus Imandars and Christ Bhaktas*, 49.

20 Shaw and Stewart, "Introduction: Problematizing Syncretism," in Shaw and Stewart, *Syncretism/Anti-Syncretism*, 1.

21 Kurt Rudolph, "Syncretism—From Theological Invective to a Concept in the Study of Religion," trans. David Warburton, in Leopold and Jensen, *Syncretism in Religion*, 71.

22 Charles Stewart, "Syncretism and Its Synonyms: Reflections on Cultural Mixture," *Diacritics* 29:3 (Fall 1999): 40.

23 Stewart, "Syncretism and Its Synonyms," 40.

24 Jørgensen, *Jesus Imandars and Christ Bhaktas*, 49; Stewart and Shaw, "Introduction: Problematizing Syncretism," in Stewart and Shaw, *Syncretism/Anti-Syncretism*, 1–2; see also Stewart, "Relocating Syncretism in Social Science Discourse," in Leopold and Jensen, *Syncretism in Religion*, 274.
25 Stewart, "Syncretism and Its Synonyms," 55.
26 Jørgensen, *Jesus Imandars and Christ Bhaktas*, 417.
27 Jørgensen, *Jesus Imandars and Christ Bhaktas*, 34; Stewart and Shaw, "Introduction: Problematizing Syncretism," in Stewart and Shaw, *Syncretism/Anti-Syncretism*, 1.
28 Eliza F. Kent, "Secret Christians of Sivakasi: Gender, Syncretism, and Crypto-Religion in Early Twentieth-Century South India," *Journal of the American Academy of Religion* 79:3 (September 2011): 677–8n2.
29 Leopold, "General Introduction," in Leopold and Jensen, *Syncretism in Religion*, 8.
30 Stewart, "Syncretism and Its Synonyms," 55.
31 Stewart, "Syncretism and Its Synonyms," 41.
32 Aylward Shorter, "Inculturation: The Premise of Universality," in *A Universal Faith: Peoples, Cultures, Religions, and the Christ*, eds. Catherine Cornille and Valeer Neckebrouck (Peeters Press: Louvain/Grand Rapids, MI: Eerdmans, 1993). Stewart points out that Edward Said, James Clifford, and Marshal Sahlins "have lifted syncretism out of the framework of acculturation" by showing that syncretism, rather than being transitional to successful assimilation, is characteristic of cultures, since hybridization simply replaces hybridization. Stewart, "Syncretism and Its Synonyms," 40. See also Stewart, "Relocating Syncretism in Social Science Discourse," in Leopold and Jensen, *Syncretism in Religion*, 274.
33 Jørgensen, *Jesus Imandars and Christ Bhaktas*, 46–8; Stewart and Shaw, "Introduction," in *Syncretism/Anti-Syncretism*, 5–6. As a global process affecting religious identities, it is helpful to relate syncretism to two similar large-scale processes studied in the social sciences under the names of *globalization* and *glocalization* (or *localization*), in which universalizing ideologies and identities creatively and destructively interact with local, indigenous reactions to globalization and with the resulting hybrids of traditional and globalizing cultures. Thus, globalization would involve processes of hybridity and departicularization, while glocalization would include fundamentalisms (or maximalisms, see Locklin and Nicholson, "The Return of Comparative Theology," 478), particularist defenses of religions, and new syntheses that retain nominal fidelity to a local tradition while incorporating elements of the newly encountered tradition or traditions. Also see Ulrike Schuerkens, "Social Transformations Between Global Forces and Local Life-Worlds: Introduction," *Current Sociology* 51:3/4 (May/July 2003): 195–7.
34 Aylward Shorter articulates the differences between inculturation, contextualization, and acculturation in "Inculturation: The Premise of Universality," in Cornille and Neckebrouck, *A Universal Faith*, 2–6. See also Jørgensen, *Jesus Imandars and Christ Bhaktas*, 69; David Mosse, "The Politics of Religious Synthesis: Roman Catholicism and Hindu Village Society in Tamil Nadu, India," in Stewart and Shaw, *Syncretism/Anti-Syncretism*, 103n1; Shaw and Stewart, "Introduction," *Syncretism/Anti-Syncretism*, 11–12; Anthony, J. Gittins, following Shorter, distinguishes between the sociological concept of acculturation and the theological concept of inculturation for which, as Gittins points out, "social scientist have no use." "Beyond Liturgical Inculturation: Transforming Deep Structures of Faith, "*Irish Theological Quarterly* 69 (2004): 49.

35 Stewart and Shaw, Introduction," in *Syncretism/Anti-Syncretism*, 11–12.

36 Koepping, "India, Pakistan, Bangladesh, Burma/Myanmar," in Phan, *Christianities in Asia*, 13–14.

37 Koepping, "India, Pakistan, Bangladesh, Burma/Myanmar," in Phan, *Christianities in Asia*, 14–17.

38 As expressed, for instance, by Felix Wilfred, "Liberation in India and the Church's Participation," in *Leave the Temple*, ed. Felix Wilfred (Maryknoll, NY: Orbis Books, 1992), 196, where he writes, "the liberating mission of the church is, then, a process of deep immersion and inculturation." Samuel Rayan expresses this view more forcefully:

> "Biblical thought . . . shocks Indian society by confronting us with a God who is one with outcasts . . . . We believe that the cross is the place where the new humanity begins to bud. It is the cross of the outcaste that bears the promise of the new earth and the new India with a human heart, a heart of flesh."

"Outside the Gate, Sharing the Insult," in Wilfred, *Leave the Temple*, 144.

39 Gavin D'Costa, for example, defines inculturation as "the use of cultures to give shape and form to the proclamation of the gospel." "Christianity and the World Religions," in D'Costa, Knitter, and Strange, *Only One Way?* 37.

40 Catherine Cornille, "Introduction," in Cornille and Neckebrouck, *A Universal Faith*, ix.

41 H. Byron Earhart, *Japanese Religion* (4th edn). (Belmont, CA: Wadsworth/Cengage Learning, 2004), 1–5, 75–8, 137–40.

42 Andrew Eungi Kim, "South Korea," in Phan, *Christianities in Asia*, 22–228.

43 Mika Vähäkangas, "Ghambageu Encounters Jesus in Sonjo Mythology: Syncretism as African Rational Action," *Journal of the American Academy of Religion* 76:1 (March 2008): 111–37; Birgit Meyer, "Beyond Syncretism: Translation and Diabolization in the Appropriation of Protestantism in Africa," in Stewart and Shaw, *Syncretism/Anti-Syncretism*, 45–68.

44 Brian Hatcher, *Bourgeois Hinduism, Or The Faith of the Modern Vedantists: Rare Discourses from Early Colonial Bengal* (New York and Oxford, 2007), 3–101.

45 See note 60.

46 Chad M. Bauman, *Christian Identity and Dalit Religion in Hindu India, 1868–1947* (Grand Rapids, MI: Eerdmans, 2008).

47 Devaka Premawardhana, "Christianity Becomes Unfamiliar," *Harvard Divinity Bulletin* 39: 1 & 2 (Winter/Spring 2011): 29–34.

48 Bauman, *Christian Identity and Dalit Religion in Hindu India*, 24; Joel Robbins, "Crypto-Religion and the Study of Cultural Mixtures: Anthropology, Value, and the Nature of Syncretism," *Journal of the American Academy of Religion* 79:2 (2011): 408–24. See also, among his other works on this topic, "What Is a Christian? Notes Toward an Anthropology of Christianity," *Religion* 33:3 (2003): 191–9. From a religious studies perspective, this move makes sense, although it remains true that the rise of this hybrid Christian movement is a result of the legacy of Western colonialism and may, therefore, have been motivated more by material than ideal interests. Consequently, despite Bauman's hopes to the contrary, hesitancy to see these religions on the same footing with indigenous religions by postcolonial scholars and anthropologists may persist, as obliquely expressed in the exclusion

of Christianity from a list of formative religious traditions in India by sociologist Kamlesh Mohan in "Cultural Values and Globalization: India's Dilemma," *Current Sociology* 59:2 (March 2011): 215.

49 Kent, "Secret Christians of Sivakasi," 679–81. Kent notes that in the late nineteenth century, prosperous Nadars in Tamil Nadu tried to raise their social status either though Christianization (southern Nadars) or sanskritization (northern Nadars) (62).

50 Jenny Daggers, "Thinking 'Religion': The Christian Past and Interreligious Future of Religious Studies and Theology," *Journal of the American Academy of Religion* 78:4 (December 2010): 962, 987.

51 Bauman, *Christian Identity and Dalit Religion in Hindu India*, 20.

52 Bauman, *Christian Identity and Dalit Religion in Hindu India*, 240–4.

53 Bauman, *Christian Identity and Dalit Religion in Hindu India*, 240–1. Bauman's approach seems designed to undermine the still important distinction between imposed religious systems and autochthonous religious systems. While Bauman claims that postmodernism teaches that no religion is purely autochthonous and, so, is a product of syncretism, it seems rash to me to conclude that the distinction between imposed and autochthonous religions is artificial and irrelevant, especially when differences in power and wealth between missionaries and potential converts favored the missionaries in colonial India, while the situation was quite the opposite in general for early Hindu missionaries and their converts in the West.

54 Jørgensen, *Jesus Imandars and Christ Bhaktas*, 437.

55 Jørgensen, *Jesus Imandars and Christ Bhaktas*, 34–45.

56 Jørgensen, *Jesus Imandars and Christ Bhaktas*, 69.

57 Jørgensen, *Jesus Imandars and Christ Bhaktas*, 2.

58 Jørgensen, *Jesus Imandars and Christ Bhaktas*, 437.

59 Jørgensen, *Jesus Imandars and Christ Bhaktas*, 27.

60 Jørgensen, *Jesus Imandars and Christ Bhaktas*, 437. This is a syncretistic trend also noticeable in North America where "nondenominational" Christians distance themselves from traditional forms of Christianity and stress instead their relationship to Jesus. This notable development can be seen as the influence in North America of Westernized versions of Hinduism and Buddhism, which stress personal inwardness at the expense of institutional forms. This Asian-influenced new religious form is traceable in the USA back to Emerson and Thoreau, both early assimilators of ideas from Asia, and it has now permeated the religious mainstream through syncretistic religious movements like theosophy, the New Thought movement, the New Age movement, and the multiple meditation and yoga movements that have spread across the USA since the days of Swami Vivekananda. As a result, many North Americans have forged novel identities by assimilating elements of Hinduism and Buddhism into their native religious identities. These movement have been chronicled in the recently published and quite absorbing accounts of the rise of these new forms of religiosity in the USA in *Philip Goldberg's American Veda* (New York: Random House, 2010), Stefanie Syman's *The Subtle Body: The Story of Yoga in America* (New York: Farrar, Straus and Giroux, 2011), Lola Williamson, *Transcendent in America: Hindu-inspired Meditation Movements as New Religion* (New York; New York University Press, 2010), and Catherine Albanese, *A Republic of Mind and Spirit: A Cultural History of American Metaphysical Religion* (New Haven, CT: Yale University Press, 2007). Peter Beyer, "Religious Diversity and

Globalization," in *The Oxford Handbook of Religious Diversity*, 192–3, summarizes scholarship charting the contemporary shift from institutionalized religious expression toward spirituality and "lived religion."

61 Jørgensen, *Jesus Imandars and Christ Bhaktas*, 437.

62 In the current climate, when the term fundamentalism has been debased through journalistic and popular abuse since September 11, 2001, and because it has become a term of abuse for a wider category of religious phenomena by the New Atheists, the neologism "maximalism" of Reid B. Locklin and Hugh Nicholson may be preferable. Locklin and Nicholson replace "fundamentalism" with "maximalism" in an attempt to undercut pejorative usages of this once very useful term. Reid and Locklin, "The Return of Comparative Theology," 478. See my discussion of *fundamentalism* in note 1 in the introduction.

63 Kraemer, *The Christian Message in a Non-Christian World*, 200, 203. Kraemer later allowed that all religions can be seen as "syncretistic to some degree," quoted in Robert D. Baird, "Syncretism and the History of Religion," in ed. Robert D. Baird, *Essays in the History of Religions* (New York: Peter Lang Publishing, 1991), 49; the quotation is taken from *Religion and the Christian Faith* (Philadelphia, PA: The Westminster Press, 1956), 397. Yet, as noted by Baird, Kraemer attempts to save his original distinction between syncretistic religions and biblical Christian faith by rejecting only a syncretism that is "a *conscious* organizing religious principle," as was the case in the religions of the Roman Empire. Ibid. But this argument ironically underscores the universality of syncretism while showing the attempted exclusion of biblical religion from a nonvirtuous form of syncretism to be a desperate, *ad hoc* defensive move.

64 Kraemer, *The Christian Message in a Non-Christian World*, 142, 144, 215–28.

65 Kraemer, *The Christian Message in a Non-Christian World*, 62, 70, 72, 143–4, 167–8.

66 Kraemer, *The Christian Message in a Non-Christian World*, 208.

67 Kraemer, *The Christian Message in a Non-Christian World*, 200, 207.

68 Kraemer, *The Christian Message in a Non-Christian World*, 211.

69 Ibid.

70 Ibid.

71 Premawardhana, "Christianity Becomes Unfamiliar," 34.

72 Ibid.

73 Premawardhana, "Christianity Becomes Unfamiliar," 29.

74 Premawardhana, "Christianity Becomes Unfamiliar," 34.

5

Hinduism, the Upaniṣads, and Apophatic Pluralism

The nonexclusive apophatic pluralism of Hinduism

Although the theory of apophatic pluralism appears justified in light of the phenomena of syncretism, religious hybridity, and departicularization, it may seem like an abstract claim to some readers unless it is brought into the arena of active, living religions. Thus, in this chapter, I will test the theory in light of the Upaniṣads (and, in Chapter 6, in light of the New Testament). Hinduism is renowned as the most tolerant of religions, and India is a land of vibrant religious activity and variety, where multiple exclusivist and inclusivist sects, as well as universalizing religious ideologies have competed with each other and modified each other for millennia. Because of this long experience with the issues and practice of religious pluralism, Hinduism and its premier mystical writings, the Upaniṣads, offer an unparalleled example of an almost systematic application of the principle of apophatic pluralism by a religious tradition, Hinduism in this case, to itself.[1]

Hinduism has not been uniformly pluralistic in its approach to other religions. In its long and rich encounter with the multiple religions that India has mothered, or that have found shelter on her soil, or that have arrived there with the goal of supplanting the other religions, Hinduism has produced multiple theologies and philosophies of religions. Although exclusivism has been rare, it can be detected in expressions such as *mlecchas* and *yavanas*[2] and in the polemics of the Mādhva school of Vedānta.[3] While a popular view of Hinduism holds that it is pluralistic, as in widespread formulas derived from the Ṛg Veda, such as "Truth is one, paths are many," some commentators on Hinduism have seen this stance as inclusivistic. Harold G. Coward has argued, for instance, that renowned Hindu philosopher Sarvepalli Radhakrishnan's "tolerance has always exclusively affirmed his own position and has protected him from the challenge of other positions."[4] Consequently, argues Coward, Radhakrishnan's stance and much of Hinduism are essentially inclusivistic insofar as

> "the Hindu approach to other religions is to absolutize the relativism implied in the viewpoint that the various religions are simply different manifestations of the one Divine. The Hindu refusal to recognize claims to exclusive truth (e.g., Christianity or Buddhism) that differ from the revelation of the Veda indicates the limited nature of Hindu tolerance."[5]

Arvind Sharma, on the contrary, holds that there is a truly pluralistic stream in Hinduism, one that includes rather than excludes inclusivism and exclusivism.[6] Sharma's simple but ingenious proposal is based on recognizing that any one of the three stances of exclusivism, inclusivism, or pluralism may be right. The logic underlying this nonexclusive pluralism is that of a nonexclusive both/and approach rather than an exclusive either/or approach to the three stances of the tripolar typology. The ingenuity of this approach is that it includes within (a nonexclusive) pluralism the possibility that either inclusivism or exclusivism may be true and that pluralism may be false.[7] On this approach, it remains a logical possibility that any of the three typical positions is correct and the others are false, despite the sincerity, conviction, and learnedness that attend the conviction that one or the other of these positions is the truth (I will argue for a similar view in a later chapter.[8])

It is along these lines, then, that Sharma discovers a genuine and ancient pluralism in Hinduism.[9] In Sharma's view, Hinduism's "encyclopedic imperative—that is, its ambition to be all things to all human beings—requires that it stick to a non-exclusive orientation."[10] This is a genuine pluralism that not only recognizes the existence of plural absolutes, but that also places itself in question. That is, it allows the coexistence of exclusivistic and nonexclusivistic claims alongside its own. Moving away from any necessary rootedness in the Vedic revelation, such a "nonexclusive" pluralism can hold open the possibility of being true to positions as widely contrary to each other as Vaiṣṇavism, Śaivism, Buddhism, Vedānta, Jainism, Mīmāṃsā, Cārvāka, and, by extension, Christianity, Islām, and Marxism.[11] Thus, Hindu pluralism is an old and settled pluralism, one that is calmly and reasonably expressed in *The Laws of Manu*: "All humans on earth should learn their own individual practices from a priest from that country."[12] So foundational is this pluralism to Hinduism—and to indigenous Indian religions in general—that, as Diana Eck points out, it is vividly expressed in the sacred geography of India, for "the pilgrim's India" is not exclusivistically oriented only to one central sacred place, but, on the contrary, is oriented to a virtual infinity of sacred places that, taken as a whole, constitute "a vivid symbolic landscape characterized not by exclusivity and uniqueness, but by polycentricity, pluralism, and duplication."[13] This stance can be found throughout the Upaniṣads, and is broader than the exclusivistic pluralism that is sometimes thought to be the final stance of these Indian mystical writings.[14]

In Sharma's view, the capacity of Hinduism to hold itself open in this way to questions about its own truth and the truth of other religions and philosophies derives from its willingness to be "a sample along with" other religions rather than insisting on making itself "the criterion" of their truth.[15] As Sharma summarizes his nonexclusive (and what I would call apophatic) pluralism: "No definition of Hinduism can be final, because within it no religious or philosophical theory or practice can be final—including this one."[16]

This Hindu apophatic pluralism (which is similar to the pluralism of Jainism, as expressed in the doctrines of *anekāntavāda* and *syādvāda*[17]) provides a compelling model of how a religious tradition can be both pluralistic and vital at the same time. One result of this ongoing vitality is that Hindu pluralism is having a global impact on other religions, as can be seen in the following comment of a Christian comparative theologian:

> "For some, at least, we may no longer be able to hear the voice of Jesus without an echo of *Gītā* 18:66. In the extreme case, we may understand the text directly enough so as to feel a call to surrender to Krishna. While it seems impossible for Christians to do this, nonetheless it may be profitable to find ourselves in so difficult a situation, for a time bereft of the fundamental certainties of our tradition."[18]

In this statement, it is clear that the nonexclusive pluralism of Hinduism has worked its way through the thinking of an orthodox Christian in a way that would have been unlikely before the 1960s and the increasingly deep Christian and especially Catholic encounter with Hinduism that has occurred since then. A major outcome of this encounter has been that Hinduism is increasingly seen as a partner in theological construction and not as an object of missionary activity. This (and not the small number of Hindu converts to Christianity) is perhaps the most notable result of the encounter between Christianity and Hinduism over the last half-millennium, since the possibility that Christianity may not be the last religious word to humanity is not an idea that comfortably surfaced in orthodox Catholic or Protestant thought before the second half of the twentieth century.

Central to this blunting of Christian particularism has been the popular reception in the West over the last two centuries of Hindu and Buddhist texts like the Bhagavad Gītā and the Dhammapada, the adoption of Hindu and Buddhist ideas and practices through the activities of missionary monks and nuns from Asia, the appreciative interpretative activity of more liberal Christian missionaries and of religious studies scholars, and the numerous meditators, yogis, and *bhaktas* who have studied with traditional teachers in Asia.[19] Less well known at the level of popular religion and spirituality but essential to this process as providing the conceptual background for classical Hinduism (and also as a part of the cultural and conceptual background of Buddhism) are the Upaniṣads, which, beginning with Schopenhauer and Emerson, have permeated Western awareness through the spread of yoga, Vedāntic philosophy, and meditation movements. The Upaniṣads have also become well known as the source of such iconic sayings as "tat tvam asi" and "neti neti." Thus, it makes sense to look to these influential texts for insights about a nonexclusive, apophatic pluralism.

The Upaniṣads and apophatic pluralism

One difficulty facing us as we approach the Upaniṣads in search of a useable pluralism is the hesitation of some scholars in identifying the stance of any contemporary religious movement or idea—pluralism, for instance—with sacred texts such as the Upaniṣads and the New Testament.[20] The danger here is that of taking one's own preferred interpretation of selected passages as the singular message of these suggestive texts. This is a legitimate concern, since sacred texts are often unsystematic expressions of multiple and competing religious and secular interests. Thus, Patrick Olivelle, an eminent translator of the Upaniṣads, questions the scholarly search for "the 'philosophy' or 'the fundamental conception' of the Upaniṣads,"[21] while Laurie Patton claims that "it is hard to place a definitive 'genre' marking upon them such as 'philosophy' rather than ritual or even poetry."[22]

Patton, however, goes on to indicate the formative significance for later Hinduism of Śaṅkara's Advaita Vedānta as "a resistant spirituality" of nineteenth-century Hindu reformers, as "the font of wisdom for many Western thinkers," and as the "bedrock of twenty-first century middle-class Hinduism."[23] Furthermore, skepticism about the philosophical meaning of the Upaniṣads is not universal among scholars of Hinduism, as indicated in the view of Henry Simoni-Wastila, who holds that "many Hindu thinkers have stressed the Vedic aphorism 'That thou art' as signifying a spiritual teaching focusing on identity, union, and nonseparation. The adage 'That thou art' serves as a goal for popular religion, yogic practice, and metaphysical speculation. The metaphysics implicit in this passage is arguably monistic, and this type of monism is also current throughout the Upaniṣads."[24]

Given their sponsorship of this and multiple other philosophical schools and movements in India, it seems disingenuous, therefore, to discount the philosophical significance of the Vedic Upaniṣads just because sections, such as the sixth chapter of the Chāndogya Upaniṣad, contain ritualistic and magical texts. Bearing these hesitations in mind, but also mindful of the strong tendency of the Upaniṣads toward nondualism, and, thus inevitably, toward an apophatic pluralism, I will approach the Upaniṣads not as a religious or philosophical sectarian in search of confirmation of my sect's teachings, but as one open to the pluralistic possibilities implicit in these ancient religious and philosophical texts. (I will take the same approach to the New Testament in the next chapter). I thus see the Upaniṣads, even when teaching magical charms and commenting on rituals, as suggesting a natural religious philosophy markedly distinct from the dualist or materialist cosmologies of the contemporary Western and Westernized world. Reading these ancient Hindu texts can awaken within us a sense of the physical and biological words as radiant expressions of an adaptive yet ultimately ineffable wisdom (*prajñā*).

The Upaniṣads and the tripolar typology

Among numerous other interests, the oldest Upaniṣads point to a transcendent dimension of being that evades our ability to speak about it even as it inspires diverse streams of revelatory language. This insight, which is vividly expressed throughout the Upaniṣads, inspires and confirms the apophatic pluralism undergirding my criticism of religious particularisms. While few readers would likely associate the Upaniṣads with exclusivism, many others might not think that they teach apophatic pluralism, thinking instead that they imply a Hindu-based pluralism oriented toward notions like brahman, ātman, and *puruṣa*. But as I have gone about the task of collecting and assigning passages in the Upaniṣads to the rubrics of pluralism, inclusivism, and exclusivism (as these terms have been clarified in the first chapter), I have found texts to exemplify each of the three positions, including exclusivism (which may surprise casual students of Hinduism), as well as many texts that appear to fall between the categories of inclusivism and pluralism, but which can be seen as actually exemplifying apophatic pluralism when subjected to deeper scrutiny. Let's now explore each of the three categories in turn in light of the major Vedic Upaniṣads in order to see if there is an Upaniṣadic tendency in favor of any one of the three categories.

Exclusivism in the Upaniṣads

If the exclusivist view of religious differences is defined as taking one of the many available bodies of religious teachings as final to the exclusion and even negation of other bodies of religious teaching, then exclusivistic passages in the Upaniṣads are very rare. The Upaniṣads clearly evince the existence of multiple competing schools and sects, but, apart from a text that suggests that people, presumably mlecchas, who dwell at the "end of the directions" are associated with evil and death (BU 1.3.10 Roebuck[25]), there seems to be little awareness of utterly alien religious others.[26] Some texts speak about the necessity of the grace of the self to attain the self (MuU 3.2.3) or of the necessity of the teacher to attain the self (MtU 4.1), while several passages in more theistic Upaniṣads like the Kaṭha and the Śvetāśvatara Upaniṣads articulate an exclusivism that is logically identical to that which underlies standard interpretations of New Testament passages such as Jn 14.6 (KJV), "Jesus saith unto him, 'I am the way, the truth, and the life: no man cometh unto the Father, but by me,'" and Acts 4.12 (KJV), "Neither is there salvation in any other: for there is none other name under heaven given among men, whereby we must be saved." Equal in ambition to these sectarian religious claims is the Śvetāśvatara Upaniṣad's stirring proclamation that no others "enjoy eternal happiness" than those who see "the one God" (*eko devaḥ*) in the self (SU 6.11-12 Olivelle[27]). And counter to the general trend of the earlier Upaniṣads, we find the jarring sectarian claim in this same Upaniṣad that "only when people will be able to roll up the sky like a piece of leather will suffering come to an end, without first knowing God (*devamavijñāya*)" (SU 6.20 O).

It seems safe to say, however, that these passages in the Upaniṣads represent a mood that owes more to the sectarian currents in India of that period, for they remain far removed in intention and mode of expression from the nondualism and daring metaphysical explorations of the older Upaniṣads. It is hard to synthesize the theism of the Kaṭha and Śvetāśvatara Upaniṣads with the radical critique of *devas* in the Bṛhadāraṇyaka Upaniṣad, where we find the bold claim that "even today, whoever knows that 'I am brahman' becomes all this. Even the gods are not able to prevent it, for he becomes their self" (BU 1.4.10 *R*). This idea is repeated in the Maitrī Upaniṣad, where Maitri teaches that the knower of brahman "reaches godhead over the gods" (MtU 4.4 *R*). Texts such as these, which are not as easily reducible to a theistic interpretation as theistic interpretations are reducible to a nondual interpretation, lend support to the central Upaniṣadic doctrine of the identity of ātman and brahman, as do texts that identify the many devas with Prajāpati, and Prajāpati, in turn, with the "field-knower" (MtU 5.2 *R*).[28] Sectarian interpretations of the Upaniṣads thrive on the coexistence of contrary religious and theological ideas like these, yet the paucity of exclusivistic, theistic texts in the Upaniṣads should call into question the advisability of attempting to erect upon them an exclusivistic, grace-based theism of a sort that is more than familiar in the religions of the West. Given that these theistic texts occur in what are generally taken by scholars as later post-Buddhist Upaniṣads, these exclusivistic theistic elements can be set aside as contrary to the more nondual stance of the earlier Upaniṣads.[29]

Exclusivistic devotion to a singular deity seems, therefore, to be an anomaly in the Upaniṣads, whose prevailing stance seems to be a posttheistic apophatic nondualism. Thus, there seems to be no place in a comprehensive understanding of the Upaniṣads for religious exclusivism. Whether they authorize inclusivism or pluralism, however, is the next question to which we must turn.

Inclusivism in the Upaniṣads

At first glance, it would seem that if exclusivism is set aside as the prevailing stance of the Upaniṣads with respect to religious diversity, then inclusivism, and not pluralism, is the only remaining possibility, since the Upaniṣads, like all religious literature are expressed in a language specific to particular religious practices and traditions. The notions of brahman, ātman, or puruṣa are, as typical expressions of Hindu religious and philosophical thought, no more universalizable than the notion of *īśvara* or the names and cults of central Upaniṣadic devas such as Rudra, Viṣṇu, or Agni. Consequently, any attempt to build a pluralistic theory of religions on notions such as brahman or ātman seems doomed from the start as an instance of an uncritically overextended inclusivism.

If inclusivism is defined as a weaker or minimal expression of particularism that takes the terminology in the home tradition as the final vocabulary to interpret all religious phenomena, then many texts in the Upaniṣads are inclusivistic. These passages, in contrast to pluralistic texts, use the religious language of the local tradition without a sense of its limitations and without that sense of the presence of contrary and irreducible religious others that motivates genuine pluralism. Thus, texts in the Upaniṣads that deploy terms like ātman and brahman without apophatic bracketing of these terms (a critical gesture that I will explore in the next section) are common.

A central inclusivistic image in the Upaniṣads is that of smoke billowing out of a fire made from wet wood, which serves as an analogy for the breathing out of all things from the "great being," or the self. So apt is this metaphor for the creative activity of the ātman that it is repeated at least three times in the Upaniṣads (BU 2.4.10, 4.6.11; MtU 6.32). The inclusivistic character of this image is suggested by the notion of entities flowing out from a central being, a notion that also animates Christian inclusivisms that see humanity and its religions as included within God's activity in Christ. The image of a productive center, whether it is called ātman, brahman, or puruṣa, is repeated throughout the Upaniṣads, as in the image of sparks from a blazing fire (MuU 2.1.1), the coming up of all breaths, worlds, Vedas, gods, and beings from the one who is in the self (MtU 6.32), and the image of the self holding together all beings as the hub and rim of a wheel holds together all the spokes of a wheel (BU 2.5.15).

Other passages vary the metaphors without departing from the idea that whatever exists can be understood as an expression of the underlying supreme reality. This self is infinite, "possessing all forms" (SU 1.9 *R*), it "faces in all directions" (SU 2.16 *R*), and is "all-pervading" (SU 3.11 *R*). As the essence of all beings, "the self is the honey of all beings, and all beings are the honey of the self" (BU 2.5.14 *R*); like butter in milk, "the self pervades everything" (SU 2.6 *R*); and, further, this self is dearer than all other beings (BU 2.4.4; 4.5.6). All worlds depend upon brahman, since *this* clearly is *that* (KaU 6.1). Rising now from concrete images to the majestic metaphysical claim that gives the Upaniṣads their undying relevance, the Chāndogya Upaniṣad declares that all of this is brahman (ChU 3.14.1). This is no mere abstraction, divorced from the living context of religious practice, since reflection upon the identity of the whole of life with the central reality evokes a potentially endless litany of forms assumed by "the one who takes all forms" (MtU 6.38–7.7 *R*). Summing up this ecstatic and inclusivistic vision of a sacred universe pervaded by a singular creative spirit, the self is eulogized as "Īśāna, Śambhu, Bhava, Rudra, Prajāpati, the All-Creator, the golden embryo, truth, breath, the goose, the teacher, Viṣṇu, Nārāyaṇa, Arka, Savitṛ, Dhātṛ, Vidhātṛ, the emperor, Indra, Indu" (MtU 6.8 *R*).

Arising as these images and speculations do from a living context of religious and spiritual practice, they retain a vital power of suggestibility that will always appeal to the human spirit, for the synthetic vision of the Upaniṣads reminds us that all things have their roots in the same source, as branches of the one "eternal *pipal* tree" (KaU 6.1 *R*). Whether there is any way to press texts using typical Hindu expressions for the ultimate into the service of pluralism is a question that will be taken up next, as will a judgment about whether inclusivism must be taken as the default view of religious diversity in the Upaniṣads.

Pluralism in the Upaniṣads

If the pluralist view of religious difference is defined minimally as the simple recognition of the existence of multiple final religious vocabularies and maximally as the refusal to take any body of religious teaching as absolutely final, then the number of passages that can be taken as pluralistic in the Upaniṣads far outnumber texts representing the other categories.

Like inclusivistic passages, many of these passages contain references to classical Hindu conceptions such as ātman, brahman, or puruṣa. Thus, these texts might conventionally be thought of as inclusivistic because they use traditional Hindu language that cannot be generalized without violating the language practices of other religious traditions (or of nonreligious ultimate views). However, when these texts invoke the apophatic strategy of "unsaying"[30] against the cataphatic, tradition-specific religious language invoked in the texts, they can be taken as unambiguously pluralistic rather than as inclusivistic. Because of the difficulty, if not impossibility, of formulating a pluralist theory of religions in a language that is not limited by its context, this may turn out to be the way that religious pluralism necessarily speaks: to indicate in our own current language that which inevitably goes beyond our own language while inspiring our language's attempts to incarnate it. For example, in the contest between Gārgya and Ajātaśatru about the character of brahman, Gārgya fell silent after saying all that he knew, and Ajātaśatru indicated that Gārgya's conventional knowledge of brahman was not sufficient for actually knowing brahman (BU 2.1.14). One can imagine this as the sort of impasse arrived at through dialogue between adherents of particularist and pluralist views about the goal of religious life, for cataphatic statements are more clearly context dependent, and thus more rapidly rendered passé than statements that merely unsay them.

Many other Upaniṣadic texts involve an apophatic denial of the forms and names used in the passage. For example, the gods were celebrating a victory of brahman when brahman appeared in the mysterious form of a *yakṣa*, which confused the gods, so they sent Agni, Vāyu, and Indra to find out what this mysterious presence was. Agni and Vāyu failed the tests given them by the yakṣa, but it disappeared from view when Indra ran up to it (KeU 3–4). This story seems to indicate that conventional approaches to brahman are insufficient, while the more successful approach to whatever it is that we call brahman is to recognize that it evades our best attempts at approaching it.

In the Maitrī Upaniṣad, brahman is said to be infinite in all directions, even though directions "do not apply to it," since it (or the self) is "inconceivable," "immeasurable, unborn, unguessable," and "unthinkable" (MtU 6.17 *R*). Again, the idea here seems to be that conventional religious language, clearly useful in its ordinary contexts, negates itself when it is examined closely.

In one of the most celebrated metaphors in the Upaniṣads, it is said that the one who knows the "divine person, [who is] higher than the highest" is "freed from name and form," just as a river loses its name and form as it flows into the ocean (MuU 3.2.8 *R* and Radhakrishnan[31]). No more apt description of the cessation of particularisms in the ground of human beatitude than this can be found in the religious literature of the world, and it foretells the fate of every contextually shaped religious teaching as self-negation in the face of the mystery that inspires religions even as it guides them from within to exceed themselves kenotically.

These texts overcome the limits of inclusivism by apophatically negating the predicates and attributes that, when not subjected to apophatic unsaying, support literalistic, realistic, overly logical, legalistic, wrongly historicized, and authoritative interpretations of religious texts and doctrines. The merest application to such teachings of rational, historical, apophatic, and other critical tools shows them to be based ultimately on authority or other persuasive or coercive means rather than on sound arguments based on verifiable, widely accepted evidence.

One may conclude, in line with Sharma's self-transcending version of Hindu pluralism outlined above, that Upaniṣadic texts that combine cataphatic imagery with apophatic negation of that imagery should be seen as implying a pluralistic rejection of the finality of any body of religious symbols and teachings. Thus, while the nonsubstantial openness toward which this radical apophaticism directs the inquirer is often called ātman, brahman, or puruṣa in the Upaniṣads, these terms need not be read inclusivistically as implying the ultimacy of Hindu teachings about specific substantial realities named in Hindu texts. On the contrary, terms like ātman, brahman, or puruṣa can be seen as self-negating vehicles of a quest for beatitude that terminates beyond the semantic range of the terms themselves. These Upaniṣadic texts can be seen as pointing toward a deeper teaching than that of ātman, brahman, and puruṣa, a teaching that perhaps can best be stated in the words of Joel Brereton: "the brahman remains an open concept. It is simply the designation given to whatever principle or power a sage believes to lie behind the world."[32] Or, in the teaching of the otherwise generally cataphatic and particularistic Śvetāśvatara Upaniṣad, they "become immortal" who know the formless reality that is higher even than the puruṣa (SU 3.10 *R*[33]).

As if in confirmation of this deeper teaching, numerous pluralistic passages in the Upaniṣads dispense as far as is possible with traditional terminology while still using language. Rather than relying on traditional names for the ultimate reality like brahman, ātman, and puruṣa, these texts either make use of abstractions like "imperishable" (BU 3.8.11 *R*), "immortal" (BU 2.3.1 *R*), "unseizable" (BU 4.2.4 *R*), "formless" (KaU 3.15 *R*), and "inconceivable" (MtU 7.17 *R*) or they veer beyond language through a gesture of linguistic self-negation, as in claims that the self is other than knowledge or ignorance (IU 10) and in the assertion that only those who don't understand brahman understand it (KeU 2.3 *R*). This latter passage can be taken as stating in the most radical terms the operating principle of a purely apophatic Upaniṣadic pluralism in which the brahman of exoteric worship, theology, and philosophy is negated in light of a transcendent, apophatically indicated brahman that is not known even by the learned (KeU 1–2). By extending this negation beyond the range of the Upaniṣads to all religious expressions, every attempt at particularistic religious hegemony is cut off at the base. It is not just Hindu, or Buddhist, or Christian language that is shown to be inadequate to the task of orienting us beyond the limitations of time, place, the senses, and the mind, but all language, religious or otherwise. The most concise expression of this apophatic pluralism is the justly famous "rule of substitution" or "symbolic statement" (*ādeśa*),[34] which is deployed through the application to all predicates of the well-known phrase *neti neti*, "not this, not this", or "'not ____, not ____.'"[35] The *ādeśa* is a tool of self-transcending religious language that inspires eulogistic litanies of negations (BU 3.8.8, 4.3.21-32) that can be quite dizzying to adherents of conventional, cataphatic, and particularistic teachings (BU 3.8.8). This apophatic pluralism is energetically and exuberantly expressed throughout the Upaniṣads, as in the teaching of Yājñavalkya to

Janaka that extols a state where there are no fathers, mothers, worlds, Vedas, thieves, murderers, Caṇḍālas, Paulkasas, *śramaṇas*, and ascetics (BU 4.3.22 *R*), and in Aśvapati Kaikeya's declaration that in his country there are no thieves, no misers, no wine drinkers, and none who are ignorant or unchaste (CU 5.11.5 *R*).

Although this second group of pluralistic texts articulates a more comprehensive pluralism than the first group, neither group of apophatic texts implies a merely negative, uncreative, and abstract spirituality, for the notion that the Upaniṣads eventuate in a radically negative apophaticism is inaccurate, as even a brief immersion in the Upaniṣads should make clear. The Upaniṣads no more terminate in an abstract negativity that is like Hegel's night in which all cows are black[36] than does the most famous apophatic mystical text in Christianity, the *Mystical Theology* of Pseudo-Dionysius, which ends with the negation of negation.[37] For prior to negation in the Upaniṣads is always that "opening" or "clearing" (*Lichtung*)[38] within which everything arises and subsides and which inspires cataphatic language in the first place, rendering the function of apophasis as the undercutting of overly literal final vocabularies rather than as the articulation of a purely negative final antivocabulary. By correlating the phrase *neti neti* of the Bṛhadāraṇyaka Upaniṣad with the phrase "made of this, made of that" (*idaṃ-mayaḥ adomaya iti*) (BU 4.4.5 *R*[39]) of that same Upaniṣad, it becomes clear that the Upaniṣads teach that brahman can be encountered both apophatically as name-and-form negating nirguṇa brahman and through the forms associated with saguṇa brahman. Disagreements about the ontological status and creative agency of brahman do not negate the fundamental Upaniṣadic insight that "all this is certainly brahman" (CU 3.14.1), whether one favors a more realistic and dualistic or a more illusionistic and nondual interpretation of the Upaniṣads.[40]

It turns out, then, that the Upaniṣads have both a cataphatic and an apophatic dimension, and that both dimensions are essential to the pluralist teaching of the Upaniṣads. For a merely cataphatic teaching, which contains expressions inevitably shaped by specific historical and linguistic contexts, cannot escape the limitations of exclusivism and inclusivism, which, in the end, are merely different degrees of particularism, while a merely apophatic teaching is incapable of finding points of contact between brahman and human experience. For example, the saying "tat tvam asi" can be seen as clearly affirmative, since it makes a claim, yet it neatly avoids particularism because, apophatically, it does not use a substantive or an adjective to denote what it is that the one who reflects upon this statement ultimately is. The neuter pronoun[41] leaves open the nature or character of the identity that makes for creaturely beatitude, thus moving beyond the notion of brahman. That the termination of wisdom in the Upaniṣads is not merely negative but also positive may be implied by the conduct of the true brahmin, who gives up both "nonsilence and silence" (BU 3.5.1 *R*).

If we take the apophatic pluralism that I have sketched here as the ultimate teaching of the Upaniṣads about the end or directionality of the human quest for beatitude, then it follows that beatitude is not a place, a person, or a thing. Beatitude is less a substance than an evasion of substance that refuses to stay confined within static bodies of teachings and nets of words and concepts. In the most radical teaching of the Upaniṣads, beatitude is a continual straining beyond the boundaries of being, language, and thought to find salvific fulfillment in a condition that animates the words and concepts that it inevitably and necessarily exceeds. This teaching surpasses any formulaic view of the Upaniṣads as terminating in the claim that an inner substance, ātman, is one with an outer substance, brahman. As indicated in the most apophatic of the above-cited Upaniṣadic texts, the directionality of Upaniṣadic beatitude is toward an ecstatic exceeding of language that encounters whatever is ultimately real just as it is apart from the distortions of contextual mediations.

It would be an error, then, to reify terms like ātman, brahman, or puruṣa as things or substances and then to assert that a nondual metaphysics based on the one true substance is the perennial goal of all religions and metaphysical systems. In contradiction of this tendency, the apophatic pluralism of the Upaniṣads points beyond a final divine substance toward a self-divesting unknowing that burrows through all language and theorizing, religious and secular, in order to track the ultimate as an nonsubstantializing openness that animates bodies of religious and philosophical teaching while not being confined or unduly detained in them.

Seen in this way, one will be hard pressed to see any real difference between the ultimate vision of the Upaniṣads and the vision of a Buddhist thinker like Tsong Khapa, who contends that "appearance dispels absolutist extremism and emptiness dispels nihilism."[42] Expanding on this terse but significant formula, Robert A. F. Thurman portrays supreme enlightened awareness as "an ability to embrace simultaneously objective existence and objective nonexistence of all things, in integrated compassion and wisdom."[43] Thus, the paired notions of "relativity" (*pratītyasamutpāda*) and "emptiness" (śūnyatā)[44] are not alien to the soteriological and philosophical aspirations of the Upaniṣads at their highest pitch, and we might view these Buddhist notions as providing less of a corrective to a supposed Upaniṣadic substantialism than as sharing in the exuberance of a ceaseless dialectic of apophasis and cataphasis, of apavāda and adhyāropa, in which the accent is now on negation and now on affirmation.

Inspired by the Upaniṣads, I propose, then, a nonsubstantialistic and nonuniversalizing attentiveness to the movement of the cataphatic and apophatic dialectic in the inner life of seekers of beatitude as the surest way toward both the highest insight available to human beings and toward a responsible religious pluralism that avoids the sterile dead ends of self-refuting and self-stultifying inclusivisms, falsely universalizing pluralisms, and self-annulling exclusivisms.

The apophatic pluralist impulse of the Upaniṣads

In this survey of the Upaniṣadic texts relating to the issue of religious differences, we see that the tendency is clearly pluralistic, though the frequent use of unavoidably tradition-specific language in some passages may lend support to persistent antipluralists who may still want to interpret these passages as evidence of a Hindu crypto-exclusivism along the lines attributed by Coward to Radhakrishnan. But since the largest number of relevant passages in the Upaniṣads appear to teach an apophatic pluralism that strains to move beyond naming and which is thus necessarily beyond the limits of any tradition or sect, the Upaniṣads can plausibly be seen as embodying a nonexclusive, self-emptying pluralism. This distinctive variety of pluralism, which is one of Hinduism's many religious gifts to humanity, has long helped Hinduism to be among the most tolerant of religions and to serve as an example of how a religion may—certainly not without struggle and lapses—overcome the noxious and inevitably false idea that it is the last indispensable religious word to humanity. There are fewer more edifying sights in the history of religions than to see a religious tradition embody the insight that it is but one expression in the pluralistic human quest for beatitude.

This insight, particularly as famously modeled in the phrase *neti neti*, has the potential to inspire critiques of overly literalistic and rigidly hierarchical religions across the globe, just as it has in Western alternative spiritual settings in the last century. In the contemporary setting of religious studies and comparative theology, the nonexclusive, apophatic pluralism of the Upaniṣads may provoke questioning of influential academic theories that imply that religious truth is isolated in diverse and walled-off bodies of teaching and practice. While such views may sometimes serve a hidden or unconscious deference to orthodoxy and traditional religious authorities, they have no place in the wider, philosophical quest for the source of human beatitude, which is the vocation of a truly global and *religious* (as opposed to a merely academic and scientific) study of the religious heritage of humanity. Rather than remaining sidelined in inclusivistically conceived traditions, we might take the lead of Upaniṣadic apophatic pluralism and see humanity's religions as unique but not exclusive ways of participating in the dialectical play of the apophatic and cataphatic dimensions of religious life, practice, and language.

Conscious as I am of the inclusivistic, constructivist, and antiuniversalistic tendencies of much theological and religious-studies scholarship in recent decades, I am pessimistic that an apophatic pluralist view will prevail in the short term, even if it seems to be the only long-term position that can endure. Inclusivist and constructivist defenders of bodies of religious doctrine and practice as impermeable realities living only in their own light will likely continue to dominate the field, at least until they are replaced by the exclusivists and inclusivists of the new forms of religion that await us over the horizon of the coming decades and centuries.

An extensive study of the religions of the world, and a deep immersion in the constructivist-essentialist and crypto-exclusivism debates have made it clear to me that no resolution of the differences between religions can be found on the level of exoteric doctrine, scripture, and symbolism.[45] No one who thinks that there can be only one incarnation can ever agree that there have been many incarnations. Yet, if the possibility of religious truth is not tied to the destiny of any particular religious language (which seems likely, since religious truth clearly predates any particular religion), then the ultimate devotion may be to cherish one's own religious language while remaining open to new religious insight. This insight has the potential to undercut theological and religious strategies attempting to preserve particular religious teachings or communities as final and, consequently, as binding upon humanity. When, like Gārgya, we have spoken all that our religions have taught us, perhaps then we will be able to agree with Ajātaśatru that "It is not known by this" (BU 2.1.14 *R*).

Notes

1 As perhaps the last gasp of Western imperialism is the postcolonialist and still hegemonic Western claim that Hinduism (and India) was the invention of the British and their Orientalist agents, beginning with the Hindu Renaissance in the late 1700s. This tendentious and implausible view has been explored by Andrew J. Nicholson in *Unifying Hinduism: Philosophy and Identity in Indian Intellectual History* (New York: Columbia University Press, 2010), 2–3, 6–9. See also Christopher Key Chapple's review of this book, *Journal of the American Academy of Religion* 80, no. 2 (June 2012): 546–9. Diana Eck contests the postcolonialist view (already an element of British imperialist discourse about India in the nineteenth century) that "India" as a cultural unity is a Western, mostly British, construct. *India: A Sacred Geography* (New York: Harmony Books, 2012), 45–8.

2 R. D. Baird, "The Response of Swami Bhaktivedanta," in *Modern Indian Responses to Religious Pluralism*, ed. Harold G. Coward (Albany, NY: State University of New York Press, 1987), 108.

3 Deepak Sarma presents a rigorous Mādhva Vedānta argument that "the doctrines, teachings, and practices" of "alien" "religions outside the Vedanta commentarial fold have no truth whatsoever." "Madhva Dialogue and Discernment," in Cornille, *Criteria of Interreligious Dialogue*, 182, 202.

4 Howard Coward, *Pluralism: Challenge to World Religions* (Maryknoll, NY: Orbis Books, 1985), 80.

5 Coward, *Pluralism*, 80. Jeffery D. Long, "(Tentatively) Putting the Pieces Together" in Clooney, *The New Comparative Theology*, 152, a Neo-Vedantic pluralist theologian of religions, articulates a version of pluralism that avoids the dangers of inclusivism and overly thin generalizations about the world's religion that this position is sometimes accused of—overly harshly and with a suspicious degree of animus by Paul J. Griffiths, who sees it as "pallid, platitudinous, and degutted." Quoted in Long, "(Tentatively) Putting the Pieces Together" in Clooney, *The New Comparative Theology*, 151–70.

6 Sharma, "Can There Be More than One Kind of Pluralism?" in Knitter, *The Myth of Religious Superiority*, 57.

7 Sharma, "Can There Be More than One Kind of Pluralism?" in Knitter, *The Myth of Religious Superiority*, 60.

8 See also Kenneth Rose, "Doctrine and Tolerance in Theology of Religions," *The Scottish Journal of Religious*, 119.

9 Hinduism's ancient pluralism "flows from its plural assumptions," because it accepts "diversity as its initial principle," according to Arvind Sharma, "A Hindu Perspective," in Meister, *The Oxford Handbook of Religious Diversity*, 310.

10 Sharma, "Can There Be More than One Kind of Pluralism?" in Knitter, *The Myth of Religious Superiority*, 60.

11 Sharma, "Can There Be More than One Kind of Pluralism?" in Knitter, *The Myth of Religious Superiority*, 59.
12 *The Laws of Manu*, trans. Wendy Doniger and Brian K. Smith (New Delhi: Penguin Books, 1991), 2.20.
13 Diana Eck, *India: A Sacred Geography* (New York, Harmony Books, 2012).
14 As expressed in passages such as BU 3.8.11, where Yājñavalkya uses a radically apophatic method to indicate through negation the unknowable character of the imperishable. Sharma's notion of nonexclusive pluralism should not be confused with the pluralistic exclusivisms described in Chapter 2 of this book, which defer the search for a principle guiding pluralism and hold the diversity of the soteriological aims of the various traditions in unresolved tension. (I use the standard abbreviations for the Upaniṣads as given in Patrick Olivelle, trans. *The Upaniṣads* [New York: Oxford University Press, 1996], xii–xiii.)
15 Sharma, "Can There Be More than One Kind of Pluralism?" in Knitter, *The Myth of Religious Superiority*, 60.
16 Sharma, "Can There Be More than One Kind of Pluralism?" in Knitter, *The Myth of Religious Superiority*, 60.
17 J. T. F. Jordens, "Gandhi and Religious Pluralism," in Coward, *Modern Indian Responses to Religious Pluralism*, 8–9.
18 Clooney, "Surrender to God Alone," in Cornille, *Song Divine*, 207. More recently, Clooney has written: "To put it more starkly: a Christian comparative theologian, or a Buddhist comparative theologian may, for good reasons that cannot be denied, cease to be exclusively Christian or exclusively Buddhist in her communal loyalties." *Comparative Theology*, 161.
19 This story has been ably evoked in numerous works including Catherine Albanese, *A Republic of Mind and Spirit: A Cultural History of American Metaphysical Religion* (New Haven: Yale University Press, 2007); Lola Williamson, *Transcendent in America: Hindu-Inspired Meditation Movements as New Religion* (New York: New York University Press, 2010); Philip Goldberg, *American Veda: From Emerson and the Beatles to Yoga and Meditation How Indian Spirituality Changed the West* (New York: Harmony, 2010); Stefanie Syman, *The Subtle Body: The Story of Yoga in America* (Farrar, Straus and Giroux, 2010); and Rick Fields, *How the Swans Came to the Lake: A Narrative History of Buddhism in America* (3rd revised edn). (Boston, MA: Shambhala, 1992). See also Howard A. Netland, *Encountering Religious Pluralism: The Challenge to Christian Faith and Mission* (Downers Grove, IL: InterVarsity Press, 2001).
20 In a review of the proposal for this book, Klaus Klostermaier wrote: "While these are sources for major religions, there is, strictly speaking, neither an Upanishadic nor a New Testament religion. There are many forms of Hinduism and many different forms of Christianity—none of these can be said to be a realization of the sources they refer to. Besides these there are many other religions that share the problematic of pluralism."
21 Olivelle, *The Upaniṣads*, lvi.
22 Laurie Patton, "Veda and Upaniṣad," in *The Hindu World*, eds. Sushil Mittal and Gene Thursby (New York: Routledge, 2004), 50.
23 Patton, "Veda and Upaniṣad," 50.
24 Henry Simoni-Wastila, "*Māyā* and Radical Particularity: Can Particular Persons be one with Brahman?" *International Journal of Hindu Studies* 6:1 (April 2002): 1.
25 Valerie Roebuck, trans. *The Upaniṣads* (New York: Penguin Books, 2003). Quotations from this translation are hereafter indicated by *R*.

26 According to William Halbfass, the Indocentrism of classical Hindu thought reduced religious others to "a faint and distant phenomenon at the horizon of the indigenous tradition." See *India and Europe: An Essay in Understanding* (Albany, NY: State University of New York Press, 1981), 58; quoted in Sharma "Can There Be More than One Kind of Pluralism?" in Knitter, *The Myth of Religious Superiority*, 58.

27 Patrick Olivelle, trans. *Upaniṣads* (New York: Oxford University Press, 1996). Quotations from this translation are hereafter indicated by O.

28 Joel Brereton, while acknowledging the susceptibility of the Vedic Upaniṣads to multiple interpretations, does concede to Śaṅkara the nondualist view that "much Upanishadic thought does stress the coherence and final unity of all things." "The Upanishads," in *Eastern Canons: Approaches to the Asian Classics*, eds. Wm. Theodore de Bary and Irene Bloom (New York: Columbia University Press, 1990), 117.

29 Brian Black, *The Character of the Self in Ancient India: Priests, Kings, and Women in the Early Upaniṣads* (Albany, NY: State University Press of New York, 2007), 4–5; Patrick Olivelle, "Introduction," in The Early Upaniṣads: Annotated Text and Translation, trans. Patrick Olivelle (New York: Oxford University Press, 1998), 12–13; and Valerie Roebuck, "Introduction," in Roebuck, The Upaniṣads, xxiv–xxvi. Eliot Deutsch holds that the early Upaniṣads "lend themselves more easily to an Advaitic interpretation than do some of the later ones." *Advaita Vedānta*, 5n4.

30 "Unsaying" is the simple but ingenious translation of *apophasis* by Michael A. Sells in *Mystical Languages of Unsaying* (Chicago, IL: The University of Chicago Press, 1994), 2–3.

31 S. Radhakrishnan, *The Principal Upaniṣads* (New York: Humanities Press, 1953).

32 Brereton, "The Upanishads," in de Bary and Bloom, *Eastern Canons*, 118.

33 Roebuck surveys competing attempts at translating this verse, which does not sit well with a purely theistic, particularistic teaching. If the verse is taken as referring to that which goes beyond theistic conceptions, then it serves to confirm the interpretation offered in this essay. Attempts to make it fit into a theistic interpretation, as indicated by Roebuck, seem to be inconclusive. *The Upaniṣads*, 453n7, 454n9.

34 The first formulation of *ādeśa* is Olivelle's; the second is Roebuck's.

35 The first translation of *neti neti* is Roebuck's; the second is Olivelle's.

36 G. W. F. Hegel, *Phänomenologie des Geistes*, eds. Hans-Friedrich Wessels and Heinrich Clairmont (Hamburg: Felix Meiner Verlag, 2006; originally published in 1807), 13.

37 " . . . for it is both beyond every assertion, being the perfect and unique cause of all things, and, by virtue of its preeminently simple and absolute nature, free of every limitation, beyond every limitation; it is also beyond every denial." Pseudo-Dionysius, *The Mystical Theology*, in Luibheid, *Pseudo-Dionysius*, 1048B.

38 Martin Heidegger, "The End of Philosophy and the Task of Thinking," in *On Time and Being*, trans. Joan Stambaugh (Chicago, IL: University of Chicago, 2002; originally published 1972), 65.

39 The Sanskrit here follows Radhakrishnan.

40 Although it is commonly thought by nonspecialists that Advaita Vedānta is thoroughly idealistic and illusionistic, it does allow for a realistic element in its epistemology, what Deutsch calls a "soft realism." *Advaita Vedānta*, 97. Śaṅkara held that the distinction between subjects and object is real, but only at the phenomenal level, a view that seems to straddle both sides of this issue. Deutsch, *Advaita Vedānta*, 94–7.

41 Patrick Olivelle agrees with Joel Brereton's arguments in "*Tat Tvam Asi* in Context" (*Zeitschrift der Deutschen Morgenländischen Gesellschaft* 136:1 [1986]: 98–109) for translating *tat tvam asi* (ChU 6.8.7–6.16.3) as "in that way you are," but he changes it to "that's how you are." *Upaniṣads*, 8.7–16.3; 387 note to 8.7–16.3. Roebuck, however, confesses herself unconvinced, pointing out that in numerous places in the Upaniṣads, the authors depart from the rules of grammatical gender, as, for example, in ChU 3.17.6, where neuter adjectives agree with a *tvam* standing in for the masculine *ātman*. *The Upaniṣads*, 423n12. Daniel Raveh, siding against Brereton here, writes: "Nevertheless, in Śaṅkara's view—as acknowledged by Brereton himself (pp. 102–3)—the particle *tat* in the *mahāvākya* refers to *sat* which denotes the *Brahman* . . . ." Daniel Raveh, "*Ayam aham asmīti*: Self-consciousness and Identity in the Eighth Chapter of the *Chāndogya Upaniṣad* vs. Śaṅkara's *Bhāṣya*," *Journal of Indian Philosophy* 36 (April 2008): 326. Laurie Patton lets the standard translation stand, "You are that," though she seems to acknowledge the intent of the translations, if not the grammatical argument of Brereton and Olivelle, when she restates Uddālaka's teaching that "*brahman* is like that . . . ." "Veda and Upaniṣad," in *The Hindu World*, eds. Sushil Mittal and Gene Thursby (New York: Routledge, 2004), 49.

42 Thurman, *The Central Philosophy of Tibet*, 170.

43 Ibid.

44 Thurman, *The Central Philosophy of Tibet*, 148–9.

45 A point conceded by Cornille, *Many Mansions?* 5, when she suggests, though without taking side in the essentialist–constructivist debate, that multiple religious belonging seems to require an essentialist view of religious teaching and experience.

6

The New Testament and Apophatic Pluralism

Turning from the Upaniṣads, which tend toward apophatic pluralism, I want now to look at the New Testament in light of the threefold typology in order to see if the New Testament promotes an exclusivism that is the natural opposite of the pluralism of the Upaniṣads. By the end of this chapter, we should be able to clearly and confidently say whether the common perception of the New Testament (at least in many of the evangelical versions of Christianity popular in the USA) as thoroughly and conclusively exclusivistic is correct or not. The outcome of this inquiry is of central importance for people shaped by Christianity and for the religious culture of the Western world, since no other scripture apart from the Hebrew Bible has so massively shaped Western religion, philosophy, and spirituality as has the New Testament over the last nearly two millennia (although in the last two centuries, Hindu and Buddhist scriptures have increasingly shaped popular Western approaches to religion and spirituality, especially in the areas of religious pluralism and contemplative practice). The interpretation of the New Testament, which is possibly the world's most overanalyzed set of writings, can be made to support a wide but not infinite number of positions, and I do not expect the following interpretation to escape criticism from many sides. Yet, because the New Testament has been widely propagated across the planet by missionaries who have often used it to promote exclusivistic religious agendas, it can be helpful to see whether it provides unambiguous support for exclusivistic views.

Rather than competing with the work of highly competent and often ingenious academic New Testament scholars, the following investigation is meant to spur further research on the New Testament in light of religious pluralism, an area that appears to be underdeveloped. In addition to looking at the New Testament to determine whether it is overwhelmingly or even predominantly exclusivistic, another intention in reading this sacred text will be to highlight what appears to be the overlooked potential of the New Testament for nonexclusivistic theologies of religions. If the New Testament can be shown as failing to support a consistently exclusivistic stance, this would be of genuine significance for further constructive Christian theological thought about the world's religions, since it would allow traditional Christians to take a more open view of other religions without exchanging a biblical starting point for a philosophical or mystical starting point. While this approach will not be necessary for religious pluralists, it may provide inspiration to potential inclusivists and pluralists in conservative Christian circles to begin moving toward less particularistic theologies of religions. At the very least, this survey of the New Testament in light of the threefold typology should place a question mark beside dogmatic claims that exclusivism or a very restrictive inclusivism are the only biblical and orthodox stances for a faithful Christian.

The principle that will guide the following interpretation of the New Testament (and which I formulated as I read the New Testament in light of the threefold typology) is that the earlier the New Testament community and its teaching, the more it expresses a traditional Jewish theocentric inclusivism that minimally leaves "the peoples" (*hoi ethnoi*, which can be translated as "the nations," "pagans," or "Gentiles") to their own devices within the broad scope of the Noahic Covenant (Gen. 9.1-17), which speaks inclusivistically of human beings as bearing the divine image,[1] or that maximally aspires to include "the peoples" within the more universalistic understanding of the Torah and of Israel as "a light for the nations" (Isa. 49.6 NRSV) that emerged in the time of Second Isaiah (after 586 BCE).[2] Conversely, the later the New Testament community and its teaching, the more it expresses a christocentric inclusivism or exclusivism.[3] Thus, the more we move away from the teachings of Jesus, a Jewish prophet and potential messiah, into the increasingly more Hellenistic teachings of the nascent Christian churches, the more the focus shifts from Jewish inclusivism to what will eventually become a particularistic teaching about Jesus Christ. Rare in the New Testament writings is pluralism of either the inclusivistic or apophatic variety, though I do point out the few places where hints of pluralism shine through its pages.

In what follows, I have tried to follow the actual historical chronology in which the New Testament books were written (more or less following the order in Gerd Theissen's *Fortress Introduction to the New Testament*[4]). I have deviated from this ordering by placing the synoptic gospels before the authentic Pauline letters, even though these letters were written before the first gospel, Mark. I have done this because the Pauline letters reflect a theology that is already more christocentric than the theocentric theology of the synoptics. The synoptic gospels seem to preserve, to a large degree, the theocentric teaching of the early communities of "followers of Jesus,"[5] which I think is due to their incorporating Q, an early collection of the sayings of Jesus that was probably composed before Paul wrote his first letter to the Thessalonians. (It seems to me that one motivation for the composition of the synoptics was to preserve the primitive teaching of the early "Jesus movement"[6] over against the newer, more syncretistic teachings of the Hellenistic churches, as reflected in the writings of Paul.)

The New Testament and the tripolar typology

Exclusivism in the New Testament

The synoptic gospels (including Q)

Among the most jarringly exclusivistic passages in the synoptic gospels are those that disparage or discountenance people who aren't Jewish: "Do not give what is holy to dogs" (*tois kusin* [Mt. 7.6 NRSV; cf. also 10.5; 15.21-28; Mk 7.27-28; Lk. 17.18]) and those that appear to make exclusivistic claims for Jesus (Mt. 10.32, 39; 11.6, 27). For instance, in Mt. 6.27 (and Lk. 10.22) Jesus uses apparently exclusivistic language that will become more familiar in the Gospel of John (cf. Jn 3.35; 10.15; 13.3; 17.25): "and no one knows the Son except the Father, and no one knows the Father except the Son and anyone to whom the Son chooses to reveal him" (NRSV). Yet, this and other similar passages do not anachronistically imply Christian exclusivism or a Jesus-centered exclusivism imposed by Jesus on his coreligionists. Rather, Jesus seems here to be offering a reinterpretation of his ancestral religion that stresses a charismatically mediated inwardness that he may have thought was lacking among his hearers. Thus, the kind of exclusivism that Jesus intends when he says that "something greater than the temple is here" can be seen as a call to his fellow religionists to focus within rather than on the externals of traditional religion. In this sense, Jesus sounds less like an exclusivistic rejecter of the rest of humanity's spiritual heritage and more like an Upaniṣadic seer criticizing overreliance on sacrificial rituals (e.g., MuU 2.7). Jesus sometimes expresses an eschatological sense of himself as what Paul Knitter calls "the final prophet"[7] of the many prophets sent to the Jewish people (as promised in Deut. 18.15-19) and, as such, thus exercises "a special, unique role in God's plan"[8] (Mt. 12.41-42; see also Lk. 10.16; 11.29-32; 12.8-9, 40; 20.17; 21.27; 22.69). Yet, the activity of these prophets would not exclusivistically eradicate the value of other religious traditions, since these Jewish prophets were enjoined to speak truthfully for the Lord and not in the name of other deities, which implies the existence of other deities and their own, non-Jewish spheres of influence. There is thus no connection between Jesus's seeing himself as a prophet or even the messiah and the exclusivistic negation of humanity's spiritual and religious heritages.

That this is the case is seen when Jesus attempts to turn away the Canaanite woman (or the Greek Syrophoenician woman in Mk 7.24-30 NRSV) by pointing out that he was "sent only to the lost sheep of the house of Israel" (Mt. 15.24 NRSV), which shows that his central concern was in ministering to his fellow religionists. This focus on the Jewish people is central in other sayings that at first glance may appear to imply Christian exclusivism, but which on closer inspection show that Jesus saw himself as indispensable for Jewish people as a figure of eschatological importance, and that he had less awareness or concern for "the peoples." Thus, Jesus speaks of himself as a "ransom for many" (*lytron anti pollōn* [Mk 10.45 NRSV]) rather than as a ransom for all, which is consistent with his focus on Jews instead of all of humanity. This view of Jesus is also consistent with one of the most solid outcomes of the so-called "third quest" for the historical Jesus, which resolutely sees Jesus as a Jewish figure.[9]

Thus, even so apparently an exclusivistic passage as Mt. 28.18-20, which portrays Jesus as having received all authority in heaven and earth and thereby charging his disciples to "make disciples of all nations" (NRSV), can be seen as arising from Jesus's now universalized sense of himself as the final prophet. But this does not imply a rejection of other people's spiritual and ethical heritages, which is confirmed in Mt. 25, where Jesus says that the Son of Man will judge "all the nations" (25.32 NRSV) on the basis of the performance of the works of mercy rather than on the basis of faith explicitly focused on Jesus or the Son of Man (25.32-46), which is a clearly nonsectarian and pluralist criterion (see "Pluralism in the New Testament" below). Thus, apparently exclusivist demands that the gospel be "proclaimed to all nations" (Mk 13.10 NRSV) can be seen as the mission of a prophet calling all people to inwardness and heroic, selfless ethical action rather than to explicit faith in that prophet as the only valid path to God. Passages such as these can be taken as endorsing a later Christian exclusivism only through a contrived and implausible hermeneutics.

The synoptics come closest to proclaiming exclusivism in the longer ending of Mark, where Jesus says to his 11 chief disciples, "Go into all the world and proclaim the good news to the whole creation. The one who believes and is baptized will be saved; but the one who does not believe will be condemned" (Mk 16.15-16 NRSV). But this anachronistic passage of extremely dubious authenticity[10] offers miraculous proofs for the validity of faith, which contradict the ethical criteria that Jesus enunciates in Mt. 25.35-36 and which are reminiscent of the similar proofs that Jesus rejects in Mt. 7.22-23, such as prophesying, casting out demons, and the performance of mighty deeds. Furthermore, the formal object of belief is left unspecified in this passage (God, Jesus, the kingdom of God?), which undercuts its value as a proof-text for later forms of Christ-centered exclusivism.

I think it is safe to say, then, that there is little explicit Christ-centered exclusivism in the synoptics. Christology in the synoptics is undeveloped, at least as far as claims that Jesus is God and is the one way of salvation, which we find in later, more elaborate Christian theologies. In the synoptics, Jesus comes across mostly as what Geza Vermes (in line with Joseph Klausner and J. B. Segal) characterizes as a "charismatic Hasid," or a Galilean holy man who is recognizably Jewish and centered upon God.[11] Indeed, Gerd Theissen holds of Jesus that "Im Kontext seiner eigenen Zeit gehört seine Ethik ins Judentum" (*In the context of his own time his ethic is part of Judaism*).[12] The later kerygmatic christologies of the Pauline–Johannine traditions are quite distinct from what Gerd Theissen calls "the Jesus tradition" of the synoptics,[13] as evidenced in the widely divergent estimates of Jesus given in the hymn about the exalted Christ in Phil. 2.6-11 (NRSV) who was "in the form of God" and the more recognizably Jewish witness to Jesus as "a prophet, mighty in deeds and words before God and all the people" in Lk. 24.19 (NRSV).[14] If we take the synoptic view as more historical, then there is nothing in principle in this picture of Jesus as a charismatic Jewish holy person that excludes the holy people of other traditions or other charismatic Jewish holy men like Honi, the Circle-Drawer, and Hanina ben Dosa, whose ministries occurred in the two centuries surrounding the beginning of the common era. Given Jesus's focus, with notable exceptions, on the people of Israel, it would be illogical to suppose that he would have rejected the validity of other religions and the holy people of other traditions in the categorical terms of contemporary Christian exclusivists.

The Pauline letters

Numerous exclusivistic passages are to be found in the letters of Paul (e.g., 1 Cor. 8.6; 12.3; 15.12-34, 47; 2 Cor. 5.10, 14, 18-19), which appear to be the result of his turning away from the theocentrism of the messianic Jesus movements of Palestine to the increasingly christocentric theologies of Hellenistic Christianities, a theological development that was ratified in the Johannine writings.[15] Because Paul promoted a liberalization and universalization of the Torah that eventually led to the (at first unforeseen) foundation of a new religion, he can hardly be seen as an exclusivist within his own natal tradition. And it certainly makes little sense to cast him as a prototype of contemporary Christian exclusivism when his own concern seems to have been to liberalize the Torah by replacing it with a faith relation to Christ (Rom. 5.20-21), which is more of a post-Jewish concern than a requirement internal to later Christian orthodoxies that rejected all other religions as false.

It is more illuminating to view Paul through the syncretistic concept of religious hybridity than as a proto-orthodox Christian exclusivist. The increasingly divine and universal Christ of his preaching can be seen as an attempt to mediate the restrictiveness of Palestinian Judaism and the universalism (or what we now call "globalization") and pluralism of Hellenistic culture. The conflict between more traditional Jewish followers of Jesus and Hellenizing Christians breaks through forcefully in Paul's letter to the Galatians, which, like much of Romans, seems to be concerned with defending the legitimacy of new, hybrid religious identities (Gal. 2.14-16). The pathos of the religiously hybrid person who is caught between two religious visions of life emerges poignantly and aggressively in Philippians ("Beware of the dogs . . . !" [3.2 NRSV]), where Paul boasts over his Jewish credentials (3.4-9) even while accounting them "as rubbish" (3.8 NRSV). This theme is also found in 2 Cor. 11.16-29, even to the point of self-caricature (11.23). One senses here the strain of a religiously hybrid person caught between lingering pride in a now-rejected religious identity and the enthusiasm of the convert to a new religious movement. This sort of syncretistic tension has become familiar again in our time in accounts of the strains and rewards of hybrid religious people engaged in mediating two or more religious traditions.

As in the hyperconnected contemporary world, with its syncretistic churning of globalizing and glocalizing currents of culture, including religion, the era of the dawn of Christianity was a period in which many local traditions, such as Palestinian Judaism, were at odds with the universalist ethos of Hellenistic culture. One response was that of Paul, when still called Saul, who retreated into a violent, fundamentalistic exclusivism. Another of Paul's responses, after his visionary conversion to the Jesus movement, was to moderate the imperatives of his local, native tradition by reframing them in light of the Hellenistic imperatives of pluralism and universalism. Just as a religiously hybrid person today may moderate the exclusivism of traditional Christianity by engaging in insight meditation or yoga, so Paul sought to overcome his own restrictive upbringing by participating in the process of replacing the Jewish law with an Hellenistic-style divinity (or what Rudolf Bultmann called a *theios anēr*, or "divine man"[16]), who could replace anxiety about sin and apostasy with a new sense of personal salvation (Rom. 8.1-4; Phil. 2.10; 3.7-14). Thus, with a mix of foreboding about his own apostasy and a desire for vindication among his former coreligionists, Paul looked forward to a day when all of his opponents would have to bend the knee to his new lord (Phil. 2.11; 2 Cor. 5.10).

Given the tortured character of Paul's hybridity, as expressed in some of the passages mentioned above, he can be seen as a tragic figure who pushed Torah-liberalizing tendencies far beyond what even the most universalizing Judaism of his time would allow.[17] He was far more radical than Jesus in this regard, who reinterpreted the Torah in a way recognizable by other Jews, while Paul wanted to replace the substance of the Torah with Jesus. Paul's ingenious, if ultimately for his own people, destructive, recasting of the Jewish law led him to the bold step of announcing to his fellow Jews that they were free of the law of Moses because of Christ (Rom. 7.4), a step that would likely have been beyond the imagination or intention of Jesus.[18] In any case, his concern in the section of Romans where this verse occurs is a theological debate with other Jews about the Torah and not with followers of other religions.

Paul's exclusivism in these letters can be seen as a sectarian matter arising from issues of identity and practice in a syncretistic, new religious movement. The viewpoints of the parties to these ancient controversies are no more universalizable and applicable to adherents of other religions than are the struggles of nineteenth-century neo-Hindu reformers in India or the doctrinal squabbling of the various sects of millenarians in nineteenth-century USA. In any case, there is no more reason to raise Paul's syncretistic reflections into a universal divine law that excludes all other religions than there would be to ratify the syncretistic musings of any other new-religious-movement founder.

The Acts of the Apostles

Although Acts can be seen as the second volume of Luke, it makes more sense to consider it here after the genuine Pauline letters rather than with the synoptics, which, because of their partial sourcing in Q, reflect more primitive theologies, while the theology of Acts is more developed than that of Q. (Nevertheless, one still detects in Acts many examples of the pre-Hellenistic and pre-Pauline theologies, which are theocentric and focused on Jesus as a Jewish prophet and possible messiah rather than upon him as an Hellenistic-style divinity, or a theios anēr.) Thus, one finds in Acts relatively sympathetic treatments of people attracted to traditional Judaism (8.26-40; 10.1-48; 16.1; 16.14; 17.4, 12; 18.7), which is consistent with the prophetic and inclusivistic Jewish understanding that the scope of God's concern is with "all flesh" (*pasa sarx*), or the whole of humanity (Acts 2.17, quoting Joel 2.28).

This openness contrasts with exclusivistic and christocentric passages that proclaim (if somewhat obliquely) that Jesus is "the Author of life" (3.15 NRSV) in whose name alone is salvation "given under heaven given among mortals" (Acts 4.12 NRSV). This is a tension that will be resolved in favor of a proto-orthodox Christian exclusivism in John, but which still seems to be unresolved in Acts. This sentiment can be seen as an expression of an enthusiasm born of the excitement of being part of a new religious movement. This mood will be familiar to anyone who has been caught up in the tremors of sectarian religiosity. It can be likened to the certainty of a child who proclaims that her father is the smartest father on the block or another child that his mother is the nicest mother on the block. Krister Stendhal, in attempting to explain the apparent exclusivism of Acts 4.12, rejects the idea that Luke, the author of Acts, is here contrasting Christianity with other religions known to him, or with religions he had likely never heard of, such as Buddhism. Instead, Stendahl thinks that this proclamation about Jesus should be seen "as love language, as caressing language."[19] It is the kind of language one might expect from lovers for their partners. And, as Stendahl points out, "the 'no other name' has no extra-Jewish referent," since it is used here by a beleaguered group of Jews to extol Jesus, a Jew, to the Temple authorities, another group of Jews.[20] It is thus intra-Jewish language that can only at the cost of hermeneutical naïveté, be pressed into the service of a later Christian exclusivism.

Attempts to defend the exclusivism of this verse by saying that it is a revealed utterance, occurring as it does in a revealed sacred text, will have to contend with the fact of plural revelations. Assertions of the universal normativity of a specific revealed text are likely to have little or no persuasive force for adherents of different and perhaps competing revealed scriptures. Since each revelation tradition has its skilled and persuasive apologists whose powers of persuasion reach only as far as the consent of those targeted for persuasion, and since it is impossible to resolve the doctrinal differences of the various religions at the level of doctrine, absolutistic claims can have no persuasive force beyond the boundaries of the communities making them or among people not inclined to be persuaded by these claims. And just as soon as a tradition begins to make use of logical and philosophical methods to clarify and justify its particular claims, it will inevitably find itself resorting to more general metaphysical and ethical views to justify its claims. But since the doctrines of other religions can also be justified to some degree by appeal to these general concepts and principles, the end result of nonapologetic appeals to philosophy and logic will be the vindication of the general truths of logic, ethics, and metaphysics rather than the vindication of the exclusive truth of the official doctrines of any specific religious tradition.

Thus, exclusivistic language in the New Testament should be seen as expressions of enthusiasm born of testimony and of polemics in the competitive, religiously plural context that Knitter calls the "classicist culture"[21] of the first and second centuries in west Asia and southern Europe. They should not, therefore, be seen as universally binding truths or laws. Religious language can at best express some aspects of the regularities of nature, the mind, and the divine, but the passage of time and the ravages of departicularization will show such expressions to be, at best, temporally limited expressions of more general truths that are better expressed through the tools and conceptualities of philosophy and the sciences.

Pseudepigraphical letters

As we move further away from the time of Paul, Christian writings become more christocentric, as in the hymn about Christ as "the image of the invisible god" (Col. 1.15 NRSV), which may go back to a genuine Pauline tradition.[22] Here, Christ is a quasiphilosophical principle in which "all the fullness of God was pleased to dwell" and through which all things are reconciled (1.19 NRSV). It is an inner mystery (1.27; 2.2), in which hide "all the treasures of wisdom and knowledge" (2.3 NRSV) and in which "the whole fullness of deity dwells bodily" (2.9 NRSV). The transformation of the Galilean prophet and possible messiah into something like the Philonic *logos* of the Johannine prologue shows us that we have moved farther away from the simpler message of the early Jesus movement. Less a man appointed by God to represent God and more a cosmic power and metaphysical principle, the Christ of this letter was constructed to appeal to people caught up in the syncretistic churning of contrasting Jewish, Hellenistic, proto-Gnostic, and local Phrygian religious practices in Colossae.[23] Similar to other universalizing principles postulated as the hidden truth of all of the religions, the claim that Christ is the summing up of the mysteries of God, humanity, and creation will be convincing only to those who are inclined to be persuaded by it.

The claim in 1 Timothy that "Christ Jesus" is the "one mediator between God and humankind" (2.5 NRSV) appears superficially to support Christian exclusivism, but its stress on Jesus's humanness ("himself human") in opposition to the singular divinity of the "one God," strikes a monotheistic Jewish theme that is clearly at odds with a Christian exclusivism in which Jesus is proclaimed to be the one way of salvation because he is said to be God in the flesh. In its actual context, this verse must rather be viewed as the supersessionist hermeneutical strategy of a new religious movement seeking a place within the Jewish Shema, or confession of faith (Deut. 6.4-5), for Jesus.[24] Its actual concern is, therefore, quite removed from that of later Christian exclusivists.

The claim in 1 Peter that "Christ also suffered for sins once for all" (*hapax*) [3.18 NRSV]) is, like the view developed in Heb. 7.27; 9.12; 10.10 and Eph. 2.15, an attempt to substitute Jesus for the Torah and its requirements, which is another example of a supersessionist, or replacement theology. This is the least externally plausible kind of exclusivism, and one that is never likely to appeal to a member of the religious tradition targeted for replacement, unless that adherent has already decided to convert to the targetting tradition.

In an attempted coup by a supersessionist theologian, Hebrews reflects a syncretistic milieu of religiously hybrid people who see a partially divinized Jesus Christ (Heb. 1.2-13, and throughout the book) as the replacement of the Jewish law (Heb. 2.17, and throughout the book; see especially Heb. 7.27). Again, this approach will only be meaningful to those who have converted from the target religion and to those who are intent on making converts, while it is inconceivable that it would be received as a plausible or even possible interpretation of the Torah by rabbinical Judaism.

The Johannine writings

The Gospel of John, when read in a literal and historical manner, appears to be one long argument for exclusive and normative claims about Jesus Christ that would evacuate all other religious traditions of their religious and spiritual values and of their religious and spiritual effectiveness, at least for people who think that this gospel is a central book in a uniquely revealed canon of sacred writings. Certainly, this has been the effect of the strategic use by Christian exclusivists over the millennia, of the famous saying in Jn 14.6, where Jesus proclaims in a manner almost wholly missing in the synoptics,

"I am the way, and the truth, and the life. No one comes to the Father except through me" (NRSV). For many exclusivists, this saying, which is thought by them to be actual words spoken by the historical Jesus in a real historical setting, is the conclusive last word of God about the negative value of the world's spiritual heritage (excluding, of course, the exclusivists' favored sectarian variants of Christianity).

But it is important to remember that much of the apparent history portrayed in this gospel is really a quasihistorical façade for a gospel that, unlike the synoptics, is a Palestinian Jewish-Christian mystical treatise designed to inspire ecstatic experiences,[25] an intention that it shares with the Pauline letters. From a purely historical standpoint, the likelihood that the historical Jesus made claims like those attributed to him in Jn 14.6 is far less than the likelihood that he spoke some of the words attributed to him in the synoptics. As New Testament scholar Bart D. Ehrman writes, "accounts of Jesus that are clearly imbued with a highly developed theology [as in John] are less likely to be historically accurate" (than Mark, Q, M, or L).[26] Or, in the words of Geza Vermes, "research has to be restricted to Mark, Matthew and Luke and to exclude John because, despite the occasional historical detail it contains, its Jesus portrait is so evolved theologically as to be wholly unsuitable for historical investigation."[27] And Gerd Theissen sees John as synthesizing the Jesus of the Jesus tradition in the synoptics and the Christ of the Pauline kerygmatic tradition by having Jesus rather than Paul make christological proclamations about himself.[28] Clearly, we see a development here away from the contrarian but thoroughly Jewish and human prophet of the synoptics to the more familiar Christian image of a semi-Hellenistic divine savior, or a theios anēr, a process that seems fully complete with the appearance of the white-haired son of man in Rev. 1.10-18.

While this imbuing of Jesus with a more divine nature may have made for effective evangelizing outside of Jewish communities, it undercuts the value of the Gospel of John as a guide to the historical Jesus. Although some recent scholarship seems ready to smooth over the differences between the Jesus of the earliest Christian communities and the Jesus of the Gospel of John,[29] the jarring differences between the two remain. Just as C. H. Dodd referred to the "strange" and the "new and unfamiliar teaching" for early Christians of the Fourth Gospel,[30] so the difference remains alive for other contemporary scholars such as Pheme Perkins,[31] and, though muted, in the writings of Raymond Brown,[32] as it does in any straightforward reading of the four gospels, which inevitably raises the question of the source of the startling differences between the synoptic Jesus and the Johannine Jesus.

The verisimilitude of historicality that wraps like an apologetic façade around this gospel (and the letter of 1 John[33]), making it a powerful piece of religious propaganda, may have been created by its author in an attempt to carve out a mediating position between the impulses that created the more prosaic and quasihistorical synoptics and those that are responsible for the clearly mystical and allegorical Gospel of Thomas. If, following Helmut Koester[34] and Richard Valantasis,[35] we take the Gospel of Thomas in its original form as the oldest available version of many of the sayings attributed to Jesus in the synoptics, and if we take the synoptics as embodying a newer gospel tradition that supplements the Thomas sayings with extended quasihistorical narratives,[36] then the Gospel of John might be seen as an attempt to combine the essentially pluralist Jesus of the Thomas tradition with the singular, quasihistorical figure of the synoptics. The purpose would have been to counter the mystagogue of the proto-Gnostic Thomas traditions with the proto-orthodox Jesus of John, who is both a mystagogue and the one quasiobjective, quasihistorical mediator of salvation for all people.[37] The success of this strategy can be seen in the ultimate success of the Jesus of John, who is much closer to the later Jesus of orthodox, particularistic Christianity than to the Jewish Jesus of the synoptics and the mystical Jesus of Thomas.[38] Thus, given the clearly polemical reinterpretation of older Jewish-Christian and "crypto-Christian" Jewish[39] views of Jesus that are on offer in John,[40] as well as the obvious attempt to use Jesus as the logos to replace the substance of the Judaism of the period, we can safely set aside the quasihistorical aspects of John and see it as a mystagogical text.[41]

Yet, by subordinating ecstatic experience to restrictive dogmatic requirements, it remains a seriously limited mystagogical text. While any mystic will immediately understand the "I am" sayings as pointing to a fundamental unity of identity between the practitioner and the divine that is achievable though mystical *gnōsis*, the attempt to subordinate this gnōsis to dogma will seem like a violation of mysticism along the lines of the persistent misunderstanding of mysticism as an expression of dogma offered by the more uncompromising contemporary constructivist theorists of mysticism. It is also reminiscent of the anxiety of later Christian mystics about the place of "the sacred humanity of Jesus" in their unitive experiences.[42]

We can also set aside as merely sectarian the many sayings of Jesus in John that might seem forbiddingly exclusivistic, if we keep in mind that the intended audience of the speeches in which they are set is Jesus's own fellow religionists who are vacillating between older and newer views of Jesus. Even if their primary audience at the time of the composition in the last decade or so of the first century was Palestinian Jewish-Christians and crypto-Christians, and even if their largest audience over the centuries has been Christians, the fact remains that Jesus is portrayed in John as having theological arguments with other Jews, which means that he can be seen, as in the synoptics, as attempting to situate himself as normative for Jews within a Jewish religious perspective. Understood in this way, as a discussion about the meaning of Judaism, Jesus's teaching in John can be seen as a local and contemporary intra-Jewish matter that has no bearing on the truth or falsity of the world's religion. A consequence for the theology of religions of this approach to the Jesus of John is that Jesus is portrayed here as negating the spirituality only of some of his fellow religionists and so the claims about himself that have been placed in his mouth by the Johannine author should not be taken as addressed to the whole of humanity, as is often done with the words of Jesus by contemporary exclusivists.[43]

Examples of apparently exclusivistic texts that can be set aside include the discourse in Chapter 5, where Jesus is portrayed as telling a Jewish audience that because they don't believe in the one (Jesus) that God has sent, they don't have God's "word abiding" in them (Jn 5.38 NRSV). He then goes on to warn an audience, broadly and anachronistically characterized as "the Jews" (5.15 NRSV), that their accuser will be Moses (5.45), thus indicating that this supposed intra-Jewish controversy is not applicable to other religions (and, I should point out, it has no relevance for the actual Judaism that exists outside of the historically damaging image of Jewish people promoted by the author of this gospel). Also in ch. 8 vv. 12-58, which is rife with historically inflammatory imagery, Jesus is engaged in a polemic with fellow religionists representing varying degrees of acceptance of the high Johannine Christology. Consequently, the condemnations placed in his mouth here should not be generalized, since they seem to proceed from a group of early, proto-orthodox exclusivistic Christians who are practicing what Raymond E. Brown characterized as a kind of Christological "one-upmanship" on more traditional Jewish Christians and on the early churches of the apostles that were open to Gentiles.[44]

This is nowhere more evident than in Jn 14.6, where Jesus is made to proclaim himself as the one way to the Father. Following the analysis of Brown,[45] this and similar Johannine statements (6.65) can be seen as polemical attempts by an exclusivist Christian sect to replace traditional Jewish institutions and teachings with a semideified Jesus. This would have been highly controversial to traditional Jews, for whom Jesus was neither the messiah nor divine, as well as for Jewish Christians and Jewish crypto-Christians who held to the lower christology evident in the synoptics (and in James and Jude). That the Johannine Christians verged on sectarian separatism in making these high christological claims did not prevent them from laying the foundation for a post-Jewish Christianity with a deified, yet still human, Jesus. Only if one identifies the historical progression of doctrine in the New Testament as a singular and exclusive divine revelation excluding other venerable traditions of revelation, might one see these Johannine controversies as the progressive unfolding of theological truth rather than as just the familiar jousting of competing religious sects. Consequently, we can safely set aside this and similar numerous "I am" sayings of the Johannine Jesus as sectarian attempts to secure a doctrinal high ground against theological opponents and not as a proclamation to the whole of humanity, whose implication is that all other religious traditions are either false or to be fulfilled in Jesus.

Other uncompromisingly exclusivist texts in the Johannine writings include Jn 1.9, which identifies Jesus with "the true light, which enlightens everyone" (NRSV), Jn 12.32, where Jesus says that after his resurrection he "will draw all people to myself" (NRSV), 1 Jn 2.2, where the writer says that Jesus Christ is "the atoning sacrifice . . . for the sins of the whole world" (NRSV), and 2 Jn 5–10, where (right after offering an almost pluralist reduction of "truth" [*aletheia*] to a walking in love, which is the commandment heard from the beginning),[46] the author immediately denounces as "the deceiver and the antichrist" one "who do[es] not confess that Jesus Christ has come in the flesh." The author also warns that people who do "not abide in the teaching of Christ," but who go beyond it, do "not have God." Consequently, people not bearing this teaching are not to be welcomed or received "into the house" (NRSV).

These texts cast a wider net than just the other sectarians of the Johannine period, but the mere statement of these ideas in a sacred text does not make them normative or universally binding, anymore than the normative claims stated in the texts of other religious traditions are universal and binding on all of humanity. It is important, when dealing with texts like this, to remember that because the quasihistorical and dogmatic character of the Johannine writings was designed to win over opposing sectarians, the view of the text is not to be uncritically taken as an instance of unquestionable divine revelation exclusively valid for all people at all subsequent times. Apart from a choice to give these writings the status of divine revelation or to limit revelation to just one of humanity's many streams of purported revelation, these are writings like any other sacred text that make claims that must be subjected to various kinds of historical, philosophical, and religious studies analyses.

Also blunting the exclusivism of the Johannine writings is its mysticism, as expressed in easily universalizable expressions such as light, love, goodness, and truth, which serves as a counterforce to their often stern dogmatics (this topic will be addressed more fully in the next section). For example, the collision of a pluralistic and/or inclusivistic stress on love, light, and goodness with the christological themes in 1 and 2 John compromises the exclusivism of the Johannine communities by revealing that in addition to the controversies over high and very high christologies that divided them, these communities also seemed to be split by universalizing celebrants of the power of love and goodness on one side and dogmatic enforcers of sectarian christologies on the other. Since 1 John seems to resolve this issue by simply placing sentiments from both sides of the controversy side by side, no clear theological claim—and certainly no universally binding theological claim—can be made on the basis of this biblical book.[47]

Inclusivism in the New Testament

The synoptic gospels (including Q)

Inclusivist passages abound in the synoptic gospels, where the teachings ascribed to Jesus are theocentric,[48] as in his famous prayer, which begins with "Father" (Lk. 11.2; Mt. 6.9-13). This address implies a personalistic and monotheistic piety that could also be consistent with a henotheistic or even polytheistic context. As the latter are inconsistent with the Judaism of Jesus's day, we can see in this prayer a monotheistic and theocentric theism colored by a strong sense of the parent/child relationship. There is nothing specifically Christian or christocentric in this prayer, which concerns itself with quotidian and weightier matters of human life. The reference to the coming kingdom does not render this a specifically Christian prayer nor does it place it beyond the bounds of traditional forms of Jewish religious inclusivism,[49] as expressed, for instance, in the idea of the Noahic Covenant (Gen. 9.1-17), which imposes upon Gentiles a simpler set of stipulations than those undertaken by Jews.

Similarly inclusivistic are the numerous parables that Jesus tells. Many of these stories, such as the parable of the sower (Mk 4.1-9), the parable of the good Samaritan (Lk. 10.29-37), the parable of the mustard seed (Lk. 13.13), the parable of the leaven (Lk. 13.20-21), the parable of the great banquet (Lk. 14.16-24), the parable of the lost coin (Lk. 15.8-10), and the parable of the lost son (Lk. 15.11-32) can be read as teaching principles of general religious or ethical significance that can, minus the explicit or implicit theism, be appropriated by people of any religious perspective. Many of Jesus's sayings, such as those collected in the Sermon on the Mount (Mt. 5–7) and in the more concise Sermon on the Plain (Lk. 6.17-49), can be seen as teaching an intense but inclusivistic Jewish piety (Mt. 5.17-48) that often veers into a potential pluralism (Mt. 5.3-7, 43-48; 6.19-22; 7.1-4) marred by an occasional ethnocentric outburst (Mt. 6.7; 7.6). This is because much of Jesus's teaching is standard spiritual fare that, though expressed in an often inimitable manner, could have been spoken by spiritual teachers of any theistic tradition.

Rather than being seen as justifying exclusivistic Christian attitudes—or, indeed, any Christian attitude, since Jesus was a Jew—much of the teaching of Jesus in the synoptics can be seen in light of Jewish piety of a distinctive type, which offered an often biting criticism of the religion of its time and place. Thus, S. Wesley Ariarajah holds that "Jesus's challenge to the religious tradition of his time" is not to be equated with Christian exclusivist rejections of other religions.[50] The Jesus of the synoptics is not a Christian exclusivist, but a clearly Jewish figure who stressed a new, more interior relationship to the religion of his ancestors. And while his focus was on other Jews, his often negative, ethnocentric view of foreigners (Mt. 15.21-28; Mk 7.24-28) was tempered by occasional praise for spiritual values that he saw as surpassing those of his own followers and Jews in general (Mt. 8.10; Lk. 7.9).[51] And even when he appears to a later Christian particularist to be establishing the basis for a new, post-Jewish religion, as when he distinguishes between his teaching and that of Moses in the antitheses in the Sermon on the Mount, he can better be seen as a Jew arguing with other Jews about the meaning of the Torah.[52]

The Pauline letters

A clearly inclusivist theism in Paul that is not yet the mature Christ mysticism of his later writings and that of the still later Johannine writings can be found in 1 Thessalonians, which is the earliest letter of Paul (written around 50 CE) and the earliest writing in the New Testament (except for "the most archaic collections"[53] in Q, which remains a hypothetical document despite the assurance of its existence provided by the discovery of the Gospel of Thomas). It is possible that the influence of the theocentric messianic traditions of Palestine still predominate over an emergent christocentrism in this letter, for Paul expresses what can be seen as an inclusivist Jew's satisfaction at the conversion of Gentiles, whom he commends for turning away from their own deities toward what Paul thinks of as "a living and true God" (1.9 NRSV). (The letter is marred by harsh references to "the Jews" that make Paul sound more like the writer of the Gospel of John than the Paul of Romans [2.14-16]). While Paul does reference *Jesus* and *Christ Jesus* at various points in this letter, he often refers merely to God (*theos*), and he uses the word *God* far more often than he uses the names *Christ* and *Jesus Christ*. Suggestive of a theistic inclusivism is his use of the phrase "the gospel of God" (*to euangelion tou theou* [2.2; 2.8; 2.9]), his recognition that the Thessalonians "have been taught by God to love one another" (4.9 NRSV), his naming God, not Christ, as "your sanctification" (4.3 NRSV), and his claim to the Thessalonians that God taught them "to love one another" (4.9 NRSV). But in 2 Thessalonians, whose

Pauline authorship is doubtful, the shift to christocentrism is dramatic, as when the author expands upon apocalyptic imagery centering on the still eagerly anticipated return of Jesus.

Underlying the sectarian polemics masking the difficulties of negotiating hybrid religious identities in Galatians (1.11-2:21; 4.21; 5.1-15) is an older Jewish inclusivism that sees the nations as justified before God if they have faith in the God of Israel (Gal. 3.6-9), a faith that does not anachronistically have Jesus Christ as its formal object, as in the Gospel of John and later expressions of Christian exclusivism. This same blending of a Jewish universalism—limited by the proscription against reverencing images for people who aren't Jews—with more sectarian concerns serves as the background in the letters to the Corinthians upon which Paul paints his increasingly christocentric theology (1 Cor. 8.6; 12.2, 3; 15.12-34, 47; 2 Cor. 5.10, 14, 19). This Pauline inclusivism, which is an apophatic blending of sapiential and pneumatological themes (1 Cor. 1.18–2.16; 3.18-20; 13.9-12), is often readily separable from the more sectarian and christological themes in these same letters (see 2.3-16a), and can thus serve as the basis for a theistic inclusivism with a Jewish coloration (i.e., the unease with other people's respect for divine images [1 Cor. 8.4-5; 10.20; 12.2]). Above all, there is the easily universalized and inclusivistic theme of love (1 Cor. 8.3; 13.1–14.1), which Paul shares with the Johannine writings, and which contributes to the essentialized popular understanding of Christianity as, above all, a religion of love.

A severe but clear inclusivism can be found at the beginning of Paul's letter to the Romans in a passage that has been overshadowed among Protestant Christians by the vastly overinterpreted Rom. 1.17, which reads in part: "The one who is righteous will live by faith" (NRSV). Immediately following this well-known proclamation, which is quoted from Hab. 2.4, Paul enters into a discussion of what is sometimes called natural theology because it is available to all human beings through reflection or general revelation (as opposed to special revelation) because God grants some degree of saving and ethical insight to humankind. Unfortunately, polemical theologians wanting to secure a favorable basis for teachings about an exclusivist kind of faith that stands aloof from all other religious and ethical possibilities have tried to reject the clear, commonsense natural theology and ethics articulated here by Paul either by refusing to acknowledge its presence in this letter, as in the case of Karl Barth,[54] or by asserting that natural theologies serve only to convict the sinner of sin, as in the case of Calvin.[55] Nevertheless, Rom. 1.18–2.16 cogently locates an ethical basis for salvation in "patiently doing good" (2.7 NRSV), which, Paul says, leads to "eternal life" (2.7 NRSV). Despite tendentious theological interpretations, in these verses Paul does not characterize all human beings as wicked and as damned, since he thinks that God delays judgment on sinners because of kindness, forbearance, and patience, which is meant to lead people to repentance, if they obey the movements of their consciences (2.4, 14-16). Nor does Paul rule out the possibility that people may "perhaps" be excused on the day of judgment (2.15-16 NRSV) if they "instinctively" (*physei*) obey the law that is "written on their hearts" (2.14-15 NRSV). Thus, Paul shows himself to be an inclusivist for whom God's mercy stretches far beyond the borders of Judaism, since God "shows no partiality" (*prosōpolēmpsia*) to Jews or to Greeks (2.9-10 NRSV). Rather than as the ultimate upholder of an anachronistic Christian exclusivism that prejudges all of humanity as lost apart from explicit faith in Jesus Christ and orthodox doctrine, Paul can, according to Gerd Theissen, be seen in his own historical context as "the leading representative of a universalistic movement of openness in Judaism" to non-Jews.[56] In his own adult religious life, Paul went from being an extremist persecutor of Jews who had crossed the boundaries of traditional Judaism to being a leading proponent of a liberal but controversial expansion of Judaism to all of humanity.

Consequently, we can view much of Romans (up through ch. 11) as a passionate and even tormented attempt on the part of a dissident Jew to make sense to himself and to his old coreligionists of his own liberalism and violation of customary Jewish practices like circumcision and *kashrut* (Rom. 9–11; see also Phil. 3.2-10; 1 Cor. 15.8-10; 2 Cor. 3.2-16; 6.4-10; 11.22-28). In the process, Paul pushed along the process of divinizing Jesus that he learned among the more Hellenistic Jewish communities in Syria in the first days after his abrupt conversion experience.[57] (It was in Syria that the Matthean view was forged of Jesus as the Shekhinah, or "the physical manifestation of the divine presence," who "replaces the Temple as the locus of divine presence."[58]) From religious dissident to new-religious movement founder, Paul can be seen as following a path that has been traced by other dissident creators of new religious movements from their birth religions (as in his dramatic autobiographical account in Gal. 1.11–2.2; 1 Cor. 15.6-10). In this regard, Paul has a similar biographical trajectory to Zoroaster, Buddha, Keshub Chunder Sen, Joseph Smith, the Bab, Charles Russell, and Sun Myung Moon. Although Paul dominated the religious life of the Christian West for upward of 15 centuries, his example and teaching is no more or less compelling in an increasingly post-Christian West than the various stories and doctrines of these other figures who were founders of new religious movements from older religious traditions.

The Acts of the Apostles

There are many expressions in Acts of theocentric Jewish inclusivism (2.16-21; 14.15-17). As in the inclusivism of the earlier Jesus traditions, this inclusivism can be seen as an intra-Jewish matter, with little relevance for people who are not Jewish (2.14-36; 3.12-26; 5.27-39). Krister Stendahl argued that the speeches in chs 2–4 are addressed by Jews to Jews—especially the Temple authorities. As he writes, "Nowhere in these chapters enter any questions about gentile gods, gentile cults or gentile religion. . . . The setting is intra-Jewish and inter-Jewish."[59] A starker christocentric focus, however, is coming into play in this book (4.8-12), which is more like the emerging concerns of the Pauline and Johannine communities, although many traces of the older theocentric view of Jesus as a prophet or perhaps even as the messiah remain (3.19-26; 7.51-56; 10.34-43; 13.6-41; 26.22-23). This, along with a broader concern for people outside the scope of the Judaism of the period (8.26-40; 10.1-48; 26.23; 28.28), gives this book a more genial tone than the Gospel of John.

A clearly inclusivistic passage in this book is Peter's declaration before the centurion Cornelius that God is impartial (*prosōpolēmptēs*, a word that is similar to *prosōpolēmpsia*, which is used by Paul in Rom. 2.11), and that "in every nation anyone who fears him and does what is right is acceptable to him" (Acts 10.34 NRSV). This is a theistic inclusivism that turns on ethical issues and the rejection of reverence for images and deities other than the God of Israel. Apart from extensive reinterpretation, this will be too restrictive an inclusivism to include all of the world's many religious traditions, but its significance for the argument of this book is that its presence in Acts undercuts claims that the New Testament teaches only Christian exclusivism or christocentric inclusivism.

A similar ethical and theocentric inclusivism is genially voiced by Barnabas and Paul in a missionary journey to Lystra, where they pointed to nature's bounty and God's forbearance as testimony to God's goodness to "all the nations," which, "in past generations," he allowed "to follow their own ways" (Acts 14.15-17 NRSV). Closely related to this genial inclusivism is the easing by the apostles in Jerusalem of the religious demands made upon people "who are turning to God" (15.19-20, 28-29; 21.25 NRSV). In Acts 17, in his speech at the Areopagus in which he quotes Greek writers who expressed ideas similar to Asian nondualisms, Paul builds common ground with his audience by appealing to a common, mystical theism with a distinctively Jewish accent (Acts 17.23-30).[60] His audience presumably found his speech attractive, at least until Paul referred to Jesus as a "man" "appointed" by God (but, significantly, not as a theios anēr, as in more christologically developed Pauline writings) whose reliability is attested by his resurrection rather than by possession of a divine status (17.31). (This passage notably expresses a very low christology.) This is consistent with a Jewish theocentric inclusivism that in that period might still have seen Jesus as a man appointed by God and certified through his resurrection to bring people who weren't Jewish into a saving relationship with the God of Israel.

Pseudepigraphical letters

A basis for a Christian inclusivism is articulated in Colossians when Christ as the hidden mystery of God is proposed as the basis of a "new self, which is being renewed in knowledge according to the image of its creator" (3.10 NRSV). In this renewed sense of self, which is purified through standard ascetical practices (3.1-10), believers discover a new identity free of ethnic, cultural, religious, and class distinctions (3.11; similar to Gal. 3.28). In principle, this inclusivism is open to all who are willing to see their old identities as taken up and fulfilled in Christ, but, as with all inclusivisms, it is an *ex post facto* apologetic device, or a theological epicycle, that will only be of use to those already predisposed to see Christ as the center of reality.

Besides articulating a similar Christian inclusivism in language that is closer to Colossians than to the authentic Pauline letters (Eph. 1.3, 9, 21-23; 2.14; 3.4, 8; 5.32), the author of Ephesians appears ready to absorb Judaism ("the commonwealth of Israel" [Eph. 2.12 NRSV]) into the orbit of the Christian churches by the gesture of abolishing the Torah and replacing it with Jesus's "flesh" (Eph. 2.14 NRSV), thereby making peace with the ancestral faith of some of the churches' members and founding figures. But the price is high, since in place of the old division between the Jewish people and people who aren't Jewish, there now will be through the blood and flesh of Christ "one new humanity in place of the two" (Eph. 2.15 NRSV) and "one God and Father of us all" (Eph. 4.6 NRSV). But as an instance of a replacement, or fulfillment, theology, this can only make sense to one of the parties in the proposed religious merger, while the other will find it utterly implausible.

The pastoral letters are riddled with theistic inclusivistic expressions, as when the view that love arises from "a pure heart, a good conscience, and sincere faith" is praised (1 Tim. 1.5 NRSV) and when Jesus Christ is carefully distinguished from the sovereign God "who dwells in unapproachable light, whom no one has ever seen or can see" (6.16 NRSV). Most striking is the universalist evangel of 1 Tim. 2.4, which proclaims that God "desires everyone to be saved and to come to the knowledge of the truth" (NRSV). Unless one supposes that either the divinity represented in this text has vain desires or would unreasonably condition the fulfillment of the divine desire upon the requirement that only those who have heard the orthodox version of the Christian gospel from orthodox preachers can be saved, then it is clear that this divine intention implies the salvific efficacy of the world's many spiritualities and humanity's ethical, aesthetic, metaphysical, and logical intuitions.[61] But to negate the idea that only Jews and Christians are among the saved, this letter categorically declares an inclusivistic (*malista pistōn*) but universal salvation: "We have our hope set on the living God, who is the Savior of all people, especially of those who believe" (*hos estin sōtēr pantōn anthrōpōn malista pistōn* [1 Tim. 4.10 NRSV]).

Some Christian exclusivists attempt to obscure the clearly inclusivistic meaning of this passage and 1 Tim. 2.3-4 ("This is right and is acceptable in the sight of God our Savior, who desires everyone to be saved and to come to the knowledge of the truth." [NRSV]) by equivocating on the meaning of the word *savior*[62] or by employing overly fine theological distinctions such as distinguishing what God has done for all human beings "without distinction" and what God does for each human being "without exception,"[63] as if God saved all people in the abstract but only those who hold to a specific version of orthodox Christian belief in actual fact. Not only do such maneuvers appear *ad hoc* and epicyclic, they also weaken the case for exclusivism. If anything, passages such as these should place a question mark next to exclusivism as an adequate interpretation of the New Testament.

By not drawing firm lines between Jews, Christians, and others who love, some pseudepigraphical writers remain faithful to the teaching, more familiar in the earlier Jesus movement, that God is the father of all people (Eph. 4.6) and not just of a favored sectarian community. Perhaps this is why the author of 1 Timothy refers to God as the savior (1 Tim. 1.1; 2.3; 4.10) and not Jesus (as in 2 Tim. 1.10; Tit. 1.4; 2.13). This ambiguity between the christologies of the two letters to Timothy is reflected perhaps in the Greek text of Tit. 2.13: *tou megalou theou kai sōtēros ēmōn Iēsou Christou*, which can be read either as distinguishing between "the great God and our Savior" [NRSV, translator's footnote f] or as identifying "our great God and Savior, Jesus Christ" [NRSV][64]. The latter texts perhaps represent a pseudepigraphical development toward a high christology and can perhaps be seen as later attempts to correct the theocentrism of 1 Timothy (yet Titus also speaks of God alone as the savior in 2.10 and 3.4, thus making one wonder if the ambiguity of Tit. 2.13 can be seen as transitional between the older theocentrism and the newer christocentrism).

The tendency to conflate Jesus and God as savior or to name Jesus as savior continues in some of the catholic letters (2 Pet. 1.1; 2.20; 3.18), which indicate that christocentrism was winning out over theocentrism as the favored view of the emerging proto-orthodox Christian tradition. Yet even here, a recognition of God's universal saving activity is not completely eclipsed, as when God is said to be "patient with you, not wanting any to perish, but all to come to repentance" (2 Pet. 3.9 NRSV).

An ethical inclusivism that is not formally grounded on references to the specific doctrines enshrined in Christian particularism can be found in Titus. This inclusivism holds that "to the pure all things are pure" (1.15 NRSV) and that the grace of "God our Savior" (2.10 NRSV), which has appeared to all people, trains "us" to live self-controlled lives (2.11-12 NRSV), a theme that is consistent with the universal Noahic Covenant.

With but two references to Jesus Christ (1.1), James expresses a purely theistic religion of good deeds that is consistent with an ethical reading of Judaism. Here, we are far from the theios anēr of Paul and the logos of John. In this letter, the focus shifts from doctrine to the simple imperatives of visiting orphans and widows (1.27), showing impartiality to the rich and the poor (2.1-7), and mercy (2.13). The focus remains firmly fixed on God, who sends gifts from above (1.17) and who is gracious to the humble (1.6).

The Johannine writings

While the explicit exclusivism that mars the Gospel of John may seem monolithic, it is often tempered by a countervailing inclusivism or even pluralism that it shares with the three Johannine letters. Earlier in the chapter in the Gospel of John, containing the uncompromising exclusivist claim that "the wrath of God" rests upon those who do "not obey the Son" (Jn 3.36 NRSV), the gospel author enunciates a more general principle than belief in a specific person as the basis for avoiding divine judgment: "But those who do what is true come to the light (ho de poiōn tēn alētheian erchetai pros to phōs), so that it may be seen clearly that their deeds have been done in God" (Jn 3.21 NRSV). The identical criterion is found in the related writing of 1 Jn 1.6: "But if we walk in the light as he himself is in the light, we have fellowship with one another, and the blood of Jesus his Son cleanses us from all sin" (1 Jn 1.7 NRSV). The last phrase, which reads like an addition to the text and which attempts to supplement an ethical criterion with a christological one, may indicate that there was a controversy among the Johannine Christians over the primacy of theological and quasihistorical criteria for salvation and ethical-mystical criteria.[65] The more mystical ethics of light and love (and goodness in 3 Jn 11), which can easily be universalized and made to serve as the basis of an inclusivistic and even pluralistic spirituality, seems to be at odds in these books with a quasihistorical christology of flesh, blood, and dogma that will inevitably lead to an orthodoxy bound to specific quasihistorical events and their dogmatic interpretations.[66]

Inclusivisms that attempt to open the door of salvation to religions other than Christianity by seeing them as avenues of God's intention to save all people through the one way of Jesus Christ seek to soften the exclusivism of Jesus's apparently ineluctably exclusivist claim to be the one way to "the Father" (14.6 NRSV) by way of the patently universalist verses in 1 Timothy that proclaim that God "desires everyone to be saved" (2.4 NRSV) and that God is the "Savior of all people" (4.10 NRSV). This approach finds support in Jesus's attempt to comfort his grieving disciples by informing them that in his "Father's house there are many dwelling places" (*monai* [4.2 NRSV]). This appears to be an explicit reference to 1 En. 39.4-5 and its vision of the "many dwelling places" or the "resting-places" of the "righteous" who eternally intercede for "the children of men" at "the ends of the heavens."[67] Even as he makes an exclusive claim for himself, the Johannine Jesus is careful to broaden it by linking himself to the saints who have eternally interceded for all of humanity, thereby crafting an inclusivism that makes the intercession of all of humanity's saints flow into his own intercessory activity.

When separated from the local controversies that shape its exclusivist polemic, the masterful use in the Johannine tradition of common images like word, water, light, bread, shepherd, door, way, and vine[68] as allegorical avenues of spiritual illumination can be seen as engendering and supporting an inclusivist mystical and sacramental spirituality grounded in personal rather than institutional religion.[69] In the application of such imagery to one's own personal experience, the mystical and allegorical dimensions of the Johannine writings come into their own and demonstrate the spiritual fruitfulness of these writings. The luminous imagery is reminiscent of other great mystical and allegorical classics like the Upaniṣads, where common aspects of the body and the world are used as the basis of an allegorizing interiorization (*upāsanā*) that leads to an illumined sense of the unity of the world, the body, and the divine. It is for this reason, perhaps, that the Johannine writings appealed to second-century Gnostics,[70] cousins to all heterodox mystics everywhere, an appeal that shows that the inner impulse of the mystical aspect of these polemical writings is toward pluralism rather than exclusivism.

One of the clearest expressions of a theistic inclusivism in the New Testament is found in Revelation in a passage that is shaped by the Jewish inclusivism and universalism of the prophets Ezekiel and Isaiah. In perhaps the most resonant and hopeful of biblical images, John the exile on Patmos (who, despite tradition, is not to be confused with the author of the Gospel of John[71]) quotes the prophet Isaiah when he declares that God will wipe every tear away from humanity's eyes (Rev. 21.3-4, and, framed exclusivistically, repeated in 7.17; see the original at Isa. 25.8). Recalling the prophet Ezekiel (37.27), the writer proclaims that in the new heaven and earth, God will dwell with humanity (*meta tōn anthrōpōn*), since all of humanity (*anthrōpoi*) will be God's "people" (or, in some ancient manuscripts, "peoples" [*laoi*, 21.4 NRSV]). Even more inclusivistically, some ancient manuscripts following Ezek. 37.27 add (see NRSV note and as reflected in the King James Version), that God will "be their God," the God, that is, of the peoples of the world. Despite the strongly exclusivistic elements of a similar passage in Revelation, which connects the redeemed nations to the Lamb (i.e., Christ [21.22–22.5]), these Johannine promises, which are derived from two of the major Jewish prophets, maintain a clearly Jewish inclusivism. As in other Johannine writings, there is a tension here between ethical and theological views of salvation, for the clearly theological reference to the servants of the Lamb in 22.3 seems to mark out an exclusive group of the saved. But they can also be seen as a special tribe of the saved rather than an exclusive group, since the criterion of judgment in the "great white throne" judgment scene in 20.11-14 is ethical (as in Mt. 25.31-46). For "the dead, great and small . . . were judged according to their works" (NRSV, *kata ta erga hautōn*).

Pluralism in the New Testament

The synoptic gospels (including Q)

The potential for a universalizing pluralism is found in the teachings of Jesus when he makes ethical treatment of others the one requisite for eternal life, as in the parable of the Good Samaritan, which Jesus tells in reply to a questioner who asked Jesus, "And who is my neighbor?" (Lk. 10.29 NRSV). Since it was the Samaritan alone among the other passersby who tended to the wounds of the man who was beaten on the road to Jericho, thereby showing true neighborliness by showing mercy, Jesus tells a questioning lawyer that this is what must be done "to inherit eternal life" (Lk. 10.25, 37 NRSV).

This same stress on ethics is graphically portrayed in the vignette of the Judgment of the Nations in Mt. 25.31-46, where Jesus distinguishes between the goats destined for eternal fire and the sheep who will inherit eternal life on the basis of works of mercy, including feeding the hungry, giving drink to the thirsty, welcoming the stranger, clothing the naked, and visiting the imprisoned. This is a purely practical teaching that involves no speculative metaphysics or theological doctrine, and if this were to be taken as Jesus's teaching about who is worthy of salvation, then notions of exclusion based on doctrine or practical religious matters would be seen as irrelevant, as is clearly shown in Jesus's warning that not all who call him Lord, prophesy, cast out demons, or do great works in his name will enter the kingdom of heaven. Indeed, he makes clear that only they who do the will of his father, as defined in the prescriptions of the Sermon on the Mount, will avoid being condemned as "evildoers" (Mt. 7.21-23 NRSV).[72]

Another strikingly pluralistic teaching of Jesus is his promise that those who seek will find, which he illustrates by reminding his hearers that no father will give a stone to a child who asks for bread (Mt. 7.9). There is no reference here to doctrine but rather to the easily universalizable moral that the father in heaven is not less likely than a human father to give good things to his children when they ask for them. Here, there is no trace of the later Christian exclusivism that would see the religions of the world as false or empty teachings rather than as gifts given in response to those who seek goodness, righteousness, and dharma.

A full-blown Christian pluralism can take as its starting point the Sermon on the Mount (Mt. 5–6), especially in sayings such as, "Blessed are the pure in heart, for they will see God" (Mt. 5.8 NRSV). Here, there is no hint of the specific doctrinal requirements of later forms of Christianity, nor is there any call to focus on Jesus as the final contemplative object of the spiritual life. The focus here is not just ethical, as in the blessings conferred upon the meek, the mourners, the merciful, and the peacemakers (Mt. 5.4, 5, 7, 9 NRSV). It is rather, contemplative, mystical, and yogic. It is no wonder, then, that this saying has been a favorite of Christian monastics and contemplatives, since it promises a direct, unmediated vision of the divine to those who cleanse their minds and hearts of all that opposes the divine. As an ascetical and contemplative practice, this call to purify one's mental stream will be instantly recognizable by ascetics and contemplatives of other traditions. A passage such as this provides strong evidence against views that too quickly claim that the New Testament exclusively teaches Christian exclusivism, since here the criterion is not doctrinal or personal but ascetical and contemplative, practices that are open to all who want to take them up, with the result that beatitude shows itself to them if they continue purifying themselves.

The Pauline letters

There is little room for pluralism in Paul's writings, which switch between a traditional theistic inclusivism and a novel christocentric exclusivism, but some traces of an inclusivistic and nontheistic pluralism of love can be found in some places (1 Cor. 8.3 and in the overly familiar boilerplate of 1 Cor. 13.1–14.1). Paul often resorts to what seem stereotyped exhortations that could have been spoken by almost any religious teacher (Gal. 5.16-25; Phil. 4.8; 11–13), which is evidence more of the practical unity of the spiritual life across the boundaries of religious traditions than of the finality of any particular set of religious doctrines. There are some clearly apophatic (and thus potentially pluralist) expressions in Paul's writings (Rom. 11.33-34; 1 Cor. 1.19; 2.9, 16; 13.9-12; 2 Cor. 3.18 ["with unveiled faces" (NRSV), or *anakekalymmenō prosōpō*]), and these are among the very few places in the New Testament where the limitations of human language and teachings about the divine are acknowledged. Perhaps because he had grappled profoundly and tragically with issues raised by religious hybridity, Paul was aware that because God's ways are "inscrutable," or better, "untraceable" (*anexichniastoi*), and his judgments are "unsearchable" (*anexeraunēta* [Rom. 11.33 NRSV]) and his are above our ways, people, at best, see the divine only as if they were gazing upon a poorly reflective mirror (2 Cor. 3.18; 1 Cor. 13.12 NRSV [*di' esoptrou en ainigmati*]). Despite this apophatic recognition of the limitations of knowledge and language, Paul's mind is aflame with the hope that he will one day see the divine with an unveiled face.

The Acts of the Apostles

There seems to be no place for pluralism (as opposed to a richly testified inclusivism) in the Acts of the Apostles, which sees Jesus as a man appointed by God and certified through his resurrection to play a central role in a universalized Jewish salvation history that reaches out to all flesh to lead it into a saving relationship with the God of Israel.

Pseudepigraphical letters

One of the most compelling apophatic passages in the New Testament appears in 1 Timothy, which extols the sovereign God "who dwells in unapproachable light, whom no one has ever seen or can see" (6.16 NRSV). This passage is remarkable for apophatically indicating that the divine light cannot be approached and that the sovereign one is alone immortal and beyond the possibility of being seen. This reference to divine ineffability, besides being clearly apophatic, is pluralistic in principle, and can, like many of the Upaniṣadic texts cited in Chapter 5, serve as a portal to pluralism for a religious tradition because it implies the relativity of the imagery and language of the supporting tradition.

When James speaks of the "royal law" of Jewish scripture as loving your neighbor as yourself, he articulates an ethical interpretation of religion that is universalizable to the point of pluralism (2.8). This teaching seems to reflect the earliest traditions of the Jesus movement and is reminiscent of the ethical teachings of Jesus in the earliest stratum of Q, teachings that seem quite distant in much of the later writings of the New Testament.[73]

The Johannine writings

These writings abound in exclusivist language, most of which can be seen as merely reflecting sectarian concerns affecting the early Jesus communities and having no applicability to other religious communities. Thus, it is not surprising that there is only one clearly pluralist verse in John (Jn 15.13), where Jesus says, "No one has greater love than this, to lay down one's life for one's friends" (NRSV), which is an ethical and not a theological criterion. In the first two of the three Johannine letters, there are a number of clearly pluralist verses. For example, 1 John, which reflects an unresolved division between christological exclusivists and inclusivist and pluralist advocates of the ethics of love, proclaims that "there is no fear in love, but perfect love casts out fear" (4.18 NRSV), while 2 John teaches that the commandment "from the beginning" is to walk in love (1.6 NRSV).[74] The clear implication of these verses is that the practice of love bypasses all forms of religious mediation, including saviors, books, or institutions. This is a pluralism that bypasses inclusivistic appeals to God. (Yet, because it remains oriented toward essentialized realities such as love, it can be seen as an inclusivistic or cataphatic form of pluralism, and thus will be more limited than an apophatic pluralism.) One can understand, if not agree with, the attempt of the conflicted Johannine community to counter this pluralist teaching with a severe christological teaching (1 Jn 2.22; 4.3; 5.12).

But in one of the most apophatic passages in the New Testament (which should be read alongside 1 Cor. 13.11-12), the Johannine writer approached a theological agnosticism that is consistent with the reduction of doctrinal issues (christology in this case) to ethical concerns: "The reason the world does not know us is that it did know him. Beloved, we are God's children now; what we will be has not yet been revealed. What we do know is this: when he is revealed, we will be like him, for we shall see him as he is" (1 Jn 3.1-2 NRSV). Although this language is inclusivistic, it seems motivated by the agnosticism that arises from the theological controversy that shapes the self-contradictory Johannine letters. It seems as if the writer of this last-quoted passage was a weary controversialist taking refuge from doctrinal strife in the platitude that even if we don't know what the right theological answer is right now, we do know that if we love, we will find ourselves united with the source of love in the end. Any mystical theologian (Meister Eckhart and Thomas Merton come to mind here) who has endured sterile doctrinal controversies with theologians who are more orthodox will recognize the mystical, agnostic mood of this passage, as will liberal Enlightenment universalists following in the train of Kant, for whom religion is, in the end, about love and how we treat others. Speaking about love as the essence of religion has become a banal cliché, yet it is a universalizing as opposed to a sectarian ethic, and so can serve as the basis for a cataphatic pluralism.[75]

In a symbol rich in apophatic significance, John of Patmos dramatically declares that when the Lamb opened the seventh seal, "there was silence (*sigē*) in heaven for about half an hour" (Rev. 8.1 NRSV). This recalls the "primeval silence" that prevailed before the creation of the world (2 Esd. 7.30 NRSV).[76] The appearance of this silence in the middle of the unfolding apocalypse appears like those moments of mystical, wordless contemplation that gently negate and relativize a religious tradition even as it provides the symbolic and practical context within which the silence arises. Thus, apophatic pluralism, which is as much a mystical insight grounded in profound and disciplined contemplation as it is a philosophical claim about doctrinal diversity instanced by the temporal limitations of language, arises within and not in opposition to the practice of a religious tradition. Rather than signifying the negation or abandonment of a religious tradition, apophatic pluralism reaffirms the significance of the tradition within which it arises by showing the tradition to be a limited indicator of that which it serves: the divine ground of life that both inspires and transcends the numberless languages that arise in its honor.

The apophatic pluralist potential of the New Testament

Although there are only a few traces of pluralism in the New Testament, the New Testament cannot be characterized as primarily promoting exclusivism, despite the presence in it of a number of well-known exclusivistic passages that play a central role in later expressions of Christian exclusivism. Especially in the earlier layers of the New Testament texts, a theistic Jewish inclusivism dominates the thought of the main figures. In this inclusivism, God is the focus and Jesus is a human being chosen by God after the manner of a prophet to renew the Torah and perhaps even to extend its range beyond Israel. Only in the later writings, which can be seen as syncretistic bridges to the proto-orthodox expressions of Hellenistic Christianity, does the focus on Jesus as a theios anēr and as the exclusive locus of salvation begin to replace the older, inclusivistic theism of the early Jesus movement.

Because the views of the early Christians were so various, they can only be approached pluralistically.[77] There is no objective basis for preferring one set of interpretations over another, since no method of justification through appeals to history, tradition, authority, experience, or outcomes is free from effective counterarguments. As the study of the history of early Christianity shows, the term *heretic* has no objective content and is merely a label applied to religious opponents. This outcome confirms the principle of apophatic pluralism, which holds that the limitations of language imply a diversity of religious teachings. While it would be wrong to say that the evidence of the New Testament is open to any interpretation (it would be impossible to claim that it argues for a purely materialist view of life, for example), the range of interpretations is wide enough to despair of finding any singular, agreed-upon meaning for all of the texts taken together (to say nothing of including all of the available noncanonical literature). Although the overall tendency of the New Testament is toward a theistic inclusivism, its diversity of views on central matters such as the significance of Jesus and the place of his followers in the commonwealth of Israel is evidence that the principle of apophatic pluralism is the future not only of religion, but of Christianity as well. Not only is this principle verified by the unsynthesizable diversity of the New Testament documents, it emerges from this study as a more ethical and theoretically sound position than the view that one religious community and one interpretation of the documents of that community can be final and normative for all human beings in all times and places. This pluralist conclusion can be avoided, for a time at least, by taking refuge in authorized and official particularistic interpretations of the New Testament. But this will be a short-term solution, since the ground upon which each authorized religious institution stands is slowly shifting beneath its feet. Even the New Testament dimly presages the inevitability of apophatic pluralism when, in a manner not wholly unlike the Upaniṣads at their most apophatic, it soars through mystical unknowing beyond traditional Jewish inclusivism and proto-orthodox Christian exclusivist polemics in order to proclaim that while it is not yet clear what we shall be when the perfect arrives, we know that they who love and do good will rise in silence with unveiled faces toward the unapproachable light while being conformed to its unknowable likeness.

Clearly, pluralistic insights such as these verge on an apophatic pluralism not unlike that found in the Upaniṣads and Christian mystics, such as Eckhart, who tend toward nondualism and in contemporary Christian theologians, such as Paul Knitter, who embrace a mystical apophaticism grounded in a nondual understanding of the world and the divine.[78] But the New Testament only rarely reaches the peak of mystical unknowing that is the beginning of postsectarian religious wisdom, while it is a main insight of the Upaniṣads. One can only imagine how it might have gone with Paul and the author of John—and how the subsequent religious history of the West might have fared—if Paul and John could have tested their insights against Yājñavalkya in the assembly of the Brāhmaṇas of the Kurus and Pāñcālas at the sacrifice of Janaka of Videha.

Christian theology and apophatic pluralism

What should have become clear in the last two chapters is that the inevitability of pluralism implies an apophatic understanding of religious language and religious teachings. (To characterize this claim as itself a covert exclusivistic or particularistic claim is theoretically clumsy,[79] since it betrays a refusal to distinguish between substantive views of the divine, which are invariably particularistic, and the critical recognition that all such claims are inevitably inadequate.) For the syncretistic churning of new religious identities and the inevitable departicularizing of religious traditions ineluctably undermine even the staunchest of particularisms. Thus, a comprehensive and nonsectarian theory of religious pluralism that respects both the changing diversity of human religious expressions and the significance of particular religions as mediating an immaterial dimension of beatitude will inevitably be apophatic and pluralistic. As we have seen in the case of the Upaniṣads, apophatic pluralism is one of the central theoretical teachings of these inspired writings, for they ever and again point out the limitations of the very language they use to orient the *upāsaka* ("worshipper") toward a beatitude beyond final naming. Even the New Testament, despite its strongly cataphatic and inclusivist bent, contains an implicit apophaticism that can be accessed by mystical Christians who have glimpsed the beatitude beyond the final naming of dogmatic theology. Consequently, the time has come to attempt to rethink orthodox Christian theology in light of the inevitability of apophatic pluralism.

This will be no easy task, since even liberal Protestant theologians have only begun to embrace pluralist theologies of religions over the last 40 years. Not even among the most liberal theologians before Vatican II and the rise of radical theologies among Protestants in the 1960s and later, could one find a genuine pluralist among Christian theologians (the older comparative theologies were invariably inclusivistic among mainstream Christian theologians). Even Paul Tillich, who is an important if often neglected bridge between the older and newer liberal theologies, remained Christocentrically inclusivist to the end (although one can perhaps see the first brightening of the pluralist dawn on the horizon in his Bampton Lectures of 1961[80]). Not until John Hick, under the influence of Wilfred Cantwell Smith, crossed the theological Rubicon and called for a Copernican revolution in theology (to mix his evocative metaphors) did liberal theology begin to shake off its inclusivist slumbers.

Among the more conservative theologians, the influence of W. C. Smith and Hick has been mixed. Indeed, one can make the case that the most militant responses to Hick's views have been among theologians who seem to have reverted to a strongly inclusivistic stance in reaction to the pluralistic theologies of more liberal theologians. But other orthodox theologians, as exemplified in the prolific and irenic writings of Oxford theologian Keith Ward,[81] have been inspired to engage in comparative theology as a response to the imperative of pluralism to acknowledge religious others.

Thus, the Christian tradition now stands at a crossroads. If human societies continue integrating at the current pace, no religious tradition will be able to maintain nonnegotiable particularist claims except at the cost of cutting off solidarity with other human beings and by retreating into ever narrower and tragically doomed forms of fundamentalism. (It is always possible, however, that a global catastrophe will propel human societies back into isolation, which is the best soil for religious particularism.) While some Christians will likely always think (as long as there is a Christianity, at least) that surrendering the claim to universal normativity will undercut the meaning and effectiveness of their religion as a spiritual path of personal and social transformation, other Christians have discovered—and many more are likely to in the future—that the surrender of this idolatry of hallowed religious language can lead to a newness of life. No doubt, this will require a major reorientation within Christianity as a whole (and other religions that resort to particularist strategies as well). While many would see such a change as equivalent to the death of Christianity or as a crisis requiring a distinction between true and false Christians,[82] others—including this writer—see it as an opportunity for Christianity to practice its own deepest kenotic and apophatic truth. Just as Jesus was said to have renounced the prerogatives of divinity (Phil. 2.6-8), so Christianity ought also to divest itself of its claims to religious sovereignty. Could Christianity survive the self-sacrificial rejection of particularism in both its inclusivist and exclusivist forms? To my mind, it could do so and thrive, for the paradox of spiritual life in all well-ordered traditions is that the surrender of the props of self-assertion leads to a more solid grounding in the ultimate, immaterial dimension of beatitude. The familiar Christian metaphor for self-abnegation is the secret of spiritual growth not only for Christianity but for all religions: "Very truly, I tell you, unless a grain of wheat falls into the earth and dies, it remains just a single grain; but if it dies, it bears much fruit. Those who love their life lose it, and those who hate their life in this world will keep it for eternal life" (Jn 12.24-25, NRSV).

Those of us who, like John Hick, can no longer see any basis for crediting the "unique superiority" of any religious tradition,[83] favor a view of religious truth that allows us to be religious (and spiritual) but not particularistic, since the retention of the particularisms of our respective traditions is no longer reasonable for spiritually mature people, no matter how genial these particularisms may be.[84] Probing and wide ranging as many inclusivistic Christian theologies of religions are, they remain bound within the limits of an improbable (even when resolutely affirmed) Christian particularism. All particularist Christian theologies without exception fail to venture deeply enough into the kenotic mystery of Christianity from which the departicularized yet genuinely apophatic and pluralist Christianities of the future may yet emerge.

Notes

1 Harold Coward characterizes the Jewish notion of the Noahic Covenant as "a simple but powerful statement of God's love for all people." Coward, *Pluralism*, 2. From early on, Jewish tradition saw the story of the Noahic Covenant as formulating a set of laws that "encompasses all of humanity." David M. Carr, note to Genesis 9:8–17, in *The New Oxford Annotated Bible: New Revised Standard Version with the Apocrypha* (3rd edn), ed. Michael D. Coogan, et al. (Oxford and New York: Oxford University

Press, 2001), 22. While a theocentric inclusivism is the default position in Judaism from the Babylonian exile until now, there have been thinkers who expressed mildly exclusivist ideas tempered by a typically inclusivist Jewish recognition that anyone who practices an ethical life with faith in the creator "will be of the children of the world to come," according to Maimonides (quoted in Coward, *Pluralism*, 5). Dan Cohn-Sherbok summarizes the mildly exclusivist yet essentially inclusivist stance of Jews over the millennia in "Judaism and other Faiths." Knitter, *The Myth of Religious Superiority*, 121–3. He moves beyond this traditional inclusivism to a genuine expression of religious pluralism that allows Judaism and other religions to retain their uniqueness as authentic expressions of "the one ultimate Reality" (Cohn-Sherbok, Ibid., 125–6). Michael S. Kogan expressed a similar pluralist view in "Toward a Pluralist Theology of Judaism," in Knitter, *The Myth of Religious Superiority*, 112–18. Pluralist interpretations of the Noahic Covenant can also be found in David M. Elcott, "Meeting the Other: Judaism, Pluralism, and Truth," in Cornille, *Criteria of Discernment in Interreligious Dialogue*, 34–5, and Jonathan Magonet, "Jews in Dialogue: Towards Some Criteria of Discernment," in Cornille, *Criteria of Discernment in Interreligious Dialogue*, 5–7.

2 Krister Stendahl, "Christ's Lordship and Religious Pluralism," in *Meanings: The Bible as Document and Guide* (Philadelphia, PA: Fortress Press, 1984), 241.

3 Ekkehard W. Stegemann and Wolfgang Stegemann describe the process of growing exclusivism that shaped the Christian communities after the destruction of the Temple in the year 70. *The Jesus Movement: A Social History of Its First Century*, trans. O. C. Dean, Jr. (Minneapolis, MN: Fortress Press, 1999), 188, 223.

4 Theissen, *Fortress Introduction to the New Testament*, trans. John Bowden (Minneapolis, MN: Fortress Press, 2003; originally published as *Das Neue Testament: Geschichte, Literature, Religion* [Munich: Verlag C. H. Beck oHG, 2001]).

5 Stegeman and Stegeman, *The Jesus Movement*, 187–220.

6 Stegeman and Stegeman, *The Jesus Movement*, 187. Burton L. Mack provides compelling evidence and arguments that the earliest strata of Q, which are themselves the earliest parts of the New Testament, portray an original Jesus movement that remembered Jesus as "a Cynic-like sage" rather than as the martyr and savior of the "Christ myth" of the later narrative gospels and the writings of Paul. *The Lost Gospel: The Book of Q and Christian Origins* (San Francisco, CA: HarperSanFrancisco, 1993), 115, 216–21.

7 Knitter, *No Other Name?* 174.

8 Knitter, *No Other Name?* 174; see also Theissen, *Fortress Introduction to the New Testament*, 23, 38.

9 John P. Meier sees one of seven of the "notable gains" of the third quest is its taking "the Jewishness of Jesus with utter seriousness" ("The Present State of the 'Third Quest' for the Historical Jesus: Loss and Gain," *Biblica* 80 (1999): 459, accessed September 9, 2011, www.bsw.org/Biblica/Vol-80-1999/The-Present-State-Of-The-145-Third-Quest-146-For-The-Historical-Jesus-Loss-And-Gain/333/article-p480.html.

10 Theissen, in commenting on Mk 16.8, holds that the original version of Mark ended at 16.8. He thinks that Mark breaks off here due perhaps to some hesitation on the part of the gospel writer to equate the pre- and postresurrection stories of Jesus. *Fortress Introduction to the New Testament*, 7, 30. Note *a* in the NRSV translation of this verse discusses the textual evidence for the view that Mark ends at 16.8.

11 Geza Vermes, *Jesus: Apocalyptic Prophet of the New Millennium* (Oxford and New York: Oxford University Press, 1999), 5–6. Theissen writes that Jesus was "a charismatic healer, of the kind we find in many cultures and also in the modern world." Theissen, *Fortress Introduction to the New Testament*, 18. Theissen affirms Jesus's full Jewish identity:

> "In other words: Jesus lived, thought, worked, and died as a Jew. One of the most important results of 200 years of modern research into Jesus is that he belongs to two religions: to Judaism, to which he was attached with all his heart, and to Christianity, whose central point of reference he became after his death—on the basis of interpretations of his person which his Jewish followers gave." (*Mit anderen Worten: Jesus lebte, dachte, wirkte und starb als Jude. Es ist eines der wichtigsten Ergebnisse von 200 Jahren moderner Jesusforschung, dass er zwei Religionen angehörte: dem Judentum, dem er von ganzem Herzen anhing, und dem Christentum, dessen zentrale Bezugsgestalt er nache seinem Tode wurde—und zwar aufgrund von Deutungen seiner Person, die ihm seine jüdischen Anhänger gaben.*)

Theissen, *The Religion of the Earliest Churches: Creating a Symbolic World*, trans. John Bowden (Minneapolis, MN: Fortress Press, 1999), 22; original version, Gerd Theissen, *Die Religonen der Ersten Christen: Eine Theorie des Urchristentums*, 2, durchgesehene Auflage (Gütersloh: Chr. Kaiser/Gütersloher Verlagshaus, 2000), 49.

12 Theissen, *Die Religionen der Ersten Christen*, 56; Bowden trans. *The Religion of the Earliest Churches*, 27.

13 Theissen, *Fortress Introduction to the New Testament*, 27–46.

14 Theissen, *Fortress Introduction to the New Testament*, 9–10, 151.

15 Stegeman and Stegeman distinguish between messianic "Jesus-followers in the land of Israel" and groups of Greek-speaking Diaspora Christians, which they call "Christ confessing communities." *The Jesus Movement*, 219–20, 251–4. Mack sees the rise of a Hellenistic Christ mythology, which, in Paul's writings began to displace the older focus on the teachings of Jesus, as occurring among groups in northern Syria and Asia Minor. Mack, *The Lost Gospel*, 2, 207–25, 246.

16 Rudolf Bultmann, *Theology of the New Testament*, trans. Kendrick Grobel (New York: Scribners, 1951), 1:35.

17 Paul can thus be understood within the larger framework characterized by Theissen: "The origin of primitive Christianity is the history of a failed attempt to universalize Judaism" (*"Die Entstehung des Urchistentums is die Geschichte eines gescheiterten Universalisierungsversuchs des Judentums"*). *The Religion of the Earliest Churches*, 165; original Theissen, *Die Religonen der Ersten Christen*, 227.

18 Bultmann pointed out that Jesus's radical reinterpretation of the Torah "stands within the scribal discussion," which is why the role of the historical Jesus is minimal in Paul and John, while "modern liberal Judaism can very well esteem Jesus as a teacher," *New Testament Theology*, 1: 35.

19 Stendahl, "Christ's Lordship and Religious Pluralism," in Stendahl, *Meanings*, 239.

20 Stendahl, "Christ's Lordship and Religious Pluralism," in Stendahl, *Meanings*, 238.

21 Knitter, *No Other Name?* 183.

22 Theissen, *Fortress Introduction to the New Testament*, 133.

23 Jennifer K. Berenson Maclean in her introduction to "The Letter of Paul to the Colossians," in Coogan et al., *The New Oxford Annotated Bible: New Revised Standard Version with the Apocrypha*, 334.

24 Margaret M. Mitchell sees the reference to the "one mediator" in this verse as "a reformulation of the Shema." *The First Letter of Paul to Timothy*, in Coogan et al., *The New Oxford Annotated Bible*, 352n2:1–18.

25 Jey. J. Kanagaraj argues for a more mystical than historical approach to the Gospel of John. *'Mysticism' in the Gospel of John: An Inquiry into Its Background* (Sheffield: Sheffield Academic Press, 1998), 9, 13, 20. Although this approach is seen as "highly questionable" by Klaus Sholtissek ("The Johannine Gospel in Recent Research," in *The Face of New Testament Studies: A Survey of Recent Research*, eds. Scot McKnight and Grant R. Osborne [Grand Rapids, MI: Baker Books, 2004], 471), Kanagaraj presents a thorough argument that John, likely a Palestinian Jew, combines themes in Hermetic and Philonic mysticism with the Merkabah mysticism of contemporary Palestinian Judaism to create a personal and communal mysticism that, instead of promoting a mysticism of abiding in God (*en theō*), cultivates a mysticism that comes from God (*ek theou*), which is achieved through faith in Jesus rather than through ascetical practices (12–13, 43–4, 46–8, 67–8, 75–7, 80–115, 202, 212–13, 311–17). (Sholtissek summarizes recent, more spiritual approaches to interpreting the Gospel of John by biblical scholars. "The Johannine Gospel in Recent Research," in McKnight and Osborne, *The Face of New Testament Studies*, 469–70.)

26 *Jesus: Apocalyptic Prophet of the New Millennium* (Oxford and New York: Oxford University Press, 1999), 88.

27 Geza Vermes, *The Religion of Jesus the Jew* (Minneapolis, MN: Fortress Press, 1993), 4.

28 Theissen, *Fortress Introduction to the New Testament*, 10, 145.

29 As indicated in summaries of recent Johannine scholarship produced by McKnight and Osborne, which favor seeing the gospel as coherent, as best read synchronically, and as in theological dialogue with other early Christian traditions rather than in conflict with them. *The Face of New Testament Studies*, 455–61.

30 C. H. Dodd, *The Interpretation of the Fourth Gospel* (Cambridge: Cambridge University Press, 1953), 6–7.

31 Pheme Perkins, *Reading the New Testament* (2nd edn). (New York: Paulist Press, 1988), 242–8.

32 Raymond E. Brown, *An Introduction to the New Testament* (New York: Doubleday, 1997), 364.

33 Pheme Perkins holds that the "opening stress [of the Johannine community in 1 John 1:1–4] on testimony to the physical reality of the word of life . . . suggests that their dispute [possibly with the Gnostic figure Cerinthus] concerned the humanity of Jesus." Introduction to *The First Letter of John* in Coogan et al., *The New Oxford Annotated Bible*, 407. If this is the case in the more theocentric 1 John, it seems even more likely in the decisively christocentric Gospel of John, as, for example in the prologue (Jn 1.1-18).

34 Helmut Koester, introduction to *The Gospel of Thomas*, in *The Nag Hammadi Library in English* (3rd edn), ed. James M. Robinson (San Francisco, CA: HarperSanFrancisco, 1990), 125.

35 Richard Valantasis, following Koester, assigns the date 60–70 CE to the oldest core sayings of the Gospel of Thomas. *The Gospel of Thomas*, trans. Richard Valantasis (London: Routledge, 1997), 13.

36 Valantasis, *The Gospel of Thomas*, 18–21.

37 See Elaine Pagels, *Beyond Belief: The Secret Gospel of Thomas* (New York: Vintage Books, 2004), 58, 67.

38 As Raymond E. Brown concluded, "the larger church did adopt Johannine pre-existence Christology." "'Other Sheep Not of This Fold': The Johannine Perspective on Christian Diversity in the Late First Century," *Journal of Biblical Literature* 97:1 (March 1978): 20, www.jstor.org/stable/3265832. Thus, despite the novelty of its high christology for early Jewish Christians and the Gentile missionary churches, the high christology of the Gospel of John and the nondocetic christology of 1 John seem to have become the basis of the christology that eventually became Nicene orthodoxy (Brown, Ibid., 21–2). Pagels alludes to this development. *Beyond Belief*, 64, 73.

39 Brown distinguished from separatist Jewish Christians a group he called "Crypto-Christians," who did not outwardly negate Jewish institutions and beliefs. "Other Sheep Not of This Fold," 11–12. Brown gives an overview of his reconstruction of the teachings of the Johannine community in *An Introduction to the New Testament*, 373–6.

40 Brown has argued that the Johannine community may have been an "alienated and exclusive conventicle" among the other early churches because of its high christology, which would also have put it in conflict with the synagogue authorities. "Other Sheep Not of This Fold," 7–8. Similarly, Theissen sees the Gospel of John as "one of the first new interpretations of Christian faith in which one notices a dissatisfaction with traditional Christianity." *Fortress Introduction to the New Testament*, 149. Paradoxically, however, this christology seems to have become the basis of the ultimately dominant but non-Jewish proto-orthodox churches. This turn away from the older Jewish Christianity of the synoptics with its lower christology can already be seen in the growing number of Samaritans who accept the Johannine teaching (Jn 4.39), which is in contrast to the ambivalent and often hostile view of Samaritans in the synoptics (e.g., Mt. 10.5; Lk. 10.33, 17.18). Theissen points out that in John, Jesus does not reject the charge of being a Samaritan (8.48), which may be reflective of some connection between this gospel and a mission to Samaria that resulted in the presence of Christians in the Samarian settlement of Sychar. *Fortress Introduction to the New Testament*, 146.

41 Theissen sees John as expressing "dissatisfaction with traditional Christianity" and, consequently, as offering an "almost mystical" reinterpretation of the *parousia*, which shifted it from a future event into the present as "a timeless confrontation with the eternal God." *Fortress Introduction to the New Testament*, 149–50.

42 Adolphe Tanquerey, *The Spiritual Life: A Treatise on Ascetical and Mystical Theology* (2nd edn), trans. Herman Branderis (Tournai, Belgium: Desclée & Co., 1930; reprinted and updated after 1954), §1486.4:698; Auguste Poulain, *The Graces of Interior Prayer: A Treatise on Mystical Theology*, trans. Leonora L. Yorke Smith (London: Kegan Paul, 1928), 14.41:188; Thomas Keating, *The Better Part: Stages of Contemplative Living* (New York and London: Continuum, 2000), 102, and Thomas Keating, *Intimacy with God* (New York: Crossroad, 1994), 36–7. While these writers

anxiously try to preserve the imagery of Jesus in the highest contemplative states, one of the earliest and most influential theorists of mystical theology, Evagrius Ponticus (fl. 344–399), argued that the highest form of contemplation moves beyond ideas and images, including "the humanity of the Savior," as noted by Louis Boyer, *Introduction to Spirituality*, trans. Mary Perkins Ryan (Collegeville, MN: Liturgical Press, 1961), 77–8. This issue is addressed without clarifying "the place of the humanity of Christ in the higher stages of the mystical life" by John Eudes Bamberger, "Introduction," in Evagrius Ponticus, *The Praktikos* and *Chapters on Prayer*, trans. John Eudes Bamberger (Kalamazoo, MI: Cistercian Publications, 1981), xciii–xciv, xcivnn291, 292.

43 A stance that evangelical theologian Amos Young tentatively attempts to change by seeing this gospel as more concerned with the relationship of the Johannine community to Jewish communities rather than as a categorical statement about all of the worlds' religions. "'The Light Shines in the Darkness': Johannine Dualism and the Challenge for Christian Theology of Religions Today," *The Journal of Religion* 89: 1 (January 2009), 35.

44 Brown, "Other Sheep Not of This Fold," 16.

45 Brown, "Other Sheep Not of This Fold," 7–8, 19.

46 There is a clear tendency in Christian theologies of religion even today to counter the sectarian distinctives of doctrine, which lead to particularism, by an appeal to love, or *agapē*, which essentializes the religious requirements for human beings and can serve as the basis for inclusivistic theologies of religions. Jacques Dupuis, for instance, holds that acts of love are the sign that God has entered the life of a person, even if it is an "anonymous" action of God and the recipient's knowledge of God is unthematized. *Toward a Theology of Christian Pluralism*, 325.

47 Peter Rhea Jones points out that scholars including Calvin, A. E. Brooks, and Bultmann "despaired of finding unity" in the interpretation of 1 John. "A Presiding Metaphor of First John," 179. Through its stress on love and God alongside christological concerns, the bolder, christological features of Johannine theology is "somewhat retracted" in 1 John, thus making the Gospel of John "acceptable to a wider Christianity," according to Theissen, *Fortress Introduction to the New Testament*, 161.

48 Theissen, *Fortress Introduction to the New Testament*, 23.

49 See Coward, *Pluralism*, 1–12.

50 S. Wesley Ariarajah, *The Bible and People of Other Faiths* (Maryknoll, NY: Orbis Books, 1989; originally published in 1985, Geneva: World Council of Churches), 35.

51 See Ariarajah, *The Bible and People of Other Faiths*, 34–5.

52 Theissen, *Fortress Introduction to the New Testament*, 19. Bultmann saw Jesus as radicalizing the Judaism of his time "in the direction of the great prophets' preaching." *Theology of the New Testament*, 1:34. Following up on a study by H. Braun on *Torahverschärfung* in the Qumran texts and the New Testament. Krister Stendahl argued that the antitheses of the Sermon on the Mount are a "sharpening of the Law," which Jesus justified by an appeal to "messianic license." "Messianic License: The Sermon on the Mount," in Stendahl, *Meanings*, 88–9, 93.

53 James M. Robinson, "The Critical Edition of Q and the Study of Jesus," in *The Sayings Source Q and the Historical Jesus*, ed. Andreas Lindemann (Leuven: Peeters Publishers, 2001), 27.

54 As Karl Barth did in "No!," his blunt attack on natural theology in a response to Emil Brunner in Brunner and Barth, *Natural Theology*, 105–6, 108–9. As Barth pungently wrote, "Only the theology and the church of the antichrist can benefit from" natural theology. Brunner and Barth, *Natural Theology*, 128.

55 Jean Calvin, *Institutes of the Christian Religion: A New Translation*, trans. Henry Beveridge (Edinburgh: Calvin Translation Society, 1845), 1.4:59–63. This is a view that is still prominent among Calvinist evangelicals like Ronald H. Nash and Bruce A. Demarest, who hold that general revelation "teaches no redemptive truths," since its purpose is to leave "the unrepentant sinner [i.e., someone, apparently, who does not hold a specific sectarian view of religious truth] without excuse." Thus, in Demarest's view, "general revelation becomes a vehicle not for salvation but for divine judgment." Bruce A. Demarest, *General Revelation* (Grand Rapids, MI: Zondervan, 1982), 246; quoted in Nash, *Is Jesus the Only Savior?*, 20–1; see also Ibid., 117–22, 159. William Lane Craig softens his philosophical defense of Christian exclusivism by allowing that the rare "anonymous Christian" might be saved on the basis of her or his response to general revelation. "No Other Name: A Middle Knowledge Perspective on the Exclusivity of Salvation through Christ," in Quinn and Meeker, *The Philosophical Challenge of Religious Diversity*, 51.

56 Theissen, *Fortress Introduction to the New Testament*, 51.

57 See Theissen, *Fortress Introduction to the New Testament*, 3–4, 47, 49–50, 51–2. See also Stegemann and Stegemann, *The Jesus Movement*, 253–4.

58 Aaron M. Gale, Introduction to "The Gospel of Matthew." In *The Annotated Jewish New Testament*, eds. Amy-Jill Levine and Marc Z. Brettler (Oxford and New York: Oxford University Press, 2011), 2.

59 Stendahl, "Christ's Lordship and Religious Pluralism," in Stendahl, *Meanings*, 238.

60 Albert Schweitzer rejected as authentic to Paul's own views the "being-in-God mysticism which our own religious sense craves," since, in Schweitzer's view, Paul advocates a Christ-mysticism as opposed to a God-mysticism. *The Mysticism of Paul the Apostle*, trans. William Montgomery (New York: The Seabury Press, 1968) 3, 8.

61 Since Vatican II, the Catholic Church seems to be heading in this direction, though its more ardent advocates, such as Jacques Dupuis and Roger Haight, have been resisted by the Vatican and writers such as Gavin D'Costa. See D'Costa's discussion of these developments in "Roman Catholic Reflections on Discerning God in Interreligious Dialogue: Challenges and Promising Answers," in Cornille, *Criteria of Discernment in Interreligious Dialogue*, 53–86.

62 Steven M. Baugh, "'Savior of All People': 1 Tim 4:10 in Context," *Westminster Theological Journal* 54:2 (Fall 1992): 333–8.

63 Nash, *Is Jesus the Only Savior?* 143. Strange makes a similar exegetical point in support of an exclusivistic view, "Daniel Strange Re-Responds to Gavin D'Costa and Paul Knitter," *Only One Way?* D'Costa et al., 215n2.

64 Many contemporary English translations favor the identification of God and Jesus Christ in their renditions of this verse, but older translations, such as the King James Version and the American Standard Version, preserve at least a hint of the ambiguity in the Greek.

65 Pheme Perkins holds that 1 John and the Gospel of John differ over whether the image of the light refers to God or to Jesus (see her introduction to *The First Letter of John*, in *The New Oxford Annotated Bible*, 406). This was likely a difficult debate since the answer one gives will lead one in either a more or less particularist direction.

66 Theodor Häring focused on an "alternation of the ethical and the christological" in his influential interpretation of the Johannine letters, according to Peter Rhea Jones, "A Presiding Metaphor of First John: μένειν ἐν," *Perspectives in Religious Studies* 37:2 (Summer 2010): 199.

67 Obery M. Hendricks, Jr., *The Gospel According to John*, in Coogan et al., *The New Oxford Annotated Bible*, 172n14:1–31. Quoted phrases from *The Book of Enoch*, trans. R. H. Charles (London: SPCK, 1917), 58.

68 Hendricks, "Introduction to *The Gospel According to John*," in Coogan et al., *The New Oxford Annotated Bible*, 146.

69 Brown holds that "there is much in Johannine theology that would relativize the importance of institution and office." "Other Sheep Not of This Fold," 17.

70 Brown disagrees with J. N. Sanders and M. R. Hillmer, who proposed that the Gospel of John was accepted by heterodox groups. "Other Sheep Not of This Fold," 6n6.

71 Theissen, *Fortress Introduction to the New Testament*, 163–4.

72 Perkins admits that the Matthew judgment scene has been read as a "parabolic affirmation" of God's "impartial judgment of all persons," but then she suggests that the scope of this otherwise universal ethical criterion may be limited by restricting the beneficiaries of the works of mercy to members of the persecuted Christian minority. "Christianity and World Religions," 375n31. This subtle suggestion makes sense in light of the reference to the "brethren" (NRSV) of the Son of man in v. 40, but it does so at the cost of limiting the scope of Jesus's words here to activity only on behalf of persecuted Christians.

73 So different are the themes of earliest strata of Q from the narrative gospels and the Pauline and Johannine christologies that Mack writes that the journey "from Q^1 to the Gospel of John is a long, long way for the imagination of any movement to journey in such a short period of time." *The Lost Gospel*, 225.

74 Brown seems to subordinate the universalist possibilities of these statements about love by seeing the scope of love as restricted to other Christians, as in Jn 13.34. *An Introduction to the New Testament*, 385.

75 Brown notes the "universalist possibilities in Johannine thought." *An Introduction to the New Testament*, 375.

76 Jean-Pierre Ruiz, "Note to Revelation 8:5." in Coogan et al., *The New Oxford Annotated Bible*, 431.

77 Haight points out the fact that "the New Testament does not contain one common Christology but a variety of different Christologies has been demonstrated by the exegetes of scripture and is commonly accepted." "Pluralist Christology as Orthodox," in Knitter, *The Myth of Religious Superiority*, 153–4. Perkins points out that "ever since Walter Bauer's *Orthodoxy and Heresy in Earliest Christianity*, students of the NT and early Christianity have been aware that detailed historical description shows Christian communities to have been regionally diverse and conceptually divided." "Christianity and World Religions," 7.

78 See, e.g., Paul Knitter, "Paul Knitter Responds to Gavin D'Costa and Daniel Strange," and "Paul Knitter Re-Responds to Gavin D'Costa and Daniel Strange," in D'Costa et al., *Only One Way?* 155, 207, 209. See also Knitter, *Without Buddha I Could Not Be A Christian*, 7, 14, 22, 139, 154–5, 157, 162. John Thatamanil also recasts Christian theology in nondualistic terms in *The Immanent Divine*, 4–5, 22–3.

79 An example is Kristin Beise Kiblinger's claim that appeals to śūnyatā by Buddhists are instances of inclusivism, a stance that fails to distinguish between substantive

claims about supposed ultimate persons, essences, realities, and so forth, and the critical negation of substantive claims. But it should be pointed out that when Buddhists speak about śūnyatā, they are no more making a substantive claim than when apophatic Christian theologians speak about divine darkness, the God beyond God, or taking leave of God for God's sake, to allude to a number of classic examples. To equate the critical notion of śūnyatā and substantive theological notions is an error like equating a substantive statement such as "being is essence" with a critical statement such as "*being* is a term whose referent eludes definition."

80 Paul Tillich, *Christianity and the Encounter of the World Religions* (New York: Columbia University Press, 1963), 35, 41, 79, 96–7.

81 Joseph Runzo characterizes Ward's generous stance toward religious diversity as "henofideism," which retains a commitment to a specific revelation—Christian, in the case of Ward—while also seeing "other world religions to be possible versions of the truth." Plurality and Relativism," in Meister, *The Oxford Handbook of Religious Diversity*, 73. This virtual pluralism (which is similar to the Christian pluralism of Roger Haight) is on display in Ward's contribution to this same volume: Keith Ward, "Religion and Revelation," in Meister, *The Oxford Handbook of Religious Diversity*, 169–82. Ward retains the theological notion of revelation as a foundational concept in his comparative theology, yet it is thoroughly pluralized through long and extensive exposure to multiple religious and philosophical traditions. Consequently, Ward seems to have moved past his earlier, very generous inclusivism into a genuine pluralism with a Christian focus. See, by contrast, Keith Ward, *Religion and Revelation: A Theology of Revelations in the World's Religions* (New York: Oxford University Press, 1994), 191, 195, 278–80.

82 D'Costa suggests that eventually pluralist theologians such as John Hick and Paul Knitter may no longer "properly be regarded as Christians." "The Impossibility of a Pluralist View of Religions," 226.

83 Hick, *A Christian Theology of Religions*, 30.

84 Hick writes respecting this choice: "We have either to seek a more comprehensive view, or else each return to the absolutism of our own tradition." *A Christian Theology of Religions*, 48.

7

The Parable of the Prisoners

Taking religious teachings seriously as religious teachings

For many religious particularists, recognizing the role that apophatic pluralism and syncretism play in the construction of religious teachings may evoke a crisis of religious meaning. The pluralism and irresolvable diversity of religious views and the turbulent processes of syncretism seem to undercut the validity of religious teachings in general and call into question whether religions actually do speak with authority about a supposed spiritual dimension of life. Some may see pluralism and syncretism as justifications for an irreligious or antireligious skepticism, while others may retreat into religious absolutism by rejecting or restricting the influence of pluralism and syncretism over their favored teachings. But another alternative is to see religious teachings, despite their diversity and constructed character, as speaking meaningfully and truthfully about an immaterial dimension of beatitude. Such a dimension will remain invisible to reductionistic, materialistic views of religion, yet only by taking the teachings of the world's religions seriously in a postsecular manner as responses to an originary and immaterial dimension of life, one that confers a sense of beatitude upon religious practitioners, will we be able to make sense, without resorting to clumsy reductionisms, of the continuing significance and persistence of religious teachings for billions of humans beings.[1] This new, postsecular view of religion was foreseen by Jürgen Habermas when he wrote:

> "philosophy, even in its postmetaphysical form, will be able neither to replace nor to repress religion as long as religious language is the bearer of a semantic content that is inspiring and even indispensable [*inspirierende, ja unaufgebbare semantische Gehalte*], for this content eludes (for the time being?) the explanatory force of philosophical language and continues to resist translation into reasoning discourses [*begründende Diskurse*]."[2]

Thus, despite every new wave of scientific and philosophical criticism, religious thought and practice thrives, likely because it answers a deep human need that cannot be met fully by science, technology, the arts, ethics, politics, entertainment, philosophy, and the delights of physical existence. As a word of reassurance to those who see pluralism as a step toward the denial of the innate meaningfulness of religious language and practice, I would say that the limitless diversity of religious teachings, identities, and institutions that emerge from and subside into the fluidic churning of syncretism does not imply that religious teachings should be seen as false, or worse, as meaningless. Indeed, it can be taken as a sign of the infinite newness of the beatific dimension of life.

This relatively unskeptical approach to the meaning of religious teachings is not blind to the major nonreligious views of religious doctrine that construe them variously as mystifications that mask the actual conditions that prevail in a society, as empirically and logically meaningless utterances, or as the grammar of language games. These approaches highlight noncognitive aspects of religious language and serve as warnings against attempts to absolutize religious language and religious claims. But if this were all that there were to religious teachings, an irreligious skepticism would be justified, and continuing to take religious teachings as cognitive or meaningful would be the mark of irrational people. Yet, religion persists, adapts, thrives, and, as Étienne Gilson observed respecting philosophy, religion "always buries its undertakers."[3] The nonreligious or antireligious critic of religion might take this as grounds for doubling down on criticism of all religious people (and not just absolutists and fanatics) as irrational. Or this might inspire an epistemological modesty and methodological pluralism that is open to other, less skeptical approaches to religious doctrine, such as viewing them as schematizations (or concrete expressions) of religious feelings, as symbols of inner experiences, as quasiphilosophical propositions, or as verbalizations of mystical insights. While none of these approaches is uncontroversial, there is no reason (barring a dogmatic and methodological materialism) why we cannot see them as also offering insights into the functions of religious doctrines.

But seeing religious teachings as meaningful or cognitive immediately raises the issue of the truthfulness of these claims. (This is a separate issue from allowing that they are meaningful, since I can claim that something is meaningful even if it is not true, as in the false but meaningful claim that the sun revolves around the earth.) Thus, the primary concern of this chapter is not with defending the cognitivity or meaningfulness of religious teachings, which I assume,[4] but with overcoming the intractable religious conflicts that arise when religious claims conflict with each other. Theravāda monks, Vedāntic *paṇḍitas*, and Christian theologians disagree in their basic doctrines and practices, but none of them as representatives of their traditions would agree that the reductionistic and noncognitive approaches to religious teachings that dominate Western explanatory enterprises, such as the social-scientific study of religion and the academic study of religion, capture the full meaning of their traditional teachings. This is a view that must be taken seriously by scholars of religion who want to understand religion *as* religion and not merely as an object of scientific or cultural study.

This stance is closer methodologically to classical theology and philosophy than to the modern academic study of religion. It takes seriously people who think that they have received revelation from a deity or have been inspired by a new and unique intuitive insight into reality and who therefore experience these inspirations as self-authenticating and as irrefutably genuine. (The fact that these experiences arise in the dynamic flow of religious syncretism does not negate their attraction and significance.) These experiences seem to come to many, though few succeed in becoming founders of enduring religious movements. Experiencing oneself as the bearer of revelation or of new liberative insights has inspired figures whose continuing importance even millennia after their deaths towers immeasurably over all of their contemporaries. This can also produce an ugly ego inflation in the new prophet or sage. Or it can create anxiety, and sometimes depression, at least at the beginning of their careers, for the new prophet or insight bearer.

While taking these teachings seriously as religious teachings, I nevertheless remain committed to apophatic pluralism, which precludes literalistic and particularistic readings of these teachings while upholding their meaningfulness in the face of the quasi skepticism of blanket, scientistic rejections of the cognitivity of religious claims. An apophatic pluralist approach also rules out seeing the world's many religious teachings as merely local and temporary expressions of generic superdoctrines or master teachings like theism or nondualism, an approach that saves the cognitivity of religious claims from skepticism by sacrificing the distinctiveness of diverse bodies of religious teaching. While granting that hardcore particularists are unlikely ever to take anything but full agreement with their views as acceptable, it is possible to work out an apophatic pluralist defense of the cognitivity of religions that does not propose its own positive teachings in place of traditional teachings, thus avoiding the misdirected charge that apophatic pluralism is itself just another form of exclusivism or inclusivism. To show how apophatic pluralism answers these needs, I offer the following thought experiment, which proposes a model for reconciling the cognitivity of diverse religious claims with apophatic pluralism.

The parable of the prisoners

When religious violence fractures the peace of an unstable country uneasily divided into multiple religious and cultural zones, six religious leaders are taken prisoner by one of the warring factions. They are imprisoned in an isolated compound, though they are allowed to associate freely with one another. Since religious conflicts are a central factor in the war raging in the surrounding countryside, the religious outlook of each of the six captives quickly emerges in their conversations. One of the prisoners is a Mormon bishop who preaches that in these latter days, God has restored the ancient revelation contained in the Book of Mormon through his servant Joseph Smith. Another prisoner is an exclusivistic evangelical Protestant pastor who believes that apart from explicit, doctrinally correct faith in the bodily risen Lord Jesus Christ, there is no salvation given to people under heaven. Still another is a *svāmin* in a Hindu Vaiṣṇava sect, who thinks that all religions culminate in the worship of the supreme personal God, Kṛṣṇa. Another Hindu prisoner is an Advaita Vedāntist monk, who teaches that through *jñāna-yoga*, the yoga of wisdom, people can realize that ātman, or the self, and brahman, or the ultimately real, are identical. Another prisoner is a Mahāyāna Buddhist nun, who has attained deep insight into the impermanence, insufficiency, and selflessness of all entities. The last prisoner is a Sunni Muslim mullā who believes that there is no God but Allāh and that Muḥammad is the last and greatest of the prophets. We can imagine the wariness or curiosity with which these religiously diverse individuals might view each other once they have adjusted physically and emotionally to their imprisonment.

Prison guards maintain security and deliver supplies, leaving the prisoners to work out how they will live together. Each of the prisoners either rejects the teachings of the others or subordinates the other teachings to his or her own teachings. But since the prisoners are committed and skilled representatives of their respective bodies of thought and practice, it is unlikely that they are going to convert one another. Yet, out of a common fascination with religious teachings and practices, they find it difficult to refrain from discussing the strengths and weaknesses of their doctrinally irreconcilable teachings. At first, some of these skilled representatives try to persuade the others of the superiority of their teachings, while others work to show the plausibility or comprehensiveness of their teachings. Although these discussions are vigorous, they fail to change any minds.

While puzzling over the futility of these doctrinal discussions, the Mormon missionary remembers a text in Cicero's *De Natura Deorum* that he had read while working on his doctorate in religious studies. With respect to the welter of contrary religious doctrines, Cicero observed that:

> "There is in fact no subject upon which so much difference of opinion exists, not only among the unlearned but also among educated men; and the views entertained are so various and so discrepant, that, while it is no doubt a possible alternative that none of them is true, it is certainly impossible that more than one should be so."[5]

At his suggestion, the other prisoners reflect together on this text, and they eventually conclude that it is logically possible that none of their views may be true objectively even though each one of these views produces a deeply felt sense of subjective certainty in its adherent. This agreement accords with the logical notion of a contrary, which implies that either one or none—but not all—of their doctrines might be true. For example, it is simply not possible to hold that both nondualism and personalistic theism are equally true. Adherents of each doctrine can marshal an impressive array of evidence to support the view that one or the other teaching is the true doctrine, and each adherent can appeal to distinctive and subjectively persuasive forms of religious experience. Each adherent can also appeal to authoritative scriptures and traditions and can call upon imposing philosophical resources to support each viewpoint. Not only this, but each adherent can also appeal to distinctive interpretations of nature, culture, and anthropology to support each view, while also offering compelling arguments showing how the competing view can be subordinated to the preferred viewpoint—all of which verifies John Locke's aphorism that "everyone is orthodox to himself."[6] Yet, despite the subjective certainty of the theist and the nondualist that they have achieved a reliable insight into the ultimate truth of religion, the objective situation remains unchanged: both of these contrary comprehensive religious visions may be false while both of them cannot objectively be true.

It thus becomes clear to the prisoners that there is no possible resolution of doctrinal issues at the level of doctrine itself, for just as nondualism and theism cannot both be objectively true (as evidenced in the dialectics of Vedānta, in which nondualists and theists trade places at the top of the hermeneutical hierarchy depending on whether it is a nondualist or a theist who is writing the scriptural commentary), so it cannot be the case that Jesus is simultaneously the second person of the Trinity, a nondivine prophet, and a possible eleventh *avatāra* of Viṣṇu. Alternatively, all of these religious doctrines could be false, since some version of materialism might be the case. And while it is logically possible that one of these teachings is true to the exclusion of the others, and thus normative for all human beings, there is no available and commonly accepted mechanism to demonstrate the truth of this doctrine to those who are not predisposed to accept it.

One positive outcome of this dialogue, which otherwise might have seemed pointless, is that even while giving no ground on the truthfulness of their incompatible beliefs, the prisoners keep discussion with the other prisoners open by agreeing as an incontestable point of logic (if not of personal conviction) that my own position may *not* be the true one despite the assurances that I derive from experience, argument, scripture, tradition, and various other sources of evidence and authentication. This practical and theoretical compromise is grounded on the recognition that because none of us actually possesses an absolute knowledge that people not disposed to agree with us will credit, we have no choice but to agree with one another that we may all be wrong or that only one of us—and who that is we can't say—may objectively be right. One of the prisoners cogently expressed this insight: "Not only could you be wrong, despite all your knowledge, experience, and sincerity—so could I." Thus, through a subtle synthesis of subjective certainty about their respective teachings and objective modesty about the possibility of demonstrating them to the unpersuaded, the prisoners discover that they can continue talking religiously to one another even while fundamentally disagreeing with each other.

But by preserving the integrity of the individual bodies of doctrine at the cost of ascribing any common meaning to diverse bodies of religious teachings, this outcome motivates a skepticism that deduces from the various, discrepant, and irreconcilable aims of the various religions that religious teachings are about nothing or are simply made up as one goes along. Sensing that the danger to religion from antireligious skepticism is greater than that posed by doctrinal disagreement among religious practitioners, the Advaita Vedāntist suggests that they work together to find a common teaching or essential truth upon which they can all agree.

For starters, the Christian, the Muslim, the Mormon, and the Vaiṣṇava suggest that the idea of a personal God inspiring the various religions could serve as a common doctrinal ground for the prisoners, but the Advaita Vedāntist and Buddhist see theism as a nonstarter, since they share a nondualist doctrine that allows no ultimate divisions between orders or kinds of being, distinctions that are essential to theism. They drive these points home in undercutting theism by reminding the Muslim that orthodox Christians seem to compromise strict monotheism with the doctrine of the Trinity. They also remind the evangelical Christian that Muslims reject as *širk*, or "association," the belief that God has a partner, that is, an incarnate son. And they remind the Muslim and the Christian that the Vaiṣṇava celebrates the adventures of a God who plays a flute while herding cows. Finally, they remind the Muslim, the Christian, and the Vaiṣṇava that God has, for many Mormons, apparently evolved into the status of deity. By thus exploiting irreconcilable differences among the theists, the Buddhist and the Advaita Vedāntist block attempts by the theist coalition to establish theism as a doctrinal common ground.

Then the Advaita Vedāntist and the Buddhist try to establish a nontheistic contemplative religion based on nondualism as the official religion of the compound, but the temporarily allied theists remind the Advaita Vedāntist that the Buddhist is a nonsubstantialist who argues that nothing has a self-nature. They also remind the Buddhist that the Advaita Vedāntist posits a quasitheistic substance, brahman, as ultimate. When the irreconcilability of these doctrines and their incapacity for reduction to a common idea or essence become clear, the nondualist alliance is also undermined.

In a somewhat desperate move, one of the prisoners suggests that they at least all believe in an ultimate divine reality, which could serve as a common ground, but the Buddhist rejects this language as betraying a lingering substantialism. Yet, when the Buddhist justifies her stance by pointing out that all religious teachings can be shown to be empty or nonultimate because they are inherently self-contradictory, some of the other prisoners reject this as a mask for skepticism and nihilism.

Other suggestions, like seeing the other prisoners as anonymous Christians, or anonymous Buddhists, and so forth, or by asserting that the beliefs of the others are fulfilled in one's own beliefs are rejected, since each of the prisoners can use these inclusivist tactics on the others with the same unconvincing results.

The prisoners eventually conclude that the quest to find a common ground fails because it fails to take the differences between the religious traditions with sufficient seriousness (which is the opposite failing of taking each body of doctrine as final in itself). For the common theism of the fundamentalist Christian, the Mormon, the Muslim, and Vaiṣṇava—when stripped of the distinctive variations of the different traditions—is not as significant to each of the theists as their distinctive and irreconcilable doctrines about a personal god. These differences loom larger for them than the vague and thin ground of a common theism or, more tenuously, of a transhistorical absolute. The differences between the Advaita Vedāntist and the Mahāyāna Buddhist on such issues as whether the Vedas are authoritative and whether an absolute spiritual substance exists are far more significant to them than their agreement on the more general doctrine of nondualism. Thus, the quest for a common ground fails, just as the attempt to preserve the integrity of each tradition at the expense of common religious meanings also failed.

Because their captivity has now continued much longer than any of them had anticipated, an unexpected turn of events occurs in their common life together. Due to the continual give and take of their discussions and the intensification of their spiritual practices amid the privations of the long days and months of their imprisonment, a new approach to doctrinal differences begins to emerge among them. Beginning quite unexpectedly with the evangelical pastor, a new sense of the limitations of religious language and doctrine begins to crop up in their discussions. In response to the Advaita Vedāntist, who had often suggested that the evangelical Christian was more interested in doctrinal correctness than spiritual experience, the evangelical pastor, who had been an undergraduate in a Reformed Christian college in the USA, begins to stress the idea of an innate sense of divinity (*sensus divinitatis*) possessed in a saving and unimpaired form only by true Christians.[7] This appeal seems to give a sturdy experiential basis to his claim that apart from doctrinally correct Christian faith, the only prospect for even the most devout non-Christians is eternal damnation. But the evangelical's victory is short lived, for the Advaita Vedāntist argues that once one takes one's stand on experience, which he agrees is the ultimate foundation for the spiritual life, then there is no way to arbitrarily rule out salvation for saints of other traditions who have also spoken from the standpoint of something like a sensus divinitatis, such as Ramakrishna, Ramana Maharshi, Kabir, and Nanak. Utterly perplexed by this comment, the evangelical pastor tries at first to double back onto the doctrinal criterion and to exclude appeals to experience, but, as a result of the dead ends in the doctrinal discussions with his fellow prisoners, and mindful of the arid discussions he had engaged in as a student in a theologically conservative seminary about Arminianism, pedobaptism, and scriptural infallibility, he now loses his conviction that the inner sense of divinity is hemmed in by just one set of words to the exclusion of all others.

Just at that point, he happens upon an anthology of Christian mystical writings in the camp library, where he reads the *Mystical Theology* of Pseudo-Dionysius, Eckhart's sermon in praise of poverty of spirit, and selections from Thomas Merton's later writings. As he reflects upon the meaning of doctrine in light of the apophatic teachings of these Christian writers, his inward sense of the divine seems to break free of the limits of specific bodies of historically conditioned doctrine into a kind of brilliant darkness beyond all expression in which this sense of beatitude no longer remains tethered to religious ideas—including notions like God or the divine. This last insight is confirmed for him in enthusiastic discussions with the Buddhist nun, for whom the word "God" is an anthropomorphic way of talking about the condition of sublime openness, wisdom, and compassion that her tradition calls śūnyatā, or "emptiness." Overhearing this discussion, the Advaita Vedāntist quickly relates it to the negative method of the Upaniṣads as codified in the classic expression *neti neti*, which suggests that no specific cataphatic religious teaching can be final because each one can be shown to be limited. The Muslim expresses interest in this approach, since there are venerable apophatic traditions in Islām, as does the Mormon missionary. The Vaiṣṇava accepts this principle, since it is found in the Upaniṣads, but advices that it must always be coordinated with positive, cataphatic descriptions of the divine.

Not wanting to relinquish the significance of personal religious experience and no longer able to hold particularistically on to the finality of any set of verbal expressions, the pastor begins to articulate the apophatic pluralist view that the finitude of language sponsors the plurality of religions. The expedient of negating particularism through the logic of contraries and the recognition that it is at least logically possible that a doctrine other than the one that one advocates may be true despite all of one's assurance to the contrary now falls away as the final epicycle of an inclusivist theology of religions. Giving up on doctrine as the most authoritative source of religious knowledge, this new convert to apophatic pluralism now subordinates doctrine to direct, contemplative insight into the nature of the ultimately real. While this insight will inevitably be expressed in the limited language of the one possessing insight, its fruit will be direct realization of the beatitude and deathlessness at the core of the spiritual experience of humanity.

Not long after this apophatic-pluralist epiphany, a peace treaty between the warring factions is signed in Geneva, and the prisoners are released from their long confinement. As is evident from the books that they write afterwards and in the initiatives that they begin in their respective traditions, they become exemplars of the apophatic pluralist outlook, which is modest about the cognitive reach of doctrine while respecting traditional religious language as the basis of community life and of vital spiritual experience.

The pluralistic moral of the parable of the prisoners

This parable portrays the emergence through interreligious discussion of a theory of religious pluralism that is both apophatic and pluralistic. This theory is a step toward one possible future in which religious people orient themselves together toward what each takes as most significant by critically relating to the many other religious teachings that human beings have created over the last 50 and more millennia. There is room in this outlook for the kind of local and modest particularism of a person who is primarily rooted in one particular religious culture, but not for a particularism that upholds one religion as final or as completing the others. Such claims can be asserted but not demonstrated, given the limitations of language and persuasion. At its worst, a theory of religious inclusivism will ratify the inveterate capacity of many religious movements to invest their own local symbols with universal finality. In these cases, even the spectacle of competing groups engaged in the same investiture of universal finality to different sets of symbols seems insufficient to call into question for them what is clearly impossible: the final adequacy of any finite set of symbols as an expression of the infinite. Almost as if it were a law governing the rise and fall of religious movements, this inadequacy will finally prevail, whether voluntarily through reflections like those portrayed in this parable or involuntarily as religious movements are eventually relieved of the sense of finality and universal normativity through the passage of time and the rise of new religious movements.

It seems self-evident, therefore, that the time has arrived for theologies of religions to take apophatic pluralism as the default view over against any form of particularism. It is simply no longer possible to maintain rationally or as a matter of faith (often the last redoubt of the nonpluralist) that in the long history of humanity (and in its possibly lengthy future) this or that religion holds some final, privileged position. Even if that were true, no group of human beings possesses a nonsubjective way of demonstrating to any other group whose faith and reason say otherwise that one tradition rather than another tradition holds the final religious truth for all of humanity. It seems undeniably true, then, that religious exclusivism and inclusivism reduce to incoherence just as soon as more than one tradition makes exclusivistic or inclusivistic claims. Clearly, then, no form of particularism can be the future of religion.

Notes

1 Rudolf Otto and Mircea Eliade, among many others, argued for a specifically religious dimension to life, which is the central concern of religion, a view that has all but been outlawed in religious studies until recently, when the turn to the postsecular in religious studies speaks to a pluralizing of theoretical perspectives and a recognition of the limits of scientistic and quasiscientific modes of analysis. See Kenneth Rose, "Faith or Hermeneutics in the Methodology of Mircea Eliade," *Journal of Alpha Theta Kappa* 18 (Fall 1994): 15–31.

2 Jürgen Habermas, *Postmetaphysical Thinking: Philosophical Essays*, trans. Mark Hohengarten (Cambridge, MA and London: MIT Press, 1992), 51. The original reads: "Solange die religiöse Sprache inspirierende, ja unaufgebbare semantische Gehalte mit sich führt, die sich der Ausdruckskraft einer philosophischen Sprache (vorerst?) entziehen und der Übersetzung in begründende Diskurse noch harren, wird Philosophie auch in ihrer nachmetaphysischen Gestalt weder ersetzen noch verdrängen können." *Nachmetaphysisches Denken: Philosophische Aufsätze* (Frankfurt am Main: Suhrkamp Verlag, 1988), 60. This theme has been provocatively treated by Habermas in *Zwischen Naturalismus und Religion: Philosophische Aufsätze* (Frankfurt am Main, Suhrkamp Verlag, 2005), 13, although in the end he still reduces the potential of religion to a concealed semantic potential that could still be rationalized, or what he in a later essay characterizes as "the unexhausted force [*das Unabgegoltene*] of religious traditions." "An Awareness of What is Missing," in Jürgen Habermas et al. *An Awareness of What is Missing: Faith and Reason in a Post-Secular Age*, trans. Ciarin Cronin (Malden, MA: Polity Press, 2010), 18. This wary recognition of the power of the sacred is traceable back to a key passage in his *The Philosophical Discourse of Modernity*, where he speaks of "the weak messianic power of the present" ("*die schwache messianische Kraft der gegenwärtigen*") as a "decentering counterpoise" to "modern time-consciousness" ("*das dezentrierende Gegengewicht gegen . . . das moderne . . . Zeitbewußtsein*"). *The Philosophical Discourse of Modernity: Twelve Lectures*, trans. Frederick Lawrence (Cambridge, MA: MIT Press, 1987), 15, 16. The original German version is *Der Philosophische Diskurs der Moderne: Zwölf Vorlesungen* (Frankfurt am Main: Suhrkamp Verlag, 1985), 25, 26. Charles Taylor defines "postsecular" as referring to "a time in which the hegemony of the mainstream master narrative of secularism will be more and more challenged." *A Secular Age* (Cambridge, MA: Harvard University Press, 2007), 535. See also Graham Ward, "The Future of Religion," *Journal of the American Academy of Religion* 74:1 (March 2006): 182. Ward has more recently contrasted what I would call the "leftist postsecularism" of Habermas with what I would call the "rightist postsecularism" of Taylor by pointing out that Habermas "views the

turn to the postsecular as a critical reflection within secularism itself," whereas for Taylor postsecularism "marks an epochal shift with respect to secularization—a shift set to continue; religion will not go away." "Theology and Postmodernism: Is It All Over?" *Journal of the American Academy of Religion* 80, no. 2 (June 2012): 467–8. Richard King, in what can be taken as a postsecular analysis of the secular discipline of academic religious studies, asks "to what extent does the secular study of religion subvert or devalue religious beliefs and explanations of the world." *Orientalism and Religion: Postcolonial Theory, India, and "The Mystic East"* (London and New York: Routledge, 1999), 43, 47.

3 Étienne Gilson, *The Unity of Philosophical Experience* (1982; repr., New York: Scribners, 1937), 306.

4 A topic that I have treated extensively in *Knowing the Real.*

5 I.II.5 (trans. Rackham).

6 John Locke, *A Letter Concerning Toleration*, ed. Charles L. Sherman (New York: D. Appleton-Century Company, 1937; Chicago, IL: Encyclopedia Britannica, Inc., 1952), 1.

7 A view expressed cogently and forcefully by Alvin Plantinga in *Warranted Christian Belief*, 175–6. See also the more pluralistic stance of Kelly James Clark and Justin L. Barrett, "Reidian Epistemology and the Cognitive Science of Religion," *Journal of the American Academy of Religion* 79:3 (September 2011): 649, 649n14.

8

Apophatic Pluralism and the Study of Religion

The theory of apophatic pluralism is not a merely negative theory that points out the nonfinality of every body of religious teachings. Although its apophatic criticism of the hegemonic pretentions of particularist forms of religion stands alone as an indefeasible critical insight, apophatic pluralism can also be taken, on the positive side, as one element in a general theory of religion that avoids secularist, scientistic, and particularist deformations of religion by arguing that religions are united in proclaiming that death is not final. This is a distinctively religious teaching, which is available in no other branch of learning apart from some classical philosophies and in some traditional expressions of the arts. Whether one accepts this perennial testimony of the religions to the deathless as a reliable insight makes little difference to the countless people in the past who have turned to religion in its many varieties for solace, hope, and insight. As long as human experience remains marked by finitude, loss, and suffering, religion will continue to thrive in unforeseeable varieties among us for just as long as it speaks about a condition of beatitude that escapes the bounds of death.

Such a boldly religious claim will undoubtedly raise criticism from many scholars in religious studies, which is currently allergic to general claims about humanity's religious heritage and which focuses instead on the particularities of individual traditions. Perhaps because it no longer sees itself as having a fundamental methodology of its own, contemporary religious studies is quick to yield to the limits on its activity implied by the methodological materialism of natural science and the cultural and biological reductionisms of anthropology. The outcome of this self-limitation by religious studies is that the discipline has dispensed with its earlier role of charting the deep structure of religious activity by distilling from the diversity of religious practices and beliefs their most fundamental intensions, or meanings, as expressed in the History-of-Religions approach of figures such as Joachim Wach and Mircea Eliade. As a result, contemporary religious studies often speaks as a distanciated and agnostic observer of religious people as they go about their mediations of the sacred. Resulting from this abandonment of its role of articulating the most general intensions of human religious activity is the contemporary irrelevance of religious studies to religion as it is practiced by most people, the inability of religious studies to articulate its own fundamental methodology, and the increasing isolation of religious studies as a marginal discipline within the academy (except, mostly, as departments offering popular elective courses to undergraduates).

This fate can be seen in the evolution of the field, which first left behind its identity as a Christian and biblically oriented study of "non-Christian" religions by becoming a discipline in search of the basic intensions of spiritual experience, as expressed above all in the project of Mircea Eliade. Revolting against the limitations of this approach, the study of religion then become a discipline in search of itself, as reflected in the increasingly sterile debate about appropriate methodologies carried out passionately but inconclusively over the last two decades.[1] Religious studies has, in the last few decades, dispensed with the nomothetic search for the general intensions that bind the religions together, and it has turned its attention away from clarifying the spiritual insights of the traditions toward reflexive and enervating inquests into the biases and interests that apparently render the study of religion an impossible discipline dedicated to the essentialized and illegitimate concept of religion. As a result, the study of religion has further marginalized itself by focusing with severe discipline on the particularities of specific religious traditions or by losing itself in suspicious critical purges of the various "discourses" that religion scholars of the past few generations have produced.[2] It is therefore an odd paradox that a discipline that dwells in the shadows of the mountains of religious traditions that have spiritually nourished billions of human beings should have almost willfully lost itself in studies that generate virtually no interest to people outside the scholar's own cohort within the academic guild of religious studies.

Contrary to these failings in contemporary religious studies, I want to argue that, alongside the ongoing ethnographic study of the world's religious traditions, religious studies should also provide a reasonable, spiritually lively, and pluralistic account of the religious view of life. Religious studies would then no longer content itself with being an appendage to anthropology made mute about its own specific religious interests, which partially but significantly transcend culture, in order to ward off a militant form of fundamentalistic scientism. Yet, for practitioners of religious studies who have restricted religious studies to thick description of specific traditions and subtraditions, which are supplemented with various forms of theorizing drawn from literary theory, cultural studies, and the social sciences, this will seem like an impermissible return to theology.[3]

In one sense, this charge would be correct, since I think the concern of theology,[4] classical philosophies, apophatic mysticisms or spiritualities, and the religious philosophies of nontheistic religions with articulating religious truth is an inalienable aspect of a full-bodied form of religious studies. Analogously, the study of religion, alongside its essential ethnographic and critical activities, could also articulate in general terms the specifically religious or spiritual insights that underlie the varied expressions of humanity's religious heritage. Its concern with these insights, moreover, should not merely be historical or phenomenological, but also soteriological. In other words, religious studies could also concern itself with orienting people to the spiritual realities that underlie human life.

To do this, it cannot be a theology in the service of one theistic religion, nor can it be a stunted philosophy or style of criticism that is subservient to the current Western hegemonic ideology of materialistic and reductionistic scientism. To go forward, we should take neither Plantinga nor Dawkins as our guides, since neither exclusivistic Christian apologetics nor intellectually naïve antireligious apologetics can articulate a general theory of religion that is true to the spiritual insights of all of humanity and is consistent with a nontotalized and nonhegemonic scientific enterprise.

We could, rather, take our cues from older, once universally admired, but now neglected, figures such as Sarvepalli Radhakrishnan, Paul Tilich, Evelyn Underhill, Rabindranath Tagore, F. H. Bradley, and Mircea Eliade, all of whom combined dazzling intellectual skills steeped in the best contemporary thought and science of their times with profound sensitivity to the universal spiritual values of humanity. Taking figures such as these as our guides, we could develop an integral style of doing religious studies, one that attends to the specifics of religious traditions, the general principles and intensions that are expressed ever and again in specific religions, and the essential spiritual practices that can be distilled from these specific and generic studies of humanity's religious expressions. In this way, perhaps, the field might move beyond the currently regnant constructivistic and tradition-centric focus, which wittingly or not, serves the interests of religious particularists.

Should it rouse itself from its particularistic slumbers, religious studies might then be able to chart the way forward to providing an intellectually satisfying account of the human religious impulse that can withstand the harsh criticism of scientistic materialism, which clothes itself in the garb of truth, but, like other ideologies, replaces the quest for truth with inflexible and inadequate dogmas.

Beyond hegemonic scientism

Without in any way encroaching upon the competence of the natural sciences to explain the physical world, I reserve to religion and philosophy a realm or dimension of insight and experience that is finally inaccessible to a scientific methodology that is limited to the physical and mathematically describable dimensions of life.[5] Despite being inaccessible to research methods designed for the physical world, the spiritual dimension of life is subject to experimentation and the reproducibility of its results, as can be seen in the instructive case of the cross-cultural similarity of the stages of meditative experience (which I will briefly consider below). Religious universals discovered through contemplation indicate that humanity possesses a mental life that, as an expression of the brain, is explicable in neurobiological terms and in light of cognitive theory. But these religious universals also spread out their own realm of experience and conviction from within human awareness. This irreducible inner awareness is the scene where our humanity is enacted through poetry, ethical deliberation, metaphysical insight, and religious dramas of salvation and liberation. Even if neurobiology and cognitive theory were to provide a complete picture of the brain and its functions, this inner, first-person realm would continue to exercise for most human beings a sovereign fascination outrivaling chemical, genetic, and neurobiological explanations of the objective, third-person realm of the physical processes of the brain. Thus, religious studies should bracket the hypothesis of the final reducibility of the mind (or, more poetically, the soul or the ātman) to the brain and continue to explore the intuitions and illuminations of the mind, especially with respect to religion and its spiritual insights.

Essential to this outlook is the rejection of inadequate views that dualistically misperceive our existence instead of seeing us as spiritual entities nondually embedded within cultural and physical worlds. We should not follow Kant in lobbing off our intellectual intuition by distinguishing between two kinds of reason, a theoretical and a practical reason, in which the operations of the first is limited to the external world and the second is limited to our ethical intuitions. Nor should we follow Stephen Jay Gould in distinguishing between what he called "the non-overlapping magisteria" of science and religion,[6] since reality isn't divided into mental and physical dimensions that are entirely distinct from each other. After 100 years in which quantum physics and hermeneutically refined philosophies and philosophies of science have taught us that we create worlds of meaning in accord with an array of interests and cultural and biological factors, it seems incurably naïve to think of the scientific view of life as anything other than one of many available models of life, one that is no less shaped by our interests than the many models of life proposed by philosophy and religion. Simply because science is effective at providing a degree of control over the physical dimension of life by uncovering the character of the physical world, does not entitle science exclusivistically to assume the finality and normativity of its naïvely realist and simplistically materialist view of life.

For example, the recent application of cognitive science to religion (which I will briefly discuss in the next section) has thrown light on the evolution of the genetic constraints that condition the kinds of religious ideas that human beings have, an approach that seems to demonstrate that, contrary to influential constructivist approaches, many religious ideas are universal. But it would be an expression of the reductive fallacy to suppose that an explanation of this sort constitutes a complete understanding of humanity's religious heritage. Pascal Boyer, the founding figure in the cognitive theory of religion, appears to be inclined in this direction when he claims that we have the kind of thoughts (including complex religious thoughts) that we do because "the mind is a complex set of machines that produces all sorts of thoughts."[7] From the standpoint of the undeniably physical aspect of human existence, this is undoubtedly true, and one can only welcome more scientific study of the genetic constraints on human thought. But if we take an explanation such as this as a complete and final explanation of humanity's inner life, then we will see that the theory is too thin, or underdetermined, to account for our mental life on its own terms. Were this speculative reinterpretation of humanity's extensive body of religious, ethical, aesthetic, metaphysical, and religious ideas conclusively verified, it would radically negate the truth of these intuitions by showing them to be, at best, adaptive fictions. But insight into the brain's processes no more invalidates the sublime insights that cap humanity's rich inner life than knowing how a computer screen works explains the images displayed on the screen as fictions devised by the machine's circuits to sell more computers and, therefore, more circuits. To insist otherwise is to display a stance logically identical to that of a religious exclusivist.

One could fill many pages with instances of the results of the reductive reinterpretation of humanity's mental life as nothing but expressions of physical processes. These accounts can be drawn from the writings not only of cognitive scientists, evolutionary psychologists, and sociobiologists, but also from science writing in the mainstream press. Only a failure of reflection or an unwillingness to critically interrogate the pretension of scientism to monological hegemony over the creation of knowledge can account for the current dominance of this banal and ham-handed view of life. It can be seen as just one more in a series of Western intellectual particularisms that have successively emerged since the time of the Constantinian Settlement in the fourth century. The West, understood in particular as the Christian and post-Christian traditions of western and northern Europe and some of its onetime colonies, has generated and forcefully propagated one hegemonic ideology after another. First, it was the exclusive truth of imperial Christianity, followed a millennium later by an exceptionalist stress on the superiority of classical Greco-Roman culture. This was succeeded by the proselytizing universalism of the Enlightenment and the revolutionary imperative of modernism to overthrow traditional social orders. This coincided with the renewal of claims for the exclusive truth of the various and competing forms of missionary Christianity, which moved alongside or in conflict with distinctive political ideologies, such as free-market capitalism, dialectical materialism, and scientific materialism. It is particularly these latter creations of the exclusivistic mentality of the West that have been supported by a monological scientism that extends its competence without warrant beyond the physical and social dimensions of life to the inner world of humanity in all of its diverse expressions. But, as with earlier Western hegemonic ideologies, hegemonic scientism should not be seen as a singular explanation for the whole of life.

And, in what is perhaps the final irony of the faded hegemonism of the West as it dissolves into the hyperconnected electronic flow of a decentered and flattened globe is the overheated, and now perhaps nostalgic, uncovering of the lingering influence of the declining West in the construction of pluralist discourse about the world's religions.[8] For it is entirely possible that in the maturing twenty-first century, as the erstwhile hegemony of the West rapidly declines before the rising New East, that such inquisitions will seem exaggerated and out of touch with the new, empirical realities of a newly dominant Asia. Thus, current criticisms of Orientalism and Western religious hegemony—while of importance when dealing with the discourses generated by the old Western imperialists and their apologists and indigenous foes in the colonial epoch, as well as in its immediate aftermath—seem unsuited to describing the current situation in which "the West" seems to be dissolving along with the idea that any one part of the planet is somehow the center and the subject of planetary history.[9] (It is also possible to see the rise of Orientalism, sufficiently broadened to include the European encounter with Asia, as a significant part of the intellectual currents that, since the eighteenth century, have created a post-Christian and religiously pluralistic West.[10])

Beyond religious constructivism

Alongside an overextended scientism (and the humanities when they are subservient to its limited view of life), religious constructivism has limited the potential of religious studies for providing a general theory of religion, one that can explain religion in spiritual and not only in scientific and cultural terms. Steven Katz, the leading constructivist theorist in the field of comparative mysticism, has argued that merely nominal differences invalidate the identification of otherwise formally identical religious objects, such as nirguṇa brahman, apophatically purified notions of God, and a view of śūnyatā that avoids the extremes of nihilism and reification. The fact, in his view, that each of these religious conceptions can be characterized as ineffable, ultimate, transcendent, and providing joy and holiness does not warrant seeing them as sharing the same "common 'object' or reality" (i.e., the concept or, more technically, the intension of an ineffable, singular ultimate), since the "experience" of the various ultimates described in different mystical traditions differ from each other.[11] In this way, Katz, in a move that has been surprisingly influential in religious studies over the last 35 years, stood the study of mysticism on its head by elevating literal, cataphatic descriptions of mystical experiences over the intension (the "object") of these descriptions, which numerous philosophically astute traditions apophatically define as ineffable (a conclusion that follows from the logical necessity that any ultimate reality must also be *simplex*). One might also say that Katz's approach to mysticism, stressing as it does cataphatic mysticism, or what he calls the "conservative character of mysticism," is almost completely innocent of the cataphatic/apophatic distinction, which would help him to see that the diversities of cataphatic mysticism are relativized (but not necessarily eliminated) in the nonexperiential, apophatic encounter with that which goes beyond naming.[12]

Michael Sells, who provides a corrective contrast to the antiapophatic views of Katz, translates the word *apophasis* with the literal and evocative expression, "unsaying."[13] This term, in Sells's view, names a style of discourse (and not merely a theory) in which the "unnameability" of the ultimate transcendent reality "is not only asserted but performed."[14] Thus, in apophatic mystical writings, "the effort to affirm transcendence leads to a continuous series of retractions," which "exerts a force that transcends normal logical and semantic structures."[15] Sells is careful to point out that apophatic discourse is not equivalent to "common [i.e., cataphatic] mystical experience."[16] This is in contrast with Katz's focus upon cataphatic mystical experiences, which, properly speaking are negated, or unsaid, in apophatic discourse.

It is not surprising then that Sallie King, one of Katz's leading critics, objected to his "excessive reliance upon the literal, referential function of language," since, as King countered in her critique of Katz's position, "for the mystic, 'God' need not necessarily be 'God,' 'Brahman' cannot be 'Brahman,' and *nirvāṇa* is certainly not *nirvāṇa*."[17] But, true to his overemphasis upon cataphatic interpretations of mysticism, Katz bluntly responded that King's "position is logically preposterous. If none of these terms is to be taken in some sense 'literally,' and 'referentially,' then they cannot be used meaningfully at all."[18] But King seems to have the better of the argument, and she demonstrates that Katz seems to favor antiapophatic, literalistic doctrinal teachings. She writes: "Katz's analysis . . . effectively empties experience of all content which does not simply reproduce what is given in the doctrine of the mystic's tradition . . . . In this sense, the content of the experience reduces to those teachings."[19] That is, as King has cogently argued in this article and elsewhere, Katz's approach "improperly reduces mystical experience to doctrine."[20] But, as we have seen in earlier chapters of this book, this is a fatal failing in Katz's approach, since there can be no hope of any sort of interreligious agreement at the level of literalistic, cataphatic readings of religious doctrines.

Thus, while Katz is correct that the *experience* of each these variously named ultimate realities is different, it does not follow from these different experiences of what each of these traditions takes as ultimately real that the ultimately real is itself a series of radically discontinuous singular cataphatic ultimates. (This view is similar to the radical pluralism of S. Mark Heim, which was discussed earlier, and which Katz seems to anticipate when he claims, quite against the actual experience of the adept on the mystical itinerary from knowing to unknowing,[21] that "mystical experience knows . . . what end it seeks from the inception of its traversal along the 'mystic's way.'"[22]) Perhaps this is why Katz is forced to misinterpret yoga as a reconditioning rather than as a deconditioning of consciousness,[23] even though the latter goal is explicitly affirmed for yoga in a foundational yogic text: *yogaś citta-vṛtti-nirodhaḥ* ("yoga is the stilling of the movement of the mind").[24] Contrary to the spirit of this yogic text, which seeks doctrine-transcending mental stillness and intuitive insight, Katz thinks that the *yogin* ultimately attains to an "experience he seeks as a consequence of the shared beliefs he holds through his metaphysical doctrinal commitments."[25] That is to say, the yogin and the mystic are really dogmatists disguised as what George Lindbeck dismissed as "experiential-expressivists."[26]

This is an unworkable stance, since it implies the simultaneous instantiation and reification as ultimate of the various cataphatic images of ultimate reality that are on offer from the world's many religious traditions. The fallacy in this view can be illustrated by noting that the experience of taking a journey to the holy city of Tiruvannamalai in southern India is different if one walks alone, walks in a group, is transported in a bullock cart, goes by taxi or rickshaw, rides on a bus, or takes the train. Despite this diversity of experiences, the city of Tiruvannamalai remains the one goal of all these diverse modes of traveling there. It makes no sense to argue that there is no common goal of the different journeys because the experiences of the different modes of transportation are different. Analogously, while the name *brahman* is not identical with the name *God*, this nominal difference, as well as the varieties of conceptual and experiential differences that attend them, does not negate the logical impossibility of there being more than one ultimate, ineffable grantor of salvation.

This logical impossibility shows up in the analysis of the concept of an ultimate reality, which indicates that there cannot be more than one ultimate reality (nor does it follow from the diversity of experiences of ultimate reality that ultimate reality must itself be diverse). One may prefer to use words such as *ultimate* and *unity* in a more metaphorical than logical way, thus allowing for a diversity of ultimates, but these differences will, in the end, be merely nominal, since the logic of ultimacy implies that these are merely varying names for the same thing: the singular ultimate reality. But if we use the idea of an ultimate reality in a conceptual rather than a metaphorical way, we will have to acknowledge that it is an abuse of clear thinking to contend that there can be two or more ultimates exemplifying identical attributes of ineffability, ultimacy, and unity simply because diverse practices of naming the ultimate have arisen in different sociocultural contexts.

Once one begins to individuate distinctive ultimates on the basis of merely nominal differences, consistency seems to demand differentiating not only between Deus, Dios, Dieu, Theos, God, and Gott as distinct and separately ultimate realties, but also between each use of a divine name, symbolized perhaps by a notation like God^1, God^2, etc., or $Brahman^1$, $Brahman^2$, etc. The futility of such an approach suggests that attempts to reconceptualize a singular ultimate reality as numerous singular, and radically discontinuous ultimate realities is a particularist strategy of preserving the finality of locally distinctive allegorical representations of a singular ultimate reality.

In contrast to this approach, which in the last generation has inspired a large body of hypernominalistic, antiuniversalizing scholarship in religious studies, there is currently a new move back toward realistic accounts of generic features of religious experience. In an influential example, the anthropologist Pascal Boyer attempts to give a causal account of why human beings have recurring religious ideas. In contrast to much of contemporary anthropology—and, I, would add, religious studies as well—Boyer argues that "important aspects of religious representations are constrained by universal properties of the mind-brain."[27] These universal constraints include "an intuitive mentalistic framework" that "accounts for other people's behavior in terms of beliefs and desires," "a mentalistic spontaneous psychology," the "ontological divide between artifact and livings beings," and "an essentialistic understanding of living kinds."[28] In other words, Boyer argues that our commonsense view of the world is genetically conditioned and is not merely the product of inductive generalizations from learning contexts, as is the view, he claims, of many cultural anthropologists.[29] These specialized cognitive constraints on learning, which can be justified through evolutionary arguments based on the selective advantage that they confer upon those who possess them,[30] are triggered by cues from empirical stimuli and play an important, constitutive role in cognitive development. Consequently, any merely empirical or inductive account of learning that fails to take into account these natural constraints on knowledge acquisition will be underdetermined, since it will not be able to account for the ability of learning subjects to acquire competence in various cognitive domains.

Boyer accordingly criticizes the "intuitive" preference of cultural anthropology for empirical, commonsense, and relativist views of the generation of religious ideas.[31] As he writes:

> "Anthropological accounts of cultural transmission are more often than not quasi-magical. They assume that exposure to cultural material will somehow generate, in the subjects concerned, the very representations that seem to inform adult competence."[32]

This approach, which Boyer calls the theory of "exhaustive cultural transmission,"[33] naïvely assumes that all ideas or representations are acquired exclusively through cultural transmission and socialization and can, therefore, be viewed as produced through "cultural construction."[34] Boyer rejects this approach as unduly empiricistic, since he thinks that the context of learning is underdetermined by the information available through sensory stimulation and socialization.[35] Since, as he argues, "there is no evidence that intuitive ontology differs from one [cultural] location to another,"[36] the central idea in contextual interpretations of religion must take into account the fact that the apparent cross-cultural diversity of religious beliefs is genetically constrained, or predetermined, by a common set of ontological assumptions that all human beings share and that are expressed with increasing complexity through the developmental process of maturation. The critical point, over against constructivists and antiessentialists in religious studies, then, is that centrally important aspects of religion are universal.[37]

Rather than provide a more detailed analysis of Boyer's theory about the recurrence of religious ideas, I want to use it to suggest a new resolution to the sterile debate within religious studies between perennialists, or essentialists, and constructivists, or contextualists. Analogously to anthropology, Boyer's nonempiricist model of cognitive development can be directed at the similarly intuitive preference in religious studies for contextual, local, and constructivist views of religious ideas, approaches that fail to recognize the constraints, long championed by essentialists, that condition the acquiring of religious ideas. Just as with anthropologists, so with religionists, for whom anthropology often serves as its foundational discipline, there is a professional tendency to emphasize cultural differences and a consequent tendency to "underestimate the recurrence of similar ideas in different cultures."[38] This leads to the even more problematic but all too common tendency of approaching any detected recurrence of ideas in different cultural settings as merely "a deceptive appearance."[39] Perhaps religious studies can take a cue from Boyer and explain the similarity of religious ideas as evidence of common intensions, or what he calls "cross-cultural universals,"[40] rather than continuing to camouflage the common intensions behind the diversity of experiences presented by the world's mystical and religious traditions. If such an approach were to gain ground in religious studies, it would spell the end of the dominance of constructivist and hypernominalistic views of religion and religious experience, which are grounded in the specious claim that merely nominal differences invalidate the identification of otherwise formally identical religious objects, such as nirguṇa brahman, apophatically purified notions of God, and a view of śūnyatā that avoids the extremes of nihilism and reification.

Rediscovering the method native to religious studies

Refuting constructivism by appealing to the recurring religious ideas discussed in the cognitive science of religion may appear to come at the high cost of tracing religious ideas to physical processes, which would, indeed, be an empty victory for religious intellectuals concerned with defending a distinctively religious understanding of the world and experience. But we can avoid the reductionism apparently implied by cognitive-scientific explanations of religion by seeing these recurring nonphysical religious ideas, or intensions, as also arising in physical processes because both the physical world and the mental world are reflections of a *dharma*, or deep sacred structure, which simultaneously radiates through the physical and mental worlds. Rather than merely explaining religion away by reducing it to biological processes, the cognitive science of religion may, as argued by Kelly James Clark and Justin L. Barrett, provide "empirical confirmation" for the tendency of human beings to produce religious accounts of the world grounded in a pluralistic sense of the divine, one that takes theistic and transtheistic forms.[41] If we assume this stance, we move simultaneously beyond the limitations of both constructivism and cognitive theory and are in a position to articulate for religious studies a method that is native to it without collapsing religious studies into theology, cultural anthropology, cultural studies, or cognitive science. This method is composed of three hierarchically related interpretative tasks:

- cataphatic thick descriptions of specific traditions
- abstracting from thick descriptions to cataphatic universals
- apophatic negation of cataphatic universals

The first task is implicitly constructivist and particularist, since it is concerned with almost ethnographic accounts of specific aspects of individual traditions; the second task is unashamedly essentialist[42] and it is aided by both cognitive science and the universalizing concerns of older forms of comparative religion; the third task is the classic and universal apophatic strategy of negating religious language in order to attain insight into reality outside of the symbolic modifications of the mind, language, culture, and the brain. Were religious studies to set out again in search of common religious realities rather than merely continuing to endlessly trace out the almost infinite particularities of thickly described[43] religious experiences and cultural contexts, it might also begin to reclaim a method distinctive to itself, one that it shares with no other faculty of human knowledge except, in part, with philosophy, classically conceived, mysticism, theologies, and the religious philosophies of the world's nontheistic religions. This would mark a partial return to the universalizing, nomothetic concerns of earlier comparative theologians and historians of religion, but with their now evident limitations—which include Eurocentrism and inclusivism—exposed and eliminated. Doubtlessly, any new attempt to discern religious universals in particulars will be subject to its own temporal and contextual limitations (as will be particularly evident to readers decades and longer into the future), but the attempt to discern the universal is always colored by the context in which it arises. This, however, no more invalidates the cognitive strategy of universalization or abstraction than does the fact that a generalization about types of available vehicles in 2012 will look remarkably different from similar generalizations made in 2062 or in 2112.

In closing, I offer a somewhat more detailed look at the application of the three interpretative tasks of the method native to religious studies.

Cataphatic thick descriptions of specific traditions

The currently dominant approach in the study of religion of idiographically[44] focusing almost exclusively upon thick descriptions of specific religious traditions or communities is traceable not only to the influence of anthropology but also to the influence of Wilfred Cantwell Smith, who, when the nomothetic History-of-Religions approach of Mircea Eliade[45] was dominant, advocated focusing upon individual religious traditions instead of generic abstractions about religion. Cantwell Smith launched an entire generation of scholarship that turned away from the quest for the generic in religion to the elevation of the individual and the unique when he claimed that "there is no *a priori* reason for holding that the unique may not be more significant, more true, than the common."[46] Studies reflecting this methodological focus on the particular and the local are now the standard in religious studies. Ironically, however, such studies serve to reinforce, whether intentionally or not, orthodox and particularist interpretations of specific religions at the expense of inquiries into the common intensions of humanity's religious experience and the apophatic relativization of the symbols through which beatific and liberative insight is expressed. Foundational and insightful as such studies are, they represent the first data-gathering step in the method native to religious studies, and, given their neglect of the larger comparative and mystical concerns that animate this project, they will not be the focus of the remaining pages of this book.

Abstracting from cataphatic thick descriptions to cataphatic universals

Besides their significance as giving voice to local religious traditions, singular cataphatic studies of individual traditions—at least when they are not too heavily in thrall to the latest academic ideology or method—are the raw material for abstracting to a general, but still cataphatic, understanding of the contours of humanity's religious experience. Certainly, any such abstraction must be provisional and subject to negotiation by all concerned parties, including those who live by the tradition, those who study it, and those who see it as an element in the global religious life of humanity. While generalizing over traditions to articulate common intensions is not now a favored method in religious studies, it remains as a significant resource not only for religious studies, but for all who concern themselves with religion. Unlike particularistic and local studies of religions, such generalizing accounts can serve as a part of a larger argument for the inherent significance of religious experience, practices, and institutions over against materialist denials of religion. They can also help people alienated from traditional religions rediscover a vital religious dimension to life.

One notable example of a religious universal is the identity of the contemplative itinerary that proceeds through the stages of *samādhi* in the Classical Yoga of

Hinduism, the multiple *jhānas* of *samatha* practice in Theravāda Buddhism, and the degrees of the *unio mystica* in Catholic mystical theology. As cogently analyzed in the *Yoga Sūtras* of Patañjali, the *Visuddhimagga* of Buddhaghoṣa, and the manuals of mystical theology assembled by A. Tanquerey and A. Poulain, the contemplative life unfolds through a deepening process of concentration, or what is called *dhyāna* in Classical Yoga, jhāna in Theravāda Buddhism, and *recueillement* ("meditation") by the Catholic manualists. Each of these sublime guides to contemplation describes in memorable terms the distinctive moment when the focused mind of the aspiring contemplative or yogin becomes fixed without distraction on the object of meditation. This palpable sign marks the transition from mental dissipation to a simplified and unified mind, which is the portal into a series of increasingly subtler and more unified mental states, which are described in strikingly similar ways in each of the three traditions. The theoretical commitments of the different mystical commentators are different and reflect their respective traditions. The Catholic manualists, for instance, attribute mystical levels of recueillement to divine grace, while the Theravāda Buddhist commentator subordinates the jhānas to liberative insight (*paññā*). Yet it remains undeniable that in each case the journey is a well-marked one that leads from distracted, sense-mediated awareness to a sublime state of heightened spiritual perception in which the mystic or yogin approaches the highest contemplative attainments of the spiritual life.

Where earlier quests for cataphatic universals focused on common conceptual, symbolic, and doctrinal elements in the world's religious traditions, this approach discovers commonalities of experience in a comparative cartography of the mystical and yogic itineraries of the world's religious traditions. If this commonality were to be accepted as an undeniable fact, then a first step toward a renewed sense of the unity of the mystical life of humanity will have been taken and religious studies will have reclaimed the second element of its native methodology, one that is captive neither to the fundamentalisms of hegemonic secularism nor of particularistic religiosity.

The apophatic negation of cataphatic universals

This search for cataphatic universals in the study of religion can break down the walls of particularism that potentially divide religious traditions and people from each other into walled and sometimes hostile camps. But to avoid an uncritical regression into modes of thought that can easily become oppressive, obscurantist, and exclusivistic, this general cataphatic theory of religion must always remain in dialectical tension with the critical, apophatic challenges emerging from new insights in the nontotalized pursuit of science, philosophy, literature, theology, religious studies, and mysticism. The choice before us is not between cataphatic spirituality and its apophatic purification, but the embrace of both. For just as apophatic theologies have ever and again departicularized literalized theologies, and negative philosophizing has always undercut overinflated cataphatic conceptions and theories, so an apophatic approach to the religious expressions of the inner, spiritual life of humanity will inevitably point out when we have extended them too far in the service of overworked, outmoded, or oppressive symbols. Without the symbolic creativity of new cataphatic visions of life, the apophatic gesture shrivels into dry skepticism, nihilism, and rejectionism, while without the skillful application of the apophatic scalpel to cataphatic teachings, symbolic exuberance gives way to fantasy and absolutism.

This dialectical interplay of the cataphatic and the apophatic is well expressed in the *Diamond Sutra*, a text that celebrates the perfection of wisdom as not merely an apophatic overcoming of cataphatic religious symbols, but as a simultaneous negating of the world of form while participating fully in it. Thus, as soon as the Buddha cataphatically promises Subhūti that he will bring the countless living beings in the universe to the overcoming of the cycle of births and deaths in nirvāṇa, he apophatically dissolves the concept of persons.[47] What he gives with one hand, he takes away with the other,[48] thus dramatically modeling the interplay of cataphatic and apophatic ways of thinking that leads to beatific insight, the highest and most enduring gift of religion to humanity. This is not a renegade apophaticism, which in a spirit of inhumane and bitter iconoclasm, negates religious language almost out of spite, but one that attends carefully to the meanings presented by traditional spirituality and lives by them, even as it understands that these forms are not and cannot be final.

Examples almost without end of the apophatic unsaying of cataphatic symbolic landscapes could be culled from all of the world's major religious traditions, and little more would be achieved than to show the ubiquity and, thus, the inevitable necessity of the apophatic dissolution of even the most beloved of sacred narratives and bodies of doctrine. When once it is acknowledged that religious language is incapable of exhausting the deathless realm of beatitude toward which the religions point in their distinctive cataphatic ways, the last step of the method native to religious studies has been employed. This does not imply the rejection of the traditions that have been unsaid, but an openness to the new insights that are yet to emerge from the inscrutable depths of the mystery of being. And it is here that the academic study of religion ends, and if academic study is our only interest, we can follow our curiosity elsewhere—or we can put down our scholarly tools and take up the *sādhana* of religion instead of just studying it.

It seems, then, that the impulse to project a cataphatic symbolic landscape before us, one that contains the sacred along with the other expressions of humankind's first-person awareness, is as unavoidable as speech and action. Just as inevitable is the apophatic impulse to subject these sacred landscapes to criticism, using all of the tools of the intellect and of critical spirituality. We need not fear that either one of these movements will prevail to the erasure of the other in the dialectic of the inner life, since the movements of the cataphatic and of the apophatic cocreate one another and succeed one another like day and night. If nothing else, the current return to the sacred after its banishment from religious studies should remind us that the castaway ideas of one intellectual generation become the seeds of revolution for another. The real challenge facing us as apophatic pluralist religious intellectuals and spiritual practitioners is to enter into the whole scientific, philosophical, literary, and religious heritage of humanity while continuing to do what we have always done: crafting ever newer and more ingenious views of life that make sense of our deepest spiritual impulses, but to do this without asserting that any of the revelations, teachings, and prophecies that have arisen in the recesses of the illumined mind are final and normative for all of humanity. If the history of religions, with its countless new teachings transformed inevitably into old teachings, teaches us anything, it should be that pluralism will always be the future of religion.

Notes

1 Richard King suggests what seems to be a workable, methodologically pluralistic solution to the fraught divide between etic and emic approaches to the study of human religiosity in its many expressions. *Orientalism and Religion*, 53–61.

2 As, for example, in Masuzawa's *The Invention of World Religions*, 13.

3 King, for instance, holds that "after the postcolonial turn" in cultural studies "religious studies as a discipline might better conceive of itself as a form of 'cultural studies' than as an offshoot of theology." *Orientalism and Religion*, 2, 60–1. He nevertheless fits this perspective within an especially cogent and forceful critique of "the irreligious dogmatism of secular reductionism," which would replace emic with etic views of religion. *Orientalism and Religion*, 47–52.

4 Or as in the concern for truth over cultural and historical matters in the naïvely realist forms of analytical theology that are now thriving in some Anglophone philosophy departments. See William Wood, "On the New Analytic Theology, or: The Road Less Traveled," *Journal of the American Academy of Religion* 77:4 (December 2009): 958.

5 Although an approach like this may be rejected as generically theological and thus as departing from the stance of religious studies (itself a thoroughly contested notion and field, as indicated in my comments under *religion* in the introduction to this book), it remains as a plausible explanation (and not merely an interpretation) of human religious activity. While not currently part of the religious studies mainstream, approaches such as this do have their devoted practitioners, including Gerhard Oberhammer, director emeritus of the University of Vienna's Indological Institute, who has pursued a comparative study of major world religions by using categories such as sacrament and revelation, which "are not reducible to sociological or even philosophical concepts," according to Francis Clooney. "Restoring 'Hindu Theology as a Category in Hindu Intellectual Discourse," in *The Blackwell Companion to Hinduism*, ed. Gavin Flood (Oxford and Malden, MA: Blackwell, 2005), 5. Numerous contemporary academic scholars of religion are moving beyond strictures limiting religious studies to methodologies imported from the sciences and literary studies. Those taking religious, mystical, spiritual, or theological approaches include, Sallie King in "A Pluralist View of Religious Pluralism," in *The Myth of Religious Superiority*; John Hick, in "The Next Step Beyond Dialogue," in *The Myth of Religious Superiority*, and John J. Thatamanil in "Comparing Professors Smith and Tillich: A Response to Jonathan Z. Smith's 'Tillich['s] Remains,'" *Journal of the American Academy of Religion* 78:4 (2010): 1171–81.

6 Stephen Jay Gould, *Rocks of Ages: Science and Religion in the Fullness of Life* (New York: Ballantine Books, 2002), 5.

7 Pascal Boyer, *Religion Explained: The Evolutionary Origins of Religious Thought* (New York: Basic Books, 2001), 95. Boyer does, however, acknowledge that "religious claims are indeed beyond verification." *Religion Explained*, 29.

8 Masuzawa eloquently uncovers what she sees as a strategy of continuing Western hegemonism in its construction over the last century or so of a pluralist "world religions discourse." *The Invention of World Religions*, xiv, 13, 22, 28–9, 33, 89–90, 97, 103, 259, 265, 267, 310–28. King's analysis of the criticism leveled against Orientalism, while of importance when dealing with the discourses generated by the old Western imperialists and their apologists and indigenous foes, seems inapt to describe the current situation in which the idea of the West seems to be dissolving along with the idea that any one part of the planet is somehow the center and the subject of planetary history.

9 See King's summary of current debates about Orientalism, *Orientalism and Religion*, 81–95.

10 Urs App argues that such a broader Orientalism played a significant role in Europe's "gradual emancipation from biblical studies" and in the West's "gradual detachment" from its traditional, biblical ideology. *The Birth of Orientalism* (Philadelphia, PA and Oxford: University of Pennsylvania Press, 2010), xiii, 3–8, 13, 31–5, 38–9, 61, 64–7, 76, 165, 238–9, 241, 259–61, 366–8, 425, 440–1, 451–79.

11 Katz, "Language, Epistemology, and Mysticism," 47–8, 50, 62. See also Steven T. Katz, "The 'Conservative' Character of Mystical Experience," in *Mysticism and Religious Traditions*, ed. Steven T. Katz (Oxford and New York: Oxford University Press, 1983), 5, 33, 40–1.

12 This accounts for Katz's attempt to render Meister Eckhart as a thoroughly orthodox and cataphatic Catholic mystic despite his condemnation and long exile from the circle of strictly orthodox thinkers. "The 'Conservative' Character of Mystical Experience," 40–1.

13 Michael A. Sells, *The Mystical Languages of Unsaying* (Chicago and London: Chicago University Press, 1994), 3.

14 Sells, *The Mystical Languages of Unsaying*, 3.

15 Sells, *The Mystical Languages of Unsaying*, 3, see also 10–13, 206–11.

16 Sells, *The Mystical Languages of Unsaying*, 216. Similarly, Denys Turner writes that for medieval Christians, apophaticism was a "practice . . . embodied in life," rather than a "mere intellectual critique of discourse," one that "consciously *organized* a strategy of disarrangement as a way of life." *The Darkness of God: Negativity in Christian Mysticism*, pb. ed. (Cambridge: Cambridge University Press, 1998), 8.

17 Sallie B. King, "Two Epistemological Models for the Interpretation of Mysticism. "*Journal of the American Academy of Religion* 56:2 (Summer 1988): 267.

18 Steven T. Katz, "On Mysticism." *Journal of the American Academy of Religion* 56:4 (Winter 1988): 757.

19 Sallie B. King, "Rejoinder to Steven T. Katz." *Journal of the American Academy of Religion* 56:4 (Winter 1988): 761.

20 King, "Two Epistemological Models for the Interpretation of Mysticism," 257.

21 This may be because Katz presumes that many of his readers will not have had personal acquaintance with a mystical experience. "Language, Epistemology, and Mysticism," 50.

22 Katz, "Language, Epistemology, and Mysticism," 62. Katz also denies the common intentionality of the various mystical traditions. "Language, Epistemology, and Mysticism," 50, 62–3.
23 Katz, "Language, Epistemology, and Mysticism," 57.
24 Patañjali, *Yoga-Sūtras* 1.2.
25 Katz, "Language, Epistemology, and Mysticism," 58. A stance seconded by Robert M. Gimello in another article in the same volume in which Katz's appeared. Gimello holds that "Buddhist mystical experiences" are "deliberately contrived exemplifications of Buddhist doctrine." This is consistent with his view that "doctrine is . . . determinative of religious experience, rather than determined by it." "Mysticism and Meditation," in Katz, *Mysticism and Philosophical Analysis*, 193. See also Robert M. Gimello, "Mysticism and its Contexts," in *Mysticism and Religious Traditions*, ed. Steven T. Katz (Oxford and New York: Oxford University Press, 1983), 63, 66, 73, 75–6, 78, 84.
26 George A. Lindbeck, *The Nature of Doctrine: Religion and Theology in a Postliberal Age* (Philadelphia, PA: The Westminster Press, 1984), 16–17, 31–2.
27 Pascal Boyer, *The Naturalness of Religious Ideas: A Cognitive Theory of Religion* (Berkeley, Los Angeles, and London: University of California Press, 1994), viii; see also 3, 17. See also Pascal Boyer, "Explaining Religious Ideas," *Numen* 39, no. 1 (April 1992): 27–57, www.jstor.org/stable/3270074; Boyer, *Religion Explained*, 2–4.
28 Boyer, *The Naturalness of Religious Ideas*, 290, 91–2, 101–2, 109–11, 123–4, 154. See also Pascal Boyer, "Explaining Religious Ideas," *Numen* 39:1 (April 1992): 278, 280, 282–3, 287–8, 291–2; Boyer, *Religion Explained*, 80–1, 87–9, 94–5, 99–101, etc.
29 Boyer, *The Naturalness of Religious Ideas*, 96, 293.
30 Boyer, *The Naturalness of Religious Ideas*, 290.
31 Boyer, *The Naturalness of Religious Ideas*, 6, 17, 25–7.
32 Boyer, *The Naturalness of Religious Ideas*, 25.
33 Boyer, *The Naturalness of Religious Ideas*, 22.
34 Ibid.
35 Boyer, *The Naturalness of Religious Ideas*, 26–7, 286.
36 Boyer, "Explaining Religious Ideas," 287.
37 An example of how cognitive science as applied to religion yields new insights into religious phenomenon is the new understanding of theism in ancient China that, beginning from the view that "belief in gods naturally arises when certain common cognitive faculties are stimulated," negates the once standard claim that ancient Chinese society was rigorously nontheistic. Kelly James Clark and Justin T. Winslett, "The Evolutionary Psychology of Chinese Religion: Pre-Qin High Gods as Punishers and Rewarders." *Journal of the American Academy of Religion* 79:4 (December 2011): 928–33. Eugene d'Aquili and Andrew Newberg similarly ground the virtual necessity with which the "mind/brain naturally posits" invisible causal agents as a function of a "causal operator," which is a "cognitive operator" that has been abundantly demonstrated by cognitive psychologists, *The Mystical Mind: Probing the Biology of Religious Experience* (Minneapolis, MN: Fortress Press, 1999), 196.
38 Boyer, *The Naturalness of Religious Ideas*, 6.
39 Ibid.
40 Boyer, *The Naturalness of Religious Ideas*, 111.

41 Kelly James Clark and Justin L. Clark and Barrett move beyond the exclusivistic Christian monotheism of Plantinga's *sensus divinitatis* to a more pluralized sense of multiple "supernatural intentional agents." "Reidian Religious Epistemology," *Journal of the American Academy of Religion* 79:3 (2011): 650, 652, 667. I, however, would replace their outmoded general category of "god" with "deities," which includes goddesses alongside gods, and I would pluralize the *sensus divinitatis* to include any apparently innate sense of a deathless realm of beatitude. I would avoid the inclusivistic move of Clark and Barrett of subordinating "the sacred dimension of life" to "clearly defined Judeo-Christian conceptions of God." Ibid., 667. By pluralizing the *sensus divinitatis*, we move beyond the limits of Reformed theology to William James's will to believe and John Hick's similar assertion of the right to believe and to trust our religious experience. Hick, *An Interpretation of Religion*, 227–8, 215, 224, 226.

42 Contrary to Masuzawa's characterization of an essentialist approach to religion as naïve (*The Invention of World Religions*, 7), I would argue that religious studies can also attend to uncovering the general themes that appear in multiple traditions, as well as attending to the spiritual dimension of religions as *spiritual* and not merely as political realities. Ibid., 20.

43 Geertz observes that thickly described "small facts speak to large issues . . . because they are made to." "Thick Description: Toward an Interpretive Theory of Culture," in Clifford Geertz, *The Interpretation of Cultures* (New York: Basic Books, 1973), 23, 222–43nn22–26.

44 The nomothetic-idiographic distinction has been traced back to Hugo Münsterberg by Russell T. Hurlburt and Terry J. Knapp, "Münsterberg in 1898, Not Allport in 1937, Introduced the Terms 'Idiographic' and 'Nomothetic' to American Psychology," *Theory & Psychology* 16 (April 2006): 287–93.

45 Steven M. Wasserstrom defines the "History of Religions" of Eliade, Henry Corbin, and Gershom Scholem as a "Life-centered idea of Religion," and "a new kind of intellectual vitalism." Wasserstrom points out that Eliade "founded what he named 'the History of Religions.'" *Religion after Religion: Gershom Scholem, Mircea Eliade, and Henry Corbin at Eranos* (Princeton, NJ: Princeton University Press, 1989), 10, 8, 10.

46 Wilfred Cantwell Smith *The Meaning and End of Religion*. 1st Paperback Edition (San Francisco: Harper & Row, 1978), 3.

47 *The Diamond Sutra*, in *The Diamond Sutra and the Sutra of Hui Neng*, trans. A. F. Price and Wong Mou-Lam (Berkeley, MA: Shambhala Publications, 1969), 26.

48 *The Diamond Sutra*, Ibid., 33.

Bibliography

Albanese, Catherine. (2007), *A Republic of Mind and Spirit: A Cultural History of American Metaphysical Religion*. New Haven, CT: Yale University Press.

Aleaz, Klarikkal P. (2005), "Pluralism Calls for Pluralistic Inclusivism." In Paul F. Knitter, (ed.), *The Myth of Religious Superiority: A Multifaith Exploration*. Maryknoll, NY: Orbis Books, pp. 162–75.

App, Urs. (2010), *The Birth of Orientalism*. Philadelphia, PA and Oxford: University of Pennsylvania Press.

Ariarajah, S. Wesley. (1989), *The Bible and People of Other Faiths*. Maryknoll, NY: Orbis Books. First published 1985 by World Council of Churches, Geneva.

—. (1991), *Hindus and Christians: A Century of Protestant Ecumenical Thought*. Amsterdam: Editions Rodopi/Grand Rapids, MI: Eerdmans.

—. (2005), "Power, Politics, and Plurality." In Paul F. Knitter, (ed.), *The Myth of Religious Superiority: A Multifaith Exploration*. Maryknoll, NY: Orbis Books, pp. 176–93.

Aristotle. (1894), *Aristotle's Ethica Nicomachea*. Edited by J. Bywater. Oxford: Clarendon Press. In *The Perseus Digital Library*. Accessed September 3, 2010. www.perseus.tufts.edu/hopper/text?doc=Perseus:text:1999.01.0053.

—. (1924), *Aristotle's Metaphysics*. Edited by W. D. Ross. Oxford: Clarendon Press. In *The Perseus Digital Library*. Accessed September 3, 2010. www.perseus.tufts.edu/hopper/text?doc=Perseus:text:1999.01.0051:book=4:section=1007b&highlight=kata/fasin,kata/fasis.

—. (1947), *Introduction to Aristotle*. Edited by Richard McKeon. New York: Modern Library.

Baird, Robert D. (1987), "The Response of Swami Bhaktivedanta." In Harold G. Coward, (ed.), *Modern Indian Responses to Religious Pluralism*. Albany, NY: State University of New York Press, pp. 105–27.

—. (1991), "Syncretism and the History of Religion." In Robert D. Baird, (ed.), *Essays in the History of Religions*. New York: Peter Lang Publishing, pp. 59–71.

Bakker, Freek L. (2010), Review of The Im-Possibility of Interreligious Dialogue, by Catherine Cornille. Exchange: *Journal of Missiological and Ecumenical Research* 39: 199–201.

Bamberger, John E. (1981), Introduction to *The Praktikos* and *Chapters on Prayer*, by Evagrius Ponticus, xxiii–xciv. Translated by John Eudes Bamberger. Kalamazoo, MI: Cistercian Publications.

Barth, Karl. (1946), "No! Answer to Emil Brunner." In Karl Barth and Emil Brunner, (eds), *Natural Theology*, translated by Peter Fraenkel. London: Geoffrey Bles: The Centenary Press, pp. 67–128.

—. (2000), *Church Dogmatics: The Doctrine of the Word of God*, vol. I.2. Translated by G. W. Bromiley, G. T. Thomson, and Harold Knight. London and New York: T&T Clark.

Bauder, Kevin T. (2011), "Fundamentalism." In Andrew David Naselli and Collin Hansen, (eds), *The Spectrum of Evangelicalism*. Grand Rapids, MI: Zondervan, pp. 19–49.

Baugh, Steven M. (Fall 1992), "'Savior of All People': 1 Tim 4:10 in Context." *Westminster Theological Journal* 54(2): 333–8.

Bauman, Chad M. (2008), *Christian Identity and Dalit Religion in Hindu India, 1868–1947.* Grand Rapids, MI: Eerdmans.

Bealar, George. (2012), "Intensional entities." In *Routledge Encyclopedia of Philosophy.* Accessed May 5, 2012. www.rep.routledge.com.read.cnu.edu/article/X019.

Becker, Karl J., Ilaria Morali, and Gavin D'Costa. (2010), *Catholic Engagement with World Religions: A Comprehensive Study.* Maryknoll, NY: Orbis Books.

Beyer, Peter. (2011), "Religious Diversity and Globalization." In Chad V. Meister, (ed.), *The Oxford Handbook of Religious Diversity.* New York: Oxford University Press, pp. 185–200.

Black, Brian. (2007), *The Character of the Self in Ancient India: Priests, Kings, and Women in the Early Upaniṣads.* Albany, NY: State University Press of New York.

Bouyer, Louis. (1961), *Introduction to Spirituality.* Translated by Mary Perkins Ryan. Collegeville, MN: Liturgical Press.

Boyer, Pascal. (April 1992), "Explaining Religious Ideas: Elements of a Cognitive Approach." *Numen* 39(fasc. 1): 27–57.

—. (1994), *The Naturalness of Religious Ideas: A Cognitive Theory of Religion.* Berkeley, Los Angeles, and London: University of California Press.

—. (2001), *Religion Explained: The Evolutionary Origins of Religious Thought.* New York: Basic Books.

Brereton, Joel. (1990), "The Upanishads." In William Theodore de Bary and Irene Bloom, (eds), *Eastern Canons: Approaches to the Asian Classics.* New York: Columbia University Press, pp. 115–35.

Brown, Raymond E. (1978), "'Other Sheep Not of This Fold': The Johannine Perspective on Christian Diversity in the Late First Century." *Journal of Biblical Literature* 97(1): 5–22.

—. (1997), *An Introduction to the New Testament.* New York: Doubleday.

Bultmann, Rudolf. (1951), *Theology of the New Testament.* Translated by Kendrick Grobel. 2 vols. New York: Scribners.

Byrne, Peter. (2011), "A Philosophical Approach to Questions About Religious Diversity." In Chad V. Meister, (ed.), *The Oxford Handbook of Religious Diversity.* New York: Oxford University Press, pp. 29–41.

Calvin, Jean. (1845), *Institutes of the Christian Religion: A New Translation.* Translated by Henry Beveridge. 2 vols. Edinburgh: Calvin Translation Society.

Carr, David M. (2001), "Introduction to Genesis 9:8–17." In Michael D. Coogan, Marc Z. Brettler, Carol A. Newsom, and Pheme Perkins, (eds), *The New Oxford Annotated Bible.* New York and Oxford: Oxford University Press, pp. 9–81.

Catholic Church. (1995), *Catechism of the Catholic Church.* New York: Doubleday.

Chapple, Christopher Key. (June 2012), Review of *Unifying Hinduism: Philosophy and Identity in Indian Intellectual History,* by Andrew J. Nicholson. *Journal of the American Academy of Religion* 80(2): 546–9.

Charles, Robert H. (1917), trans. *Book of Enoch.* London: SPCK.

Cicero, Marcus T. (1979), *On the Nature of the Gods. Academics.* Translated by H. Rackham. Cambridge, MA: Harvard University Press.

Clark, Kelly J. and Justin L. Barrett. (2011), "Reidian Epistemology and the Cognitive Science of Religion." *Journal of the American Academy of Religion* 79(3): 639–75.

Clark, Kelly J. and Justin T. Winslett. (2011), "The Evolutionary Psychology of Chinese Religion: Pre-Qin High Gods as Punishers and Rewarders." *Journal of the American Academy of Religion* 79(4): 928–33.

Clooney, Francis X. (2001), *Hindu God, Christian God: How Reason Helps Break Down the Boundaries Between Religions*. Oxford: Oxford University Press.

—. (2005a), *Divine Mother, Blessed Mother: Hindu Goddesses and the Virgin Mary*. Oxford and New York: Oxford University Press.

—. (2005b), "Restoring 'Hindu Theology' as a Category in Hindu Intellectual Discourse." In Gavin Flood, (ed.), *The Blackwell Companion to Hinduism*. Oxford and Malden, MA: Blackwell, pp. 447–77.

—. (2006), "Surrender to God Alone: the Meaning of Bhagavad Gītā 18:16 in Light of Śrīvaiṣṇava and Christian Tradition." In Catherine Cornille, (ed.), *Song Divine: Christian Commentaries on the Bhagavad Gītā*. Leuven: Peeters/Grand Rapids, MI: W. B. Eerdmans, pp. 191–207.

—. (2010a), *Comparative Theology: Deep Learning Across Religious Borders*. Malden, MA and Oxford: Wiley-Blackwell.

—, (ed.). (2010b), *The New Comparative Theology: Interreligious Insights from the Next Generation*. New York: T&T Clark.

—. (2010c), "Response." In Francis X. Clooney, (ed.), *The New Comparative Theology*. New York: T&T Clark, pp. 191–200.

Coakley, Sarah. (2011), "Prayer as Crucible: How My Mind Has Changed." *The Christian Century* 128(6): 32–3.

Cohn-Sherbok, Dan. (2005), "Judaism and other Faiths." In Paul F. Knitter, (ed.), *The Myth of Religious Superiority*. London: Palgrave Macmillan, pp. 119–32.

Congregation for the Doctrine of the Faith. (1997), "Notification on the book *Toward a Christian Theology of Religious Pluralism*, Orbis Books: Maryknoll, New York by Father Jacques Dupuis, S. J.," January 24, 2001. Accessed December 26, 2011. www.va/roman_curia/congregations/cfaith/documents/rc_con_cfaith_doc_20010124_dupuis_en.html.

—. (2000), "Declaration *Dominus Iesus* On the Unicity and Salvific Universality of Jesus Christ and the Church," August 6, 2000. Accessed May 19, 2012, www.vatican.va/roman_curia/congregations/cfaith/documents/rc_con_cfaith_doc_20000806_dominus-iesus_en.html.

Coogan, Michael D., Marc Z. Brettler, Carol A. Newsom, and Pheme Perkins, (eds). (2001), *The New Oxford Annotated Bible: New Revised Standard Version with the Apocrypha* (3rd edn). Oxford and New York: Oxford University Press.

Cornille, Catherine. (1992), "Introduction to Cornille and Neckebrouck." In *A Universal Faith: Peoples, Cultures, Religions, and the Christ*. Peeters Press: Louvain/Grand Rapids, MI: Eerdmans, pp. vii–x.

—. (2002), "The Dynamics of Multiple Belonging." In Catherine Cornille, (ed.), *Many Mansions? Multiple Religious Belonging and Christian Identity*. Maryknoll, NY: Orbis Books, pp. 1–6.

—. (2008), *The Im-Possibility of Interreligious Dialogue*. New York: Crossroad.

—, (ed.). (2009), *Criteria of Discernment in Interreligious Dialogue*. Eugene, OR: Cascade Books.

Cornille, Catherine and Valeer Neckebrouck, (eds). (1993), *A Universal Faith: Peoples, Cultures, Religions, and the Christ*. Peeters Press: Louvain/Grand Rapids, MI: Eerdmans.

Coward, Harold G. (1985), *Pluralism: Challenge to World Religions*. Maryknoll, NY: Orbis Books.

—, (ed.). (1987), *Modern Indian Responses to Religious Pluralism*. Albany, NY: State University Press of New York.
Cracknell, Kenneth. (2005), *In Good and Generous Faith: Christian Responses to Religious Pluralism*. Peterborough: Epworth.
Craig, William L. (2000), "No Other Name: A Middle Knowledge Perspective on the Exclusivity of Salvation through Christ." In Phillip L. Quinn and Kevin Meeker, (ed.), *The Philosophical Challenge of Religious Diversity*. New York, Oxford: Oxford University Press, pp. 38–53.
Daggers, Jenny. (December 2010), "Thinking 'Religion': The Christian Past and Interreligious Future of Religious Studies and Theology." *Journal of the American Academy of Religion* 78(4): 961–90.
d'Aquili, Eugene and Andrew Newberg. (1999), *The Mystical Mind: Probing the Biology of Religious Experience*. Minneapolis, MN: Fortress Press.
Davies, Oliver. (2006), *God Within: The Mystical Tradition of Northern Europe* (revised edn). Hyde Park, NY: New City Press.
D'Costa, Gavin. (July 1984), "John Hick's Copernican Revolution: Ten Years After." *New Blackfriars* 65: 323–31.
—. (1987), *John Hick's Theology of Religions: A Critical Evaluation*. Lanham, MD: University Press or America.
—, (ed.). (1990), *Christian Uniqueness Reconsidered: The Myth of a Pluralistic Theology of Religions*. Maryknoll, NY: Orbis Books.
—. (1990a), "Christ, the Trinity, and Religious Pluralism." In Gavin D'Costa, (ed.), *Christian Uniqueness Reconsidered: The Myth of the Pluralistic Theology of Religions*. Maryknoll: Orbis Books, pp. 3–29.
—. (1990b), "Preface to D'Costa." In Gavin D'Costa, (ed.), *Christian Uniqueness Reconsidered: The Myth of the Pluralistic Theology of Religions*. Maryknoll, NY: Orbis Books, pp. vii–xxii.
—. (June 1996), "The Impossibility of a Pluralist View of Religions." *Religious Studies* 32(2): 223–32.
—. (2000), *The Meeting of Religions and the Trinity*. Maryknoll, NY: Orbis Books.
—. (2003), "Christ, Revelation and the World Religions." In T. W. Bartel, (ed.), *Comparative Theology: Essays for Keith Ward*. London: SPCK, pp. 33–43.
—. (2009), *Christianity and World Religions: Disputed Questions in the Theology of Religions*. Oxford, Chichester, UK, and Malden, MA: Wiley-Blackwell.
—. (2010), "Pluralist Arguments: Prominent Tendencies and Methods." In Karl J. Becker, Ilaria Morali, and Gavin D'Costa, (eds), *Catholic Engagement with World Religions*, Maryknoll, NY: Orbis Books, pp. 329–44.
—. (2011a), "Christianity and the World Religions: A Theological Appraisal." In Gavin D'Costa, Paul F. Knitter, and Daniel Strange, (eds), *Only One Way? Three Christian Responses on the Uniqueness of Christ in a Religiously Plural World*. London: SCM Press, pp. 3–46.
—. (2011b), "Theology Amid Religious Diversity." In Chad V. Meister, (ed.), *The Oxford Handbook of Religious Diversity*. Oxford and New York: Oxford University Press, pp. 142–53.
D'Costa, Gavin, Paul F. Knitter, and Daniel Strange. (2011), *Only One Way? Three Christian Responses on the Uniqueness of Christ in a Religiously Plural World*. London: SCM Press.

de Andia, Ysabel. (2005), "Negative Theology." In *Encyclopedia of Christian Theology*, vol. 1, edited by Jean-Yves Lacoste and translated by Antony Levi, New York: Routledge, pp. 1109–13.

Demarest, Bruce A. (1982), *General Revelation*. Grand Rapids, MI: Zondervan.

Deutsch, Eliot. (1969), *Advaita Vedānta: A Philosophical Reconstruction*. Honolulu: The University Press of Hawai'i.

Dionysius Areopagita, Pseudo-. (1857), *De Mystica theologia*. Edited by Balthasaris Corderius. In Jacques-Paul Migne, (ed.), *Patrologiae Cursus Completus, Series Graeca*, vol. 3. Paris: J. P. Migne, pp. 997A–1048B.

—. (1987), *The Mystical Theology*. In *Pseudo-Dionysius: The Complete Works*, translated by Colm Luibheid. Mahwah, NJ: Paulist Press, pp. 133–41.

Dodd, Charles H. (1953), *The Interpretation of the Fourth Gospel*. Cambridge: Cambridge University Press.

Doniger, Wendy and Brian K. Smith. (1991), *The Laws of Manu*. New Delhi: Penguin Books.

Dupuis, Jacques. (1991), *Jesus Christ at the Encounter of World Religions*. Maryknoll, NY: Orbis Books.

—. (2001), *Toward a Christian Theology of Pluralism*. Maryknoll, NY: Orbis Books. First published 1997 by Orbis Books.

Earhart, H. Byron. (2004), *Japanese Religion* (4th edn). Belmont, CA: Wadsworth/Cengage Learning.

Eck, Diana L. (July 1988), "The Religions and Tambaram." *International Review of Mission* 77: 375–89.

—. (2003), *Encountering God: A Spiritual Journey from Bozeman to Banaras*. Boston, MA: Beacon Press. First published 1993 by Beacon Press.

—. (2012), *India: A Sacred Geography*. New York: Harmony Books.

Eckhart, Meister. (1994), *Meister Eckhart: Selected Writings*. Translated by Oliver Davies. New York: Penguin Books.

Ehrman, Bart D. (1999), *Jesus: Apocalyptic Prophet of the New Millennium*. Oxford and New York: Oxford University Press.

Elcott, David M. (2009), "Meeting the Other: Judaism, Pluralism, and Truth." In Catherine Cornille, (ed.), *Criteria of Discernment in Interreligious Dialogue*. Eugene, OR: Cascade Books, pp. 26–49.

Emerson, Ralph W. (1940), "An Address." In Brooks Atkinson, (ed.), *The Complete Essays and Other Writings of Ralph Waldo Emerson*. New York: The Modern Library, pp. 67–84.

Farley, Wendy. (2005), *The Wounding and Healing of Desire: Weaving Heaven and Earth*. Louisville, KY: Westminster John Knox Press.

Fields, Rick. (1992), *How the Swans Came to the Lake: A Narrative History of Buddhism in America* (3rd revised edn). Boston, MA: Shambhala.

Forrester, Duncan B. (1976), "Professor Hick and the Universe of Faiths." *Scottish Journal of Theology* 29: 65–72.

Fredericks, James L. (1999), *Faith Among the Faiths: Christian Theology and Non-Christian Religions*. New York/Mahwah, NJ: Paulist Press.

—. (2004), *Buddhist and Christians: Through Comparative Theology to Solidarity*. Maryknoll, NY: Orbis Books.

—. (2010), "Introduction." In Francis X. Clooney, (ed.), *The New Comparative Theology: Interreligious Insights from the Next Generation*. New York: T&T Clark, pp. ix–xix.

Gale, Aaron M. (2011), "Introduction to 'The Gospel of Matthew'." In Amy-Jill Levine and Marc Z. Brettler, (eds), *The Annotated Jewish New Testament*. Oxford and New York: Oxford University Press, pp. 1–2.

Geertz, Clifford. (1973), *The Interpretation of Cultures*. New York: Basic Books.

Gibson, David. "The Vatican Levies Further Penalties on Roger Haight, S. J." *dotCommonweal*, January 2, 2009. Accessed June 5, 2012. www.commonwealmagazine.org/blog/?p=2644.

Gilkey, Langdon. (1987), "Plurality and its Theological Implications." In John Hick and Paul F. Knitter, (eds), *The Myth of Christian Uniqueness: Toward a Pluralistic Theology of Religions*. Maryknoll NY: Orbis Books, pp. 37–50.

Gilson, Étienne. (1937), *The Unity of Philosophical Experience*. New York: Scribners. Reprint, Westminster, MD: Christian Classics, 1982.

Gimello, Robert M. (1978), "Mysticism and Meditation." In Steven Katz, (ed.), *Mysticism and Philosophical Analysis*. London: Oxford University Press, pp. 170–99.

—. (1983), "Mysticism and its Contexts." In Steven Katz, (ed.), *Mysticism and Religious Traditions*. New York: Oxford University Press, pp. 61–88.

Gittins, Anthony J. (2004), "Liturgical Inculturation: Transforming Deep Structures of Faith." *Irish Theological Quarterly* 69: 47–72.

Godlove, Jr., Terry F. (December 2010), "Religion in General, not in Particular: A Kantian Meditation." *Journal of the American Academy of Religion* 78(4): 1025–47.

Goldberg, Philip. (2010), *American Veda*. New York: Random House.

Gould, Stephen J. (2002), *Rocks of Ages: Science and Religion in the Fullness of Life*. New York: Ballantine Books.

Griffiths, Paul J. (2001), *Problems of Religious Diversity*. Malden, MA: Blackwell.

—. (2006), "On the Future of the Study of Religion in the Academy." *Journal of the American Academy of Religion* 74(1): 66–74.

Grimes, John. (1996), *A Concise Dictionary of Indian Philosophy*. Albany, NY: State University of New York Press.

Gross, Rita M. (2005), "Excuse me, but What's the Question? Isn't Religious Diversity Normal?" In Paul F. Knitter, (ed.), *The Myth of Christian Uniqueness: Toward a Pluralistic Theology of Religions*. Maryknoll, NY: Orbis Books, pp. 75–87.

Habermas, Jürgen. (1985), *Der Philosophische Diskurs der Moderne: Zwölf Vorlesungen*. Frankfurt am Main: Suhrkamp Verlag.

—. (1987), *The Philosophical Discourse of Modernity: Twelve Lectures*. Translated by Frederick Lawrence. Cambridge, MA: MIT Press.

—. (1988), *Nachmetaphysisches Denken: Philosophische Aufsätze*. Frankfurt am Main: Suhrkamp Verlag.

—. (1992), *Postmetaphysical Thinking: Philosophical Essays*. Translated by Mark Hohengarten. Cambridge, MA and London: MIT Press.

—. (2005), *Zwischen Naturalismus und Religion: Philosophische Aufsätze*. Frankfurt am Main: Suhrkamp Verlag.

—. (2010), "An Awareness of What is Missing." In *An Awareness of What is Missing: Faith and Reason in a Post-Secular Age*. Translated by Ciarin Cronin. Malden, MA: Polity Press, pp. 15–23.

Haight, Roger. (1987), "Pluralist Christology as Orthodox." In Paul F. Knitter, (ed.), *The Myth of Christian Uniqueness: Toward a Pluralistic Theology of Religions*. Maryknoll, NY: Orbis Books, pp. 151–61.

—. (1999), *Jesus: Symbol of God*. Maryknoll, NY: Orbis Books.
—. (2005), *The Future of Christology*. New York: Continuum.
Halbfass, William. (1981), *India and Europe: An Essay in Understanding*. Albany, NY: State University of New York Press.
Hart, Kevin. (1989), *The Trespass of the Sign: Deconstruction, Theology, and Philosophy*. Cambridge: Cambridge University Press.
Hatcher, Brian. (2007), *Bourgeois Hinduism, Or The Faith of the Modern Vedantists: Rare Discourses from Early Colonial Bengal*. New York and Oxford: Oxford University Press.
Hegel, G. W. F. (2006), *Phänomenologie des Geistes*. Edited by Hans-Friedrich Wessels and Heinrich Clairmont. Hamburg: Felix Meiner Verlag, First published 1807.
Heidegger, Martin. (2002), "The End of Philosophy and the Task of Thinking." In *On Time and Being*, translated by Joan Stambaugh, 55–73. Chicago: University of Chicago, First published 1972 by Harper & Row.
Heim, S. Mark. (1995), *Salvations: Truth and Difference in Religion*. Maryknoll, NY: Orbis Books.
—. (2001), *The Depth of the Riches: A Trinitarian Theology of Religious Ends*. Grand Rapids, MI: Eerdmans.
Hendricks, Jr., Obery M. (2001), "Introduction and Notes to *The Gospel According to John*." In Michael D. Coogan, Marc Z. Brettler, Carol A. Newsom, and Pheme Perkins, (eds), *The New Oxford Annotated Bible*. New York: Oxford University Press, pp. 146–7.
Henrici, Peter. (2010), "The Concept of Religion from Cicero to Schleiermacher: Origins, History, and Problems with the Term." In Karl J. Becker, Ilaria Morali, and Gavin D'Costa, (eds), *Catholic Engagement with World Religions*. Maryknoll, NY: Orbis Books, pp. 1–22.
Hick, John. (1973a), *God and the Universe of Faiths: Essays in the Philosophy of Religion*. London: Macmillan.
—. (1973b), "The Copernican Revolution in Theology." In John Hick, (ed.), *God and the Universe of Faiths: Essays in the Philosophy of Religion*. London: Macmillan, pp. 120–32.
—. (1982), *God Has Many Names*. Philadelphia, PA: The Westminster Press.
—. (1985), "Religious Pluralism and Absolute Claims." In John Hick, (ed.), *Problems of Religious Pluralism*. London: Macmillan Press, pp. 46–66.
—. (1987), "The Non-Absoluteness of Christianity." In John Hick and Paul F. Knitter, (eds), *The Myth of Christian Uniqueness: Toward a Pluralistic Theology of Religions*. Maryknoll, NY: Orbis Books, pp. 16–36.
—. (1989), *An Interpretation of Religion: Human Responses to the Transcendent*. New Haven, CT and London: Yale University Press.
—. (1991), Foreword by John Hick in *The Meaning and End of Religion*, 1st Fortress Press ed., by Wilfred Cantwell Smith. Minneapolis, MN: Fortress Press.
—. (1995), *A Christian Theology of Religions: The Rainbow of Faiths*. Louisville, KY: Westminster John Knox Press.
—. (1997), "The Possibility of Religious Pluralism: A Reply to Gavin D'Costa." *Religious Studies* 33(2): 161–6.
—. (2004), *An Interpretation of Religion: Human Responses to the Transcendent* (2nd edn). New Haven, CT and London: Yale University Press.
—. (2005), "The Next Step Beyond Dialogue." In Paul F. Knitter, (ed.), *The Myth of Christian Superiority: A Multifaith Exploration*. Maryknoll, NY: Orbis Books, pp. 3–12.

—. (2006), "Exclusivism versus Pluralism in Religion: A Response to Kevin Meeker." *Religious Studies* 42: 207–8.
—. (2009), "A Brief Response to Aimee Upjohn Light." *Journal of Ecumenical Studies* 44(4): 691–2.
Hick, John and Paul F. Knitter, (eds). (1987), *The Myth of Christian Uniqueness: Toward a Pluralistic Theology of Religions*. Maryknoll, NY: Orbis Books.
Hodgson, Peter C. (2005), "The Spirit and Religious Pluralism." In Paul F. Knitter, (ed.), *The Myth of Religious Superiority: A Multifaith Exploration*. Maryknoll, NY: Orbis Books, pp. 135–50.
—. (2007), *Liberal Theology: A Radical Vision*. Minneapolis, MN: Fortress Press.
Hurlburt, Russell T. and Terry J. Knapp. (2006), "Münsterberg in 1898, Not Allport in 1937, Introduced the Terms 'Idiographic' and 'Nomothetic' to American Psychology." *Theory & Psychology* 16: 287–93.
International Theological Commission of the Roman Curia's Pontifical Commission. "The Hope of Salvation for Infants Who Die Without Being Baptised." Rome, April 19, 2007. Accessed April 27, 2011. www.vatican.va/roman_curia/congregations/cfaith/cti_documents/rc_con_cfaith_doc_20070419_un-baptised-infants_en.html.
Jones, Peter R. (Summer 2010), "A Presiding Metaphor of First John: μένειν ἐν." *Perspectives in Religious Studies* 37(2): 179–93.
Jordens, J. T. F. (1987), "Gandhi and Religious Pluralism." In Harold G. Coward, (ed.), *Modern Indian Responses to Religious Pluralism*. Albany: State University Press of New York, pp. 3–17.
Jørgensen, Adelin. (2008), *Jesus Imandars and Christ Bhaktas: Two Case Studies of Interreligious Hermeneutics and Identity in Global Christianity*. Frankfurt am Main: Peter Lang.
Kanagaraj, Jey J. (1998), '*Mysticism' in the Gospel of John: An Inquiry into Its Background*. Sheffield: Sheffield Academic Press.
Kärkkäinen, Veli-Matti. (2003), *An Introduction to the Theology of Religions: Biblical, Historical, and Contemporary Perspectives*. Downers Grove, IL: InterVarsity Press.
Katz, Steven T. (1978), "Language, Epistemology, and Mysticism." In Steven T. Katz, (ed.), *Mysticism and Philosophical Analysis*. New York, Oxford University Press, pp. 22–74.
—. (1983), "The 'Conservative' Character of Mystical Experience." In Steven T. Katz, (ed.), *Mysticism and Religious Traditions*. Oxford and New York: Oxford University Press, pp. 3–60.
—, (ed.). (1978), *Mysticism and Philosophical Analysis*. New York: Oxford University Press.
—, (ed.). (1983), *Mysticism and Religious Traditions*. Oxford and New York: Oxford University Press.
—. (Winter 1988), "On Mysticism." *Journal of the American Academy of Religion* 56(4): 751–7.
Kaufman, Gordon D. (1972), *God the Problem*. Cambridge, MA: Harvard University Press.
—. (1987), "Religious Diversity, Historical Consciousness, and Christian Theology." In John Hick and Paul F. Knitter, (eds), *The Myth of Christian Uniqueness: Toward a Pluralistic Theology of Religions*. Maryknoll, NY: Orbis Books, pp. 3–15.
—. (1996), *God, Mystery, Diversity: Christian Theology in a Pluralistic World*. Minneapolis, MN: Fortress Press.
Keating, Thomas. (1994), *Intimacy with God*. New York: Crossroad.
—. (2000), *The Better Part: Stages of Contemplative Living*. New York and London: Continuum.

Kent, Eliza F. (September 2011), "Secret Christians of Sivakasi: Gender, Syncretism, and Crypto-Religion in Early Twentieth-Century South India." *Journal of the American Academy of Religion* 79(3): 676–705.

Kiblinger, Kristin B. (2010), "Relating Theology of Religions and Comparative Theology." In Francis X. Clooney, (ed.), *The New Comparative Theology: Interreligious Insights from the Next Generation*. New York: T&T Clark, pp. 21–42.

Kim, Andrew E. (2011), "South Korea." In Peter C. Phan, (ed.), *Christianities in Asia*. Malden, MA and Oxford: Wiley-Blackwell, pp. 22–228.

King, Richard. (1999), *Orientalism and Religion: Postcolonial Theory, India, and the "Mystic East"*. London and New York: Routledge.

King, Sallie B. (Winter 1988a), "Rejoinder to Steven T. Katz." *Journal of the American Academy of Religion* 56(4): 759–61.

—. (Summer 1988b), "Two Epistemological Models for the Interpretation of Mysticism." *Journal of the American Academy of Religion* 56(2): 257–79.

—. (2005), "A Pluralist View of Religious Pluralism." In *The Myth of Religious Superiority: A Multifaith Exploration*. Maryknoll, NY: Orbis Books, pp. 88–101.

Klostermaier, Klaus K. (Summer 2009), "Facing Hindu Critique of Christianity." *Journal of Ecumenical Studies* 44: 461–6.

Knitter, Paul F. (1985), *No Other Name? A Critical Survey of Christian Attitudes Toward the World Religions*. Maryknoll, NY: Orbis Books.

—. (2002), *Introducing Theologies of Religions*. Maryknoll, NY: Orbis Books.

—. (2005a), "Is the Pluralist Model a Western Imposition? A Response in Five Voices." In Paul F. Knitter, (ed.), *The Myth of Religious Superiority: A Multifaith Exploration*. Maryknoll, NY: Orbis Books, pp. 28–42.

—, (ed.). (2005b), *The Myth of Religious Superiority: A Multifaith Exploration*. Maryknoll, NY: Orbis Books.

—. (2007), "My God is Bigger than Your God! Time for Another Axial Shift in the History of Religion." *Studies in Interreligious Dialogue* 17(1): 100–18.

—. (2009a), "Review of *The Im-Possibility of Interreligious Dialogue*, by Catherine Cornille." *Theological Studies* 70(4): 952–4.

—. (2009b), *Without Buddha I Could Not Be a Christian*. Oxford: One World.

—. (2011a) "Paul Knitter Responds to Gavin D'Costa and Daniel Strange." In Gavin D'Costa, Paul F. Knitter, and Daniel Strange, (eds), *Only One Way? Three Christian Responses on the Uniqueness of Christ in a Religiously Plural World*. London: SCM Press, pp. 153–66.

—. (2011b), "Paul Knitter Re-Responds to Gavin D'Costa and Daniel Strange." In Gavin D'Costa, Paul F. Knitter, and Daniel Strange, (eds), *Only One Way? Three Christian Responses on the Uniqueness of Christ in a Religiously Plural World*. London: SCM Press, pp. 199–212.

Koepping, Elizabeth. (2011), "India, Pakistan, Bangladesh, Burma/Myanmar." In Peter C. Phan, (ed.), *Christianities in Asia*. Malden, MA and Oxford: Wiley-Blackwell, pp. 9–42.

Koester, Helmut. (1990), trans. *The Gospel of Thomas*. In James M. Robinson, (ed.), *The Nag Hammadi Library in English* (3rd edn). San Francisco, CA: HarperSanFrancisco, pp. 124–38.

Kogan, Michael S. (2005), "Toward a Pluralist Theology of Judaism." In Paul F. Knitter, (ed.), *The Myth of Religious Superiority: A Multifaith Exploration*. Maryknoll, NY: Orbis Books, pp. 112–18.

Kraemer, Hendrik. (1947), *The Christian Message in a Non-Christian World* (2nd edn). New York and London: International Missionary Council.
—. (1956), *Religion and the Christian Faith*. Philadelphia, PA: The Westminster Press.
Lemesurier, Peter. (1990), *This New Age Business*. Forres: Findhorn Press.
Leopold, Anita M. and Jeppe S. Jensen, (eds). (2005), *Syncretism in Religion: A Reader*. New York: Routledge. First published 2004 by Equinox Publishing, London.
Leuba, James H. (1912), *The Psychological Study of Religion: Its Origin, Function, and Future*. New York: Macmillan.
Light, Aimee U. (Summer 2009), "Harris, Hick, and the Demise of the Pluralistic Hypothesis." *Journal of Ecumenical Studies* 44(3): 467–70.
Lindbeck, George A. (1984), *The Nature of Doctrine: Religion and Theology in a Postliberal Age*. Philadelphia, PA: The Westminster Press.
Lipner, Julius. (1977), "Does Copernicus Help? Reflections for a Christian Theology of Religions." *Religious Studies* 13: 243–58.
Locke, John. (1937), *A Letter Concerning Toleration*. Edited by Charles L. Sherman. New York: D. Appleton-Century Company. First published 1952 by Encyclopedia Britannica, Chicago.
Locklin, Reid B. and Hugh Nicholson. (2010), "The Return of Comparative Theology." *Journal of the American Academy of Religion* 78(2): 477–514.
Long, Jeffrey. (2010), "Tentatively Putting the Pieces Together: Comparative Theology in the Tradition of Sri Ramakrishna." In Francis X. Clooney, (ed.), *The New Comparative Theology: Interreligious Insights from the Next Generation*. New York: T&T Clark, pp. 151–70.
Mack, Burton L. (1993), *The Lost Gospel: The Book of Q and Christian Origins*. San Francisco, CA: HarperSanFrancisco.
Maclean, J. K. B. (2001), "Introduction and Notes to *The Letter of Paul to the Colossians*." In Michael D. Coogan, Marc Z. Brettler, Carol A. Newsom, and Pheme Perkins, (eds), *The New Oxford Annotated Bible*. New York and Oxford: University Press, pp. 334–5.
Magonet, Jonathan. (2009), "Jews in Dialogue: Towards Some Criteria of Discernment." In Catherine Cornille, (ed.), *Criteria of Discernment in Interreligious Dialogue*. Eugene, OR: Cascade Books, pp. 3–25.
Markham, Ian S. (2011), "A Religious Studies Approach to Questions about Religious Diversity." In Chad V. Meister, (ed.), *The Oxford Handbook of Religious Diversity*. Oxford and New York: Oxford University Press, pp. 21–8.
Marsden, George M. (1991), *Understanding Fundamentalism and Evangelicalism*. Grand Rapids, MI: Eerdmans.
Marty, Martin E. and R. Scott Appleby. (1991), *The Fundamentalism Project*. Chicago: University of Chicago Press.
Masuzawa, Tomoko. (2005), *The Invention of World Religions: Or, How European Universalism was Preserved in the Language of Pluralism*. Chicago: University of Chicago Press.
McKnight, Scot and Grant R. Osborne, (eds). (2004), *The Face of New Testament Studies: A Survey of Recent Research*. Grand Rapids, MI: Baker Academic.
McRoberts, Omar M. (2011), "Growth in Secular Attitudes Leaves Americans Room for Belief in God," *UChicago News*. Accessed October 24, 2011. www.news.uchicago.edu/article/2009/10/23/growth-secular-attitudes-leaves-americans-room-belief-god.

Meier, John P. (1999), "The Present State of the 'Third Quest' for the Historical Jesus: Loss and Gain." *Biblica* 80: 459–87. Accessed September 9, 2011. www.bsw.org/Biblica/Vol-80–1999/The-Present-State-Of-The-145-Third-Quest-146-For-The-Historical-Jesus-Loss-And-Gain/333/article-p480.html.

Meister, Chad. (2011), "Introduction to Meister." *The Oxford Handbook of Religious Diversity*. Oxford and New York: Oxford University Press, pp. 3–6.

—, (ed.). (2011), *The Oxford Handbook of Religious Diversity*. Oxford and New York: Oxford University Press.

Merton, Thomas. (1971), *Contemplative Prayer*. New York: Doubleday.

Meyer, Birgit. (1994), "Beyond Syncretism: Translation and Diabolization in the Appropriation of Protestantism in Africa." In Charles Stewart and Rosalind Shaw, (eds), *Syncretism/Anti-Syncretism*. London and New York: Routledge, pp. 45–68.

Mitchell, Margaret M. (2001), "Introduction to *The First Letter of Paul to Timothy*." In Michael D. Coogan, Marc Z. Brettler, Carol A. Newsom, and Pheme Perkins, (eds), *The New Oxford Annotated Bible*. Oxford and New York: Oxford University Press, pp. 350–1.

Mohan, Kamlesh. (2011), "Cultural Values and Globalization: India's Dilemma." *Current Sociology* 59(2): 214–28.

Mohler R. Albert. (2012), "The Subtle Body—Should Christians Practice Yoga?" *Albertmohler. com*. Accessed May 19, 2012. www.albertmohler.com/2010/09/20/the-subtle-body-should-christians-practice-yoga/.

Monier-Williams, Monier. (2008), *Monier-Williams Sanskrit-English Dictionary* 2008 online revision. www.sanskrit-lexicon.uni-koeln.de/monier/.

Moser, Paul K. (2011), "Religious Exclusivism." In Chad V. Meister, (ed.), *The Oxford Handbook of Religious Diversity*. Oxford and New York: Oxford University Press, pp. 77–88.

Mosse, David. (1994), "The Politics of Religious Synthesis: Roman Catholicism and Hindu Village Society in Tamil Nadu, India." In Charles Stewart and Rosalind Shaw, (eds), *Syncretism/Anti-Syncretism*. London and New York: Routledge, pp. 85–107.

Nāgārjuna. (1986), *Mūlamadhyamakakārikā of Nāgārjuna: The Philosophy of the Middle Way*. Translated by David J. Kalupahana. Albany, NY: State University of New York Press.

Nash, Ronald H. (1994), *Is Jesus the Only Savior?* Grand Rapids, MI: Zondervan.

Netland, Howard A. (2001), *Encountering Religious Pluralism: The Challenge to Christian Faith and Mission*. Downers Grove, IL: InterVarsity Press.

Nicholson, Andrew J. (2010), *Unifying Hinduism: Philosophy and Identity in Indian Intellectual History*. New York: Columbia University Press.

Nicholson, Hugh. (2010), "The New Comparative Theology and the Problem of Hegemonism." In Francis X. Clooney, (ed.), *The New Comparative Theology: Interreligious Insights from the Next Generation*. New York: T&T Clark, pp. 43–62.

—. (2011), *Comparative Theology and the Problem of Religious Rivalry*. New York: Oxford University Press.

Nicholson, Hugh and Locklin, Reid. (2010), "The Return of Comparative Theology." *Journal of the American Academy of Religion* 78(2): 477–514.

Nikhilananda, Swami, trans. (2002), *Vedānta-Sāra (The Essence of Vedānta) of Sadānanda Yogīndra* (2nd edn). Kolkata: Advaita Ashrama. First published 1974.

Olivelle, Patrick, (ed.). (1986), "Tat Tvam Asi in Context." *Zeitschrift der Deutschen Morgenländischen Gesellschaft* 136(1): 98–109.

—. (1996), *Upaniṣads*. Oxford and New York: Oxford University Press
—. (1998), Introduction to *The Early Upaniṣads: Annotated Text and Translation*. Translated by Patrick Olivelle. New York: Oxford University Press, pp. 3–27.
Pagels, Elaine. (2004), *Beyond Belief: The Secret Gospel of Thomas*. New York: Vintage Books.
Patton, Laurie. (2004), "Veda and *Upaniṣad*." In Sushil Mittal and Gene Thursby, (eds), *The Hindu World*. New York: Routledge, pp. 37–51.
Paul VI (pope). (1964a), *Ecclesiam Suam*. Rome: The Vatican, August 6, 1964. Accessed May 19, 2011, www.vatican.va/holy_father/paul_vi/encyclicals/documents/hf_p-vi_enc_06081964_ecclesiam_en.html.
—. (1964b), *Lumen Gentium*. Rome: The Vatican, November 21, 1964. Accessed May 19, 2012, www.vatican.va/archive/hist_councils/ii_vatican_council/documents/vat-ii_const_19641121_lumen-gentium_en.html.
—. (1965), "Declaration on the Relationship of the Church to Non-Christian Religions." Rome: The Vatican, October 26, 1965. Accessed December 26, 2011. www.vatican.va/archive/hist_councils/ii_vatican_council/documents/vat-ii_decl_19651028_nostra-aetate_en.html.
Perkins, Pheme. (1986), "Christianity and World Religions: New Testament Questions." *Interpretation* 50(4): 367–78.
—. (1988), *Reading the New Testament* (2nd edn). New York: Paulist Press.
—. (2001), "Introduction to *The First Letter of John*." In Michael D. Coogan, Marc Z. Brettler, Carol A. Newsom, and Pheme Perkins, (eds), *The New Oxford Annotated Bible*. New York and Oxford: Oxford University Press, pp. 406–7.
Phan, Peter C. (ed.). (2011), *Christianities in Asia*. Malden, MA and Oxford: Wiley-Blackwell.
Pinnock, Clark H. (1992), *A Wideness in God's Mercy: The Finality of Jesus Christ in a World of Religions*. Grand Rapids, MI: Zondervan.
Plantinga, Alvin. (1974), *God, Freedom, and Evil*. Grand Rapids, MI: Eerdmans.
—. (2000), *Warranted Christian Belief*. New York: Oxford University Press.
Plato. (1961), *Theatetus*. Translated by Francis Macdonald Cornford and Benjamin Jowett. In Edith Hamilton and Huntington Cairns, (eds), *The Collected Dialogues of Plato Including the Letters*. Princeton, NJ: Princeton University Press, pp. 847–919.
Poulain, Auguste. (1928), *The Graces of Interior Prayer: A Treatise on Mystical Theology*. Translated by Leonora L. Yorke Smith. London: Kegan Paul.
Pratt, Douglas. (1999), "The Dance of Dialogue: Ecumenical Interreligious Engagement." *The Ecumenical Review* 51: 274–87.
Premawardhana, Devaka. (Winter/Spring 2011), "Christianity Becomes Unfamiliar." *Harvard Divinity Bulletin* 39(1–2): 29–34.
Price, A. F., and Wong Mou-Lam, trans. (1969), *The Diamond Sutra and the Sutra of Hui Neng*. Berkeley, CA: Shambhala Publications.
Race, Alan. (1982), *Christians and Religious Pluralism*. Maryknoll, NY: Orbis Books.
Radhakrishnan, Sarvepalli. (1953), *The Principal Upaniṣads*. New York: Humanities Press.
Ratzinger, Joseph C. (2004), "Notification on the book 'Jesus Symbol of God' by Father Roger Haight S. J." Rome: The Congregation for the Doctrine of the Faith, December 13, 2004. Accessed October 7, 2011. www.vatican.va/roman_curia/congregations/cfaith/documents/rc_con_cfaith_doc_20041213_notification-fr-haight_en.html.

Raveh, Daniel. (2008), "*Ayam aham asmīti*: Self-consciousness and Identity in the Eighth Chapter of the *Chāndogya Upaniṣad* vs. Śaṅkara's *Bhāṣya*." *Journal of Indian Philosophy* 36: 319–33.

Rayan, Samuel. (1992), "Outside the Gate, Sharing the Insult." In Felix Wilfred, (ed.), *Leave the Temple: Indian Paths to Human Liberation*. Maryknoll, NY: Orbis Books, pp. 125–45.

Rescher, Nicholas. (1985), *The Strife of Systems*. Pittsburgh, PA: Pittsburgh University Press.

Robbins, Joel. (2003), "What Is a Christian? Notes Toward an Anthropology of Christianity." *Religion* 33(3): 191–9.

—. (2011), "Crypto-Religion and the Study of Cultural Mixtures: Anthropology, Value, and the Nature of Syncretism." *Journal of the American Academy of Religion* 79(2): 408–24.

Robinson, James M. (2001), "The Critical Edition of Q and the Study of Jesus." In Andreas Lindemann, (ed.), *The Sayings Source Q and the Historical Jesus*. Leuven: Peeters Publishers, pp. 27–52.

Roebuck, Valerie, trans and ed. (2003), "Introduction to Roebuck." In *The Upaniṣads*. London: Penguin Books, pp. xv–xli.

Rorty, Richard. (1989), *Contingency, Irony, and Solidarity*. Cambridge: Cambridge University Press.

Rose, Kenneth. (Fall 1994), "Faith or Hermeneutics in the Methodology of Mircea Eliade." *Journal of Alpha Theta Kappa* 18: 15–31.

—. (Autumn 1996a), "Doctrine and Tolerance in Theology of Religions: On Avoiding Exclusivist Hegemonism and Pluralist Reductionism." *The Scottish Journal of Religious Studies* 17(2): 109–21.

—. (1996b), *Knowing the Real: John Hick on the Cognitivity of Religions and Religious Pluralism*. New York: Peter Lang Publishing.

—. (1998), "Keith Ward's Inclusivist Theology of Revelations." *New Blackfriars* 79: 164–76.

—. (Winter 2004), "Is Christianity the Most Universal Faith? Response to Tillich and the World Religions: Encountering Other Faiths Today by Robison B. James." *The Bulletin of the North American Paul Tillich Society* 30: 15–19.

—. (2007), "'Interspirituality': When Interfaith Dialogue Is but a Disguised Monologue." *Hinduism Today*. October/November/December, p. 54.

—. (Winter 2011), "Toward an Apophatic Pluralism: Beyond Confessionalism, Epicyclism, and Inclusivism in Theology of Religions." *Journal of Ecumenical Studies* 46(1): 67–75.

—. (2012), "Interspirituality and Unsaying: Apophatic Strategies for Departicularizing Christ and the Church in Current Roman Catholic Mystical Movements." *Mysticism: The Mysticism Group of the American Academy of Religion*. Accessed May 10, 2012. www.aarmysticism.org/documents/Rose03.pdf.

Rudolph, Kurt. (2005), "Syncretism—From Theological Invective to a Concept in the Study of Religion," trans. David Warburton. In Anita Maria Leopold and Jeppe Sinding Jensen, (eds), *Syncretism in Religion: A Reader*. New York: Routledge, pp. 68–85. First published 2004 by Equinox Publishing, London.

Ruiz, Jean-Pierre. (2001), "Note to Revelation 8:5." In Michael D. Coogan, Marc Z. Brettler, Carol A. Newsom, and Pheme Perkins, (eds), *The New Oxford Annotated Bible*. Oxford and New York: Oxford University Press, p. 431.

Runzo, Joseph. (2011), "Plurality and Relativism." In Chad V. Meister, (ed.), *The Oxford Handbook of Religious Diversity*. Oxford and New York: Oxford University Press, pp. 61–76.

Sarma, Deepak. (2009), "Madhva Dialogue and Discernment." In Catherine Cornille, (ed.), *Criteria of Interreligious Dialogue*. Eugene, OR: Cascade Books, pp. 182–202.

Schilbrack, Kevin. (2010), "Religions: Are There Any?" *Journal of the American Academy of Religion* 78(4): 1112–38.

Schleiermacher, Friedrich. (1988), *On Religion: Speeches to its Cultured Despisers*. Translated by Richard Crouter. Cambridge: Cambridge University Press.

Schmidt-Leukel, Perry. (2005), "Exclusivism, Inclusivism, Pluralism: The Tripolar Typology—Clarified and Reaffirmed." In Paul F. Knitter, (ed.), *The Myth of Religious Superiority: A Multifaith Exploration*. Maryknoll, NY: Orbis Books, pp. 13–27.

Schuerkens, Ulrike. (2003), "Social Transformations Between Global Forces and Local Life-Worlds: Introduction." *Current Sociology* 51(3–4): 195–7.

Schweitzer, Albert. (1968), *The Mysticism of Paul the Apostle*. Translated by William Montgomery. New York: The Seabury Press.

Sells, Michael A. (1994), *Mystical Languages of Unsaying*. Chicago: The University of Chicago Press.

Sharma, Arvind. (2005), "Can There Be More than One Kind of Pluralism?" In Paul F. Knitter, (ed.), *The Myth of Religious Superiority: A Multifaith Exploration*. Maryknoll, NY: Orbis Books, pp. 56–61.

—. (2011), "A Hindu Perspective." In Chad V. Meister, (ed.), *The Oxford Handbook of Religious Diversity*. Oxford and New York: Oxford University Press, pp. 309–20.

Sholtissek, Klaus. (2004), "The Johannine Gospel in Recent Research." In Scot McKnight and Grant R. Osborne, (eds), *The Face of New Testament Studies: A Survey of Recent Research*. Baker Academic: Grand Rapids, pp. 444–71.

Shorter, Aylward. (1993), "Inculturation: The Premise of Universality." In Catherine Cornille and Valeer Neckebrouck, (eds), *A Universal Faith: Peoples, Cultures, Religions, and the Christ*. Peeters Press: Louvain/Grand Rapids: Eerdmans, pp. 1–19.

Simoni-Wastila, Henry. (2002), "*Māyā* and Radical Particularity: Can Particular Persons be One with Brahman?" *International Journal of Hindu Studies* 6(1): 1–18.

Smith, Jonathan Z. (1982), *Imagining Religion: From Babylon to Jonestown*. Chicago: University of Chicago Press.

—. (2003), "Religion and Religious Studies: No Difference at All." In Carl Olsen, (ed.), *Theory and Method in the Study of Religion: A Selection of Critical Readings*. Belmont, CA: Wadsworth/Thomson Learning, pp. 25–9.

—. (2010), "Tillich['s] Remains . . ." *Journal of the American Academy of Religion* 78(4): 1139–70.

Smith, Wilfred C. (1978), *The Meaning and End of Religion* (1st pb. ed). San Francisco, CA: Harper & Row.

—. (1981), Towards *a World Theology: Faith and the Comparative History of Religion*. Philadelphia, PA: Westminster Press.

—. (1987), "Idolatry: In Comparative Perspective." In John Hick and Paul F. Knitter, (eds), *The Myth of Christian Uniqueness: Toward a Pluralistic Theology of Religions*. Maryknoll, NY: Orbis Books, pp. 53–68.

Stegemann, Ekkehard W. and Wolfgang Stegemann. (1999), *The Jesus Movement: A Social History of Its First Century*. Translated by O. C. Dean, Jr. Minneapolis, MN: Fortress Press.

Stendahl, Krister. (1984a), "Christ's Lordship and Religious Pluralism." In Krister Stendhal, (ed.), *Meanings: The Bible as Document and Guide*. Philadelphia, PA: Fortress Press, pp. 233–44.

—. (1984b), "Messianic License: The Sermon on the Mount." In Krister Stendahl, (ed.), *Meanings: The Bible as Document and Guide*. Philadelphia, PA: Fortress Press, pp. 85–97.
—, (ed.). (1984c), *Meanings: The Bible as Document and Guide*. Philadelphia, PA: Fortress Press.
Stewart, Charles. (2005), "Relocating Syncretism in Social Science Discourse." In Anita Maria Leopold and Jeppe Sinding Jensen, (eds), *Syncretism in Religion*. New York: Routledge, pp. 264–85. First published 2004 by Equinox Publishing, London.
—. (Autumn 1999), "Syncretism and Its Synonyms: Reflections on Cultural Mixture." *Diacritics* 29(3): 40–62.
Stewart, Charles and Rosalind Shaw. (1994), "Introduction: Problematizing Syncretism." In Charles Stewart and Rosalind Shaw, (eds), *Syncretism/Anti-Syncretism*. London and New York: Routledge, pp. 1–26.
—, (eds). (1994), *Syncretism/Anti-Syncretism*. London and New York: Routledge.
Stolz, Fritz. (2001), "Synkretismus, I Religionsgeschichtlich." In Gerhard Müller, (ed.), *Theologische Realenzyklopädie*, vol. 32. Berlin and New York: Walter de Gruyter, pp. 527–30.
Strange, Daniel. (2011a), "Daniel Strange Re-Responds to Gavin D'Costa and Paul Knitter." In Gavin D'Costa, Paul F. Knitter, and Daniel Strange, (eds), *Only One Way? Three Christian Responses on the Uniqueness of Christ in a Religiously Plural World*. London: SCM Press, pp. 213–28.
—. (2011b), "Perilous Exchange, Precious Good News: A Reformed 'Subversive Fulfillment' Interpretation of Other Religions." In Gavin D'Costa, Paul F. Knitter, and Daniel Strange, (eds), *Only One Way?Three Christian Responses on the Uniqueness of Christ in a Religiously Plural World*. London: SCM Press, pp. 91–136.
Streiker, Lowell. (1990), *New Age Comes to Main Street*. Nashville, TN: Abingdon Press.
Sugirtharajah, Sharada. (2012), "Introduction: Religious Pluralism—Some Issues." In Sharada Sugirtharajah, (ed.), *Religious Pluralism and the Modern World: An Ongoing Engagement with John Hick*. Houndmills: Palgrave Macmillan, pp. 1–16.
Syman, Stefanie. (2011), *The Subtle Body: The Story of Yoga in America*. New York: Farrar, Straus and Giroux.
Tanquerey, Adolphe. (1930), *The Spiritual Life: A Treatise on Ascetical and Mystical Theology* (2nd edn). Translated by Herman Branderis. Tournai, Belgium: Desclée & Co. Reprinted and updated after 1954.
Taves, Ann. (2011), "'Religion' in the Humanities and the Humanities in the University." *Journal of the American Academy of Religion* 79(2): 287–314.
Taylor, Charles. (2007), *A Secular Age*. Cambridge, MA: Harvard University Press.
Teasdale, Wayne. (1995), "Bede Griffiths as Mystic and Icon of Reversal." *America* 173(9): 22–3.
—. (1999), *The Mystic Heart: Discovering a Universal Spirituality in the World's Religions*. Novato, CA: New World Library.
—. (2002), *A Monk in the World: Cultivating a Spiritual Life*. Novato, CA: New World Library.
—. (2003), *Bede Griffiths: An Introduction to His Interspiritual Thought*. Woodstock, VT: SkyLight Paths Publishing.
Thatamanil, John J. (2006), *The Immanent Divine: God, Creation, and the Human Predicament*. Minneapolis, MN: Fortress Press.

—. (2010), "Comparing Professors Smith and Tillich: A Response to Jonathan Z. Smith's 'Tillich['s] Remains.'" *Journal of the American Academy of Religion* 78(4): 1171–81.
Theissen, Gerd. (1999), *The Religion of the Earliest Churches: Creating a Symbolic World*. Translated by John Bowden. Minneapolis, MN: Fortress Press.
—. (2000), *Die Religonen der Ersten Christen: Eine Theorie des Urchristentums*. 2 durchgesehene Auflage. Gütersloh: Chr. Kaiser/Gütersloher Verlagshaus.
—. (2001), *Das Neue Testament: Geschichte, Literature, Religion*. Munich: Verlag C. H. Beck oHG.
—. (2003), *Fortress Introduction to the New Testament*. Translated by John Bowden Minneapolis, MN: Fortress Press.
Thurman, R. A. F., trans. (1991), *The Central Philosophy of Tibet: A Study and Translation of Jey Tsong Khapa's Essence of True Eloquence* (1st pb. ed). Princeton, NJ: Princeton University Press. First published 1984 as *Tsong Khapa's Speech of Gold in the "Essence of True Eloquence"* by Princeton University Press.
Tiessen, Terrance L. (2004), *Who Can be Saved? Reassessing Salvation in Christ*. Downers Grove, IL: Inter-Varsity Press.
Tillich, Paul. (1963), *Christianity and the Encounter of the World Religions*. New York: Columbia University Press.
—. (2000), *The Courage to Be* (2nd edn). New Haven, CT: Yale University Press.
Toner, Patrick. (1910), *The Catholic Encyclopedia*, vol. 9. *New Advent*. New York: Robert Appleton Company. Accessed April 27, 2011. www.newadvent.org/cathen/09256a.htm.
Torrey, Reuben A., Charles Lee Feinberg, and Warren W. Wiersbe, (eds). (1990), *The Fundamentals: The Famous Sourcebook of Foundational Biblical Truths*. Grand Rapids, MI: Kregel Publications.
Tracy, David. (1987), "Theology: Comparative Theology." In Mircea Eliade, (ed.), *Encyclopedia of Religion*, vol. 14. New York: Macmillan, pp. 446–55.
Troeltsch, Ernst. (1971), *The Absoluteness of Christianity and the History of Religions*. Translated by David Reid. Richmond, VA: John Knox Press. First German publication 1929 by J. C. B. Mohr, Tübingen.
Tsoukalas, Steven. (2006), *Kṛṣṇa and Christ: Body-Divine Relation in the Thought of Śaṅkara, Rāmānuja, and Classical Christian Orthodoxy*. Milton Keynes: Paternoster.
Turner, Denys. (1998), *The Darkness of God: Negativity in Christian Mysticism* (pb. ed). Cambridge: Cambridge University Press.
Vähäkangas, Mika. (2008), "Ghambageu Encounters Jesus in Sonjo Mythology: Syncretism as African Rational Action." *Journal of the American Academy of Religion* 76(1): 111–37.
Valantasis, Richard, trans. (1997), *The Gospel of Thomas*. London: Routledge.
Vermes, Geza. (1993), *The Religion of Jesus the Jew*. Minneapolis, MN: Fortress Press.
—. (1999), *Jesus: Apocalyptic Prophet of the New Millennium*. Oxford and New York: Oxford University Press.
Vroom, Hendrik. (1996), *No Other Gods: Christian Belief in Dialogue with Buddhism, Hinduism, and Islam*. Translated by Lucy Jansen. Grand Rapids, MI: Zondervan.
Ward, Graham. (2006), "The Future of Religion." *Journal of the American Academy of Religion* 74(1): 179–86.
—. (2012), "Theology and Postmodernism: Is It All Over?" *Journal of the American Academy of Religion* 80(2): 466–84.
Ward, Keith. (1994), *Religion and Revelation: A Theology of Revelations in the World's Religions*. New York: Oxford University Press.

—. (2011), "Religion and Revelation." In Chad V. Meister, (ed.), *The Oxford Handbook of Religious Diversity*. Oxford and London: Oxford University Press, pp. 169–82.

Wasserstrom, Steven M. (1989), *Religion after Religion: Gershom Scholem, Mircea Eliade, and Henry Corbin at Eranos*. Princeton, NJ: Princeton University Press.

Wilfred, Felix. (1992a), "Liberation in India and the Church's Participation." In Felix Wilfred, (ed.), *Leave the Temple: Indian Paths to Human Liberation*. Maryknoll, NY: Orbis Books, pp. 175–97.

—, (ed.). (1992b), *Leave the Temple: Indian Paths to Human Liberation*. Maryknoll, NY: Orbis Books.

Williams, Rowan. (2007), "Christian Identity and Religious Plurality." In Luis N. Rivera-Pagán, (ed.), *God, in your Grace . . .: Official Report of the Ninth Assembly of the World Council of Churches*. Geneva: WCC Publications, World Council of Churches, pp. 179–86.

Williamson, Lola. (2010), *Transcendent in America: Hindu-inspired Meditation Movements as New Religion*. New York: New York University Press.

Wood, William. (2009), "On the New Analytic Theology, or: The Road Less Traveled." *Journal of the American Academy of Religion* 77(4): 941–60.

Wuthnow, Robert. (2005), *America and the Challenges of Religious Diversity*. Princeton, NJ and Oxford: Princeton University Press.

Young, Amos. (2009), "'The Light Shines in the Darkness': Johannine Dualism and the Challenge for Christian Theology of Religions Today." *The Journal of Religion* 89(1): 31–56.

Index

Lightning Source UK Ltd.
Milton Keynes UK
UKOW05f2015030217
293569UK00022B/442/P

9 781628 925265